Sri Lanka

Since Independence, Sri Lanka has been engulfed by political tragedy, as successive governments have failed to settle the grievances of the Tamil minority in a way acceptable to the majority Sinhala population. The new Premadasa presidency faces huge economic and political problems and continued violent unrest in all areas of the country.

This book is not a conventional political history of Sri Lanka. It employs historical and anthropological evidence to challenge the widely-held belief that conflict in Sri Lanka is simply the continuation of centuries of animosity between Sinhala and Tamil. Instead, the authors show how modern ethnic identities have been refashioned since the colonial period. The war between Tamils and the Sinhala-dominated government has been accompanied by rhetorical wars over archaeological sites, place-name etymologies and the political use of the national past. The book is also one of the first attempts to focus on local perceptions of the crisis and draws on a broad range of sources, from village fieldwork to newspaper controversies. Its interest extends beyond contemporary politics to history, anthropology and development studies.

The Editor

Jonathan Spencer is a lecturer in the Department of Social Anthropology at the University of Edinburgh.

Sri Lanka

History and the Roots of Conflict

Edited by

Jonathan Spencer

ROUTLEDGE

London and New York

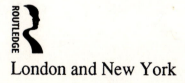

First published 1990
by Routledge
11 New Fetter Lane, London EC4P 4EE

Simultaneously published in the USA and Canada
by Routledge
a division of Routledge, Chapman and Hall, Inc.
29 West 35th Street, New York, NY 10001

Reprinted 1995, 1997

Typeset by LaserScript Limited, Mitcham, Surrey
Printed and bound in Great Britain by
George Over Limited, London and Rugby

British Library Cataloguing in Publication Data

Spencer, Jonathan
Sri Lanka: history and the roots of conflict.
1. Sri Lanka. Political events
I. Title
954.9303

ISBN 0–415–04461–8

Library of Congress Cataloging in Publication Data

Sri Lanka: history and the roots of conflict / edited by Jonathan Spencer.
p. cm.
Includes bibliographical references.
ISBN 0–415–04461–8 : 49.95
1. Sri Lanka—Ethnic relations. 2. Sri Lanka—Politics and government.
I. Spencer, Jonathan, 1954– .
DS489.2.S74 1990
305.8′0095493—dc20 90–31654
CIP

To the memory of
Newton Gunasinghe
and
Serena Tennekoon

Contents

Contributors ix

Acknowledgements xi

Abbreviations xii

1. Introduction: the power of the past 1
Jonathan Spencer

Part I: Colonialism, history and racism

2. The generation of communal identities 19
Elizabeth Nissan and R.L. Stirrat

3. The people of the lion: the Sinhala identity and ideology in history and historiography 45
R.A.L.H. Gunawardana

4. Historical images in the British period 87
John D. Rogers

5. The politics of the Tamil past 107
Dagmar Hellmann-Rajanayagam

Part II: History at a moment of crisis

6. Nationalist rhetoric and local practice: the fate of the village community in Kukulewa 125
James Brow

7. A compound of many histories: the many pasts of an east coast Tamil community 145
Mark P. Whitaker

8. Rural awakenings: grassroots development and the cultivation of a national past in rural Sri Lanka 164
Michael D. Woost

Part III: The politics of the past

9. J.R. Jayewardene: righteousness and *realpolitik* 187
Steven Kemper

10. Newspaper nationalism: Sinhala identity as historical discourse 205
Serena Tennekoon

11. Afterword: scared places, violent spaces 227
E. Valentine Daniel

Index 247

Contributors

JONATHAN SPENCER is Lecturer in Social Anthropology at the University of Edinburgh and author of *A Sinhala Village in a Time of Trouble: Politics and Change in Rural Sri Lanka* (1990).

R. L. STIRRAT is a Lecturer in Social Anthropology at the University of Sussex and author of *On the Beach* (1989) and numerous articles on religion and economics in Sri Lanka.

ELIZABETH NISSAN was until 1988 a Lecturer in Anthropology at the University of Durham.

R. A. L. H. GUNAWARDANA is Professor of History at the University of Peradeniya (Sri Lanka) and the author of *Robe and Plough* (1979).

JOHN D. ROGERS has a Ph.D. in history from the School of Oriental and African Studies, London, and is the author of *Crime, Justice and Society in Colonial Sri Lanka* (1987).

DAGMAR HELLMANN-RAJANAYAGAM is a Research Fellow at the German Historical Institute, London, and the author of a number of articles on Tamil nationalism in Sri Lanka.

JAMES BROW is Associate Professor of Anthropology at the University of Texas, Austin, and the author of *Vedda Villages of Anuradhapura* (1978).

MARK WHITAKER has a Ph.D. from Princeton University and has taught at Drew University and is Professor of Anthropology at Skidmore College.

MICHAEL WOOST is completing a Ph.D. in anthropology at the University of Texas, Austin.

STEVEN KEMPER is Professor of Anthropology at Bates College, and author of *A History of Representations: Chronicles, Politics, and Culture in Sinhala Life* (forthcoming).

SERENA TENNEKOON, anthropologist and feminist activist, was completing a Ph.D. in anthropology at Cornell University and had published a number of articles on politics and culture in Sri Lanka before her death in 1989.

E. VALENTINE DANIEL is Professor of Anthropology at the University of Michigan and author of *Fluid Signs: Being a Person the Tamil Way* (1984).

Acknowledgements

The idea for this book came from discussions at a conference on Sri Lanka at the University of Sussex in 1987, although only one of the papers collected here was actually presented there. The School of African and Asian Studies at Sussex, Richard Brown, Irene Sheard, and Tony Stevenson all gave help and support at the time. The idea of a book on this theme was first suggested by James Manor. Earlier versions of the introduction and the papers by Brow, Woost and Whitaker were presented at a session of the American Anthropological Association in Phoenix in 1988; special thanks are due to Valentine Daniel for his comments at the time. Nick Wedd helped with hardware for the final editing, and Katherine Manville and Bridget Morris retyped three of the chapters. Throughout the preparation of this book Jock Stirrat and Liz Nissan have been the source of endless good advice and encouragement. In a moment of great adversity, my wife Julia Swannell was to be seen copying diacritics on to the manuscript; this was the most tangible but by no means most important of her contributions. I am also grateful to Jennifer Robertson for her help in the preparation of Serena Tennekoon's chapter.

Earlier versions of the chapters by Gunawardana and Tennekoon were published in *The Sri Lanka Journal of the Humanities*, Social Scientists' Association *Ethnicity and Social Change in Sri Lanka* (Colombo, 1984), and *South Asia Bulletin*.

Abbreviations

The following abbreviations have been used in the notes and references.

Mv.	*The Mahavamsa or Great Chronicle of Ceylon*, translated and edited by Wilhelm Geiger (London, 1912)
Cv.	*The Culavamsa being the More Recent Part of the Mahavamsa*, translated and edited by Wilhelm Geiger, 2 vols. (London, 1929–30)
CJHSS	*Ceylon Journal of Historical and Social Studies*
CSSH	*Comparative Studies in Society and History*
ESC	Social Scientists' Association *Ethnicity and Social Change in Sri Lanka* (Colombo, 1984)
EZ	*Epigraphica Zeylanica*
JAS	*Journal of Asian Studies*
JRASCB	*Journal of the Royal Asiatic Society (Ceylon Branch)*
MAS	*Modern Asian Studies*

Chapter one

Introduction: the power of the past[1]

Jonathan Spencer

> Many people – many nations – can find themselves holding, more or less wittingly, that 'every stranger is an enemy'. For the most part this conviction lies deep down like some infection; it betrays itself only in random, disconnected acts, and does not lie at the base of a system of reason. But when this does come about, when the unspoken dogma becomes the major premiss in a syllogism, then, at the end of the chain, there is the Lager.
>
> Primo Levi[2]

In 1948 the colony of Ceylon was granted independence by Britain. Forty years later the island (renamed Sri Lanka in 1972) lurches from political crisis to political crisis. Large sections of its territory in the north and east have been under the *de facto* control of troops of the Indian Peace Keeping Force (IPKF), although that control was still regularly threatened by the activities of various militant Tamil separatist groups. The Colombo government has remained in charge of the populous south and west, but here normal administration has been subject to constant violent disruption by a group of Sinhala militants known as the Janata Vimukti Peramuna (JVP or People's Liberation Front). As a result of new elections in late 1988 and early 1989, the veteran President J.R. Jayewardene of the United National Party (UNP) was replaced by his former Prime Minister, Ranasinghe Premadasa. The new government, it is generally agreed, faces huge economic and political problems.

The single most obvious factor in the decline into political crisis has been the failure of successive governments to settle the grievances of the minority Tamil population in a way that is nevertheless acceptable to the majority Sinhala population.[3] Historically, the Tamil heartland of the Jaffna peninsula has provided a steady stream of educated émigrés – lawyers, teachers, civil servants, doctors – who not only filled many posts in the bureaucracy of colonial Ceylon but also moved further afield to Malaysia, Singapore, and India, and, more recently, Britain,

Canada and the USA. Since the 1950s the availability of government employment within Sri Lanka has gradually dried up. In 1956 the sitting government was defeated in a general election by a coalition of Sinhala-dominated parties, led by the charismatic S.W.R.D. Bandaranaike of the Sri Lanka Freedom Party (SLFP). The new coalition was elected on a wave of Buddhist nationalism which demanded, amongst other things, that the Sinhala-Buddhist majority should receive its 'rightful' share of official employment. Within months of its election two things had happened: legislation was passed making Sinhala the sole official language; and communal rioting broke out between Sinhala and Tamil in the east of the country.[4]

Since 1956 there have been repeated attempts to achieve a political solution to the problem, none of them so far successful. These attempts were punctuated by occasional outbreaks of violence between the two groups. In the mid-1970s Tamil frustration at what was felt to be continued discrimination turned to militancy of a new kind. Talk of separatism and the founding of a new state of 'Eelam' in the 'traditional homelands' of the north and east became commonplace even amongst conservative Jaffna politicians and was adopted as official policy by the main Tamil political party, the Tamil United Liberation Front (TULF), which formed the official opposition to Jayewardene's regime after the 1977 election. But the TULF found itself outflanked by the rise of new groups of young armed militants prepared to fight for their independence. From the mid-1970s these groups – of which the Liberation Tigers of Tamil Eelam (LTTE or the Tigers) have been most consistently threatening – embarked on a policy of terrorist attacks against any representative of the Sinhala-dominated government.[5] The government responded with counter-terror of its own. The situation escalated until 1983, when thousands of Tamils were killed in rioting in the Sinhala-dominated south after a massacre of government soldiers in the north.[6] Soon after, the militant groups started to operate in the Tamil areas of the east, and attacks on state personnel were replaced by massacres and counter-massacres of civilians in border areas between the two ethnic blocks.

In 1987 the government attempted a major military *putsch* in the Jaffna peninsula. The Indian government, which had harboured and covertly supported the Tamil militants in the past, made it clear that it would no longer tolerate the continued instability off its southern shore. In a bewildering volte-face, and under heavy pressure, the Colombo government signed an agreement with India, conceding a degree of political devolution to Tamil areas, and agreeing to the entry of Indian forces as guarantors of peace in the contested areas. The agreement was unpopular on both sides of the ethnic divide. Within months the Indian forces were embroiled in new fighting with their erstwhile protégés in the LTTE, while Sinhala opposition became manifest in a series of assassinations and attacks attributed to the JVP.

This book is an attempt to shed fresh light on the sources of the political tragedy that has engulfed Sri Lanka in the past decade. The conflict between the majority Sinhala population and the minority Tamil population is often presented, not least by the antagonists themselves, as the inevitable outcome of centuries of hostility. Political rhetoric in Sri Lanka is dense with historical allusion, as many of the papers in this book illustrate. The Buddhists of the majority Sinhala population are usually represented as heirs to an ancient tradition of Sinhala-Buddhist nationalism, dormant during the colonial period, but aggressively rejuvenated in the era of mass politics; the Tamils are similarly presented as their ancient enemies.

The contributors to this book, while differing considerably in their individual interpretations of the sources of conflict, nevertheless share a common aim. This is to expose the inadequacy of explaining conflicts like those in Sri Lanka as the inevitable working out of immanent – 'primordial' – cultural forces. Rather, the historical arguments so often heard in Sri Lankan politics have themselves to be understood as products of their own peculiar history. In the light of Indian intervention and the continuing violence in the south it may seem that academic arguments about the past are of little relevance, but the demonstration that the crisis itself has been made by the actions of particular men and women, and is not the outcome of inherited destiny, can only encourage those who want to believe that because past mistakes were avoidable there is still hope for the future.

The most prominent view of the national past in modern Sri Lanka is that held by the majority Sinhala population, who have exercised ever tighter control over national government since Independence. According to this view, the Buddha himself entrusted the island's destiny to the Sinhala people as guardians of his teaching. This view is now insistently proclaimed in the press, in the speeches of politicians, and in school-books and history lessons. In the face of these Sinhala-Buddhist claims on the national past, alternative Tamil histories have been put together and propagated in the Tamil-speaking north and east of the island. Both 'official history' and 'opposition history' agree on the basic terms of the argument: present conflicts can only be explained by reference to the past. The war which has been fought between the armed Tamil separatists and the Sinhala-dominated government has been accompanied by rhetorical wars fought over archaeological sites, place-name etymologies, and the interpretation of ancient inscriptions.

There are several things which this book is not. It is not a conventional political history of the current conflict. A number of such accounts already exist, albeit of highly variable quality.[7] Nor is its content quite as specialized as the discussion of history might imply. In looking at the sources of current versions of the national past, and the ways in which such versions are disseminated and contested, the contributors have assembled a remarkably broad account of the cultural politics of the ethnic crisis. The historians (Gunawardana, Rogers, Hellmann-Rajanayagam) have provided rich, detailed accounts of the making or remaking of modern ethnic identities during the colonial period. The anthropologists (Whitaker, Brow, Woost) have detailed the processes by which those identities are now being reproduced among Sri Lanka's predominantly rural population. Other contributors, whose chapters escape easy disciplinary pigeon-holing, describe changes in the larger political structure (Nissan and Stirrat), the political use of the past (Kemper), and the effects of recent challenges to the hegemonic interpretation of the past (Tennekoon). In place of that kind of political history which is based almost entirely on English-language sources and seeks its explanations only within the actions of the English-speaking élite, the history in this volume employs local sources and attends to the voices of people many miles from the capital. These are the sort of people who have usually been in the front line of the conflict, and they are the people who will decide the fate of all attempts to find a peaceful settlement.

This book, most definitely, is not an attempt to rewrite Sri Lanka's national past. The aim is not to disprove or discredit any particular view of the national past. Nor is there any intention to put forward the absurd argument that the categories 'Sinhala' and 'Tamil' are somehow colonial inventions, or that modern conflicts were created *ex nihilo* by Machiavellian colonialists in a spirit of divide and rule. Instead the book seeks to analyse the appeal and effect in the present of certain dominant interpretations of Sri Lankan history, and the way in which modern ethnic identities have themselves been shaped by political circumstances. The roots of present understandings of ethnic identity in Victorian Orientalist scholarship, described below by Rogers and Gunawardana, and the current self-consciousness about the distortions of Orientalist work in general,[8] make any further attempt to rewrite the past from outside Sri Lanka especially inappropriate. The broad orientation of this volume is toward the asking of new and unfamiliar questions about past, present, and future in Sri Lanka, not the provision of fixed and definite answers.

The roots of ethnic identity

The opening chapter by Nissan and Stirrat provides an overview of the history of the present conflict which is at once analytic and yet remarkably comprehensive. Drawing on recent theories of nationalism and a wide range of comparative material, they argue that the present conflict, and the ethnic identities on which it is based, are radically different from earlier conflicts and identities. In particular, they point out that the pre-colonial states in Sri Lanka were based on kingship and a political structure which was indifferent to the cultural or linguistic constitution of the population. Even colonial conflict between different ethnic groups, as manifest in a spate of riots and disturbances in the late nineteenth and early twentieth centuries, was markedly different from post-colonial conflict. Colonial disturbances were usually aligned on religious lines – Sinhala Buddhist attacking Sinhala Catholic; Tamil Hindu attacking Tamil Catholic; Buddhist, Catholic or Hindu attacking Muslim; and Muslims attacking all back in return. The first modern evidence of Tamil–Sinhala conflict, defined in terms of linguistic group, comes from 1956, the year when major national language reforms were introduced. In simple terms Sinhala–Tamil conflict is a product of modern politics. To interpret the history of the pre-colonial kingdoms in terms of 'nationalism' – a distinctive ideology of the modern nation-state – is anachronistic and therefore misleading. But this has not prevented a host of earlier scholars from doing just that, and the question of how this came about is addressed in the next three papers, those of Gunawardana, Rogers, and Hellmann-Rajanayagam.

The understanding of the national past as a history of warring 'communities', 'races', or 'ethnic groups' is a product of colonial readings of the available sources on the Sri Lankan past. The most important of these, the Buddhist chronicle the Mahavamsa, is a remarkable document which is alluded to throughout this volume. Usually referred to these days as Sri Lanka's 'national chronicle', it is a work in Pali verse written by Buddhist monks from the sixth century AD onwards. It provides an unbroken chronicle of kings, monks, wars, rebellions, and acts of piety from the time of the Buddha in the fifth century BC to the fourth century AD. Subsequent additions (translated as the Culavamsa) brought the story up to the arrival of the British in the Kandyan kingdom in 1815. In the last decade, as Kemper describes below, the government has sponsored a further updating of the chronicle to bring it up to our own times, although not without new stylistic and intellectual problems.

Despite the miraculous nature of much of its content, the Mahavamsa has provided a sure chronological frame for historians working in both Sri Lanka and India. Rogers describes how, after initial scepticism from colonial historians, the Mahavamsa gradually became central to the colonial understanding of the Sri Lankan past, and then how this understanding was itself adapted by members of the Sri Lankan élite of the time. The process he describes is of great importance because the Mahavamsa, and specifically the colonial interpretation of its content, was a vital ingredient in the polemics of early cultural nationalists. As their understanding of Sinhala-Buddhist identity was appropriated and exploited by politicians from the 1930s onwards, the Mahavamsa provided both content and legitimation for an increasingly strident Sinhala nationalism.

The importance of the Mahavamsa in modern Sinhala nationalism is twofold. As an apparently authentic text it was especially well suited to colonial preconceptions about the relationship between history and identity. But the stories it contains, and the presuppositions upon which it is based, would inevitably push any later ideological use of it in some directions and not in others; a nationalism based upon the Mahavamsa would have to be a Buddhist nationalism with little space for non-Buddhist identities.

The history in the Mahavamsa is a didactic history, as Kemper explains in his chapter.[9] Its purpose is to demonstrate the virtues and rewards of a particular political relationship between Buddhism and the pre-colonial polity. The king protects and supports the sangha (the order of Buddhist monks); the sangha preserves the teaching of the Buddha and acts as a 'field of merit' for both the king and the people; the people prosper when the king governs righteously and provides proper protection for the sangha. The ideal king is the unifying conqueror who can unite the island under one rule. It is this ideology, asserted and demonstrated throughout the chronicle, which has been used by recent writers as evidence of early 'nationalism'.

Such a view implicitly conflates the crucial difference between 'king' and 'people', while assuming that the interpretations put forward by the chroniclers were shared by all the actors in the events described, at the time at which they occurred. Neither of these criticisms could be regarded as especially novel in other areas of historical scholarship, yet they have rarely been aired in Sri Lanka. The fact is that the investigation of the history of ethnic identity in Sri Lanka has barely begun. We do know that key episodes from the Mahavamsa were the subject of poems and songs collected in the nineteenth century, but in many cases written earlier, though there has been no systematic attempt to investigate the salience and significance of ethnic and other categories found in these sources. We also have evidence of the importance of local stories of the times of the kings from the work of anthropologists, although these stories may collapse the scrupulous chronology of the chronicles into a shorter 'mythical' time-frame.[10] But if there is any evidence for popular historical consciousness of some sort before the spread of modern nationalism, events of the early colonial period suggest that Sinhala identity was not considered a necessary attribute of legitimate rule: the last kings of the pre-colonial kingdom were Tamil-speakers, and the pretenders who challenged British rule in Sinhala-speaking areas in the early nineteenth century affected to belong to the same Tamil-speaking line. What marked legitimacy above all was support and protection for Buddhism, regardless of the ruler's ethnic identity.[11] This suggests that the linking thread between past and present is not nationalism as such but the legitimating force of Buddhism.

Gunawardana's chapter is a revised version of an essay first published in Sri Lanka in 1979. It was subsequently reprinted in a collection on ethnicity published in 1984, but this is the first time it has been made widely available outside Sri Lanka. Gunawardana directly challenges the widely-held view that the chronicles provide evidence for a 2,000-year history for Sinhala nationalism. As a distinguished medieval historian, Gunawardana is singularly well qualified for the task he has set himself. In place of popular anachronisms, Gunawardana provides a wealth of evidence for the changing connotations and uses of the term 'Sinhala' from the early chronicles up to modern histories, while pointing out how racist readings of Sri Lankan history, first found in colonial historiography, have been carried over into much modern scholarship. What is remarkable, given the criticism Gunawardana has directed at nationalist historiography, is how little his findings have been challenged in Sri Lanka.

Like Rogers and Nissan and Stirrat, Gunawardana directs our attention to the reinterpretation of the chronicles and the subtle reworking of ideas of ethnicity and identity in the colonial period. Gradually the Sinhala people became known as an 'ancient race', descendants of 'Indo-Aryan' settlers from North India, and as such different in 'blood', origins, and kind from their Tamil neighbours.

Hellmann-Rajanayagam describes parallel processes in the making of Tamil history. What was lacking here was a single clear historical source of Tamil identity equivalent to the Buddhist militancy of the Mahavamsa. The historiography of the major areas of Tamil settlement, the east coast and the Jaffna peninsula, is at once shallower and more obviously problematic than that provided by the Mahavamsa. Was there a Tamil kingdom in Jaffna? Was the east coast ruled from Kandy? Modern nationalists have tried to answer questions like these which, along with the contentious search for 'traditional homelands', have come to dominate recent writing on the Tamil past. But, as Hellmann-Rajanayagam makes clear, one reason why Tamil nationalist historiography is less strident than Sinhala nationalist historiography is that Tamil identity can be sought in a much wider range of cultural resources, Indian as well as Sri Lankan.

The same pattern can be seen in Whitaker's vivid report from an east coast village where multiple, alternative understandings of the past can be drawn on in different situations. Put crudely, there is simply so much Tamil culture in the world, that a relative paucity of historical sources (of the type likely to impress colonial historians) may pose little problem for the constructors of national identity. Even so, the rise of Tamil nationalism in Sri Lanka has received far less scholarly attention than the parallel rise of Sinhala nationalism, and the contributions here only scratch the surface of this crucial problem. Even more remote is the prospect of a detailed historical comparison of the very different fates of Tamil nationalism in Sri Lanka and in India; such a comparison would, I believe, reveal important general lessons for the conduct of post-colonial politics.

The roots of ethnic conflict

Today's ethnic alignments cannot simply be read off from the animosities identified in different parts of the chronicles. The main formal criterion of membership of the rival Sinhala and Tamil communities today is linguistic, but in the colonial period the most salient identities – at least as far as riots and disturbances were concerned – were religious. Catholics, who were pitted against Buddhists and Hindus in colonial conflicts, are now divided into Sinhala Catholics and Tamil Catholics.[12] Yet Muslims, a group who are predominantly Tamil-speaking, and as such might be thought to have suffered as much as anyone from linguistic discrimination since 1956, have stubbornly maintained their ethnic separateness from their fellow Tamil-speakers and have pursued their own distinctive political course in recent years, while remaining aloof until very recently from the central ethnic conflict. In fact, the peculiar assembly of 'races' identified in the census of Sri Lanka, based upon a *mélange* of religious, linguistic, and geographical criteria, can only be explained through a detailed account of the politics of identity.

A schematic explanation of the immediate historical roots of the current tragedy would have to start in what Rogers describes as the 'age of mature colonialism', the late nineteenth and early twentieth century. Victorian racial theory held that the world was divided into distinct races or kinds of people, and both Rogers and Gunawardana trace the growing dominance of this assumption in both colonial and Sri Lankan understandings of the island's history. As Sri Lankans were gradually admitted to the higher levels of colonial government, it was assumed that each section of the population could only be effectively represented by a person of the same 'kind'. So, for example, in the 1880s a move to allow separate representation for Muslims on the Legislative Council was opposed by a leading Tamil figure who argued that they were 'really' only Tamils; the Muslims responded with arguments 'proving' their Arabian descent.[13] The incident displays in exemplary form the effect of a particular set of colonial assumptions which linked the possibility of access to political power to racial criteria, and looked to history as the arbiter of racial authenticity.

What the colonial assumptions ignored was the huge social and cultural gap which existed between the small élite of wealthy English-educated Sri Lankans – supposedly the natural representatives of their various 'races' – and the mass of the population. The second factor in the making of the modern politics of identity is the composition of Sri Lanka's political class and its enduring relationship with its political subjects.[14] In other colonial contexts the political ambitions of the élite forced them to build an anti-colonial alliance with the population. As Nairn puts it in his analysis of the global rise of nationalism, 'The new middle-class intelligentsia of nationalism had to invite the masses into history; and the invitation-card had to be written in a language they understood'.[15] Exactly how that invitation-card was written, just what this mutually intelligible language consisted of, varied with the particular context of different nationalisms. In India, Congress had to win the population's participation in a mass struggle against a government reluctant to hand over power. For Congress leaders like Gandhi and Nehru, this meant using symbols and rhetoric which would, they hoped, appeal to all sections of the population. The fact that – for all the trials, tribulations, problems of regional opposition, and recent dangerous toying with the forces of internal division – Congress is still seen to some extent as the embodiment of the national political will is a measure of their achievement. In Sri Lanka there was no such mass struggle against colonial rule. The colony was granted universal franchise in 1931 to the dismay of at least some elements within the political élite. This élite had to enlist the new voters – the masses – not in order to forge the widest possible alliance against the colonial ruler, but instead in order to win over sections to support their own particular local candidature. Almost immediately politicians started to accuse their opponents of communalism while pursuing similar divisive strategies themselves.[16] By the handover of power in 1948 a tradition of regional Tamil opposition to the dictates of Colombo was firmly established. In the years of crisis there has been no overarching image of Sri Lankan national identity to hold Tamil sentiment back from the path to separatism; the only images available link the nation to one group, the Sinhala people, and one religion, Buddhism.

I stress this historical point because it has been frequently argued that the rise of Bandaranaike's Sinhala-Buddhist populism in the mid-1950s represented a radical break in the island's political history in which power passed from the hands of the old Anglophone élite into those of the new rising Sinhala middle-classes.[17] But Bandaranaike was himself a member of that old élite, while even the first government of Independent Ceylon led by D.S. Senanayake deprived most of the Indian

Tamil population of citizenship at a stroke after Independence. Indeed, if we look more closely at pre-1956 politics, it is possible to discern the contours of attitudes and policies which still persist today and are still the focus of bitter complaint by the minorities. These attitudes and policies draw heavily on the colonial understanding of the past described by Rogers, using it now as a blueprint for the present and the future.

Central to this blueprint is the ideal of the nation as a collection of villages, each with its irrigation tank, its temple, and its swathe of paddy-fields.[18] Senanayake was captivated by this vision, and, as a minister in the 1930s, encouraged the peasant colonization of the sparsely populated Dry Zone. This area was the heartland of the old kingdoms of Anuradhapura and Polonnaruva, and colonization policy was explicitly presented as the reconstruction of past glory. The policy has persisted and grown; the UNP's major development effort in the 1980s has been the massive Mahaväli scheme, designed to provide hydro-electric power and create new irrigated land for settlers. But the overall effect of successive colonization schemes – recently supported by apparently unwitting Western governments – has been the settlement of thousands of Sinhala peasants in the hinterland of the main centres of Tamil population in the north and the east. Here is one source of the characteristically Tamil concern with space – the delineation of the 'homelands' – rather than time; identity is a matter of belonging to a place as much as having a history,[19] and that is what has been threatened by Sinhala efforts to rebuild in what they take to be the image of the island's past.

Nationalism as process

This reconstruction of the island's society in the form of an idealized national past is still going on and its effects in the 1980s are documented in the chapters by Brow and Woost. Their evidence exemplifies Gellner's suggestion that nationalism 'is not what it seems, and above all it is not what it seems to itself. The cultures it claims to defend and revive are often its own inventions, or are modified out of all recognition.'[20] Much of the invention and modification takes place in the schoolroom, or through the medium of print and radio, but a great deal comes through the efforts of politicians. One feature of rural society in Sri Lanka in the 1980s which is at once self-evident yet elusive is what could be called ideological over-production. The news is full of the speeches of local and national politicians, political meetings and rallies are (or were in the early 1980s) the biggest public events in most areas, while each village has its political parties, often bitter political divisions, and countless opportunities for village leaders to articulate their own local version of the dominant ideology.

Both cases involve situations in which local circumstances are at obvious variance with outsiders' interpretations. The villages are divided rather than united, local identities are more confused and specific than nationalist ideology suggests. In Brow's case the memory of Vedda identity and a local idiom of belonging is invoked when the intervention of national politics splits the village; the politicians' rhetoric of the glorious Sinhala-Buddhist past is forgotten as community division becomes a threat to all. In Woost's chapter, a new and heterogeneous community is selected for attention by a group of Colombo intellectuals with their own ideals of rural life. The villagers allow them their fantasies, especially as their acquiescence brings the possibility of short-term political reward. But when their failure to live up to the intellectuals' ideal is threatened with public exposure they hasten to fabricate evidence of the development the intellectuals so badly want to see. Their efforts succeed when the village is the site of a public meeting at which powerful local politicians celebrate its new place in national history.

What these examples show is that nationalism in rural Sri Lanka is not a pre-existent fact, a 'given' upon which politics builds; it is a process, characterized by argument and assertion, itself deeply tied to local politics. The expanding place of the state in everyday life is accompanied by an ever more insistent rhetoric which argues that the state is 'our' state. Outside the Sinhala areas, the place of the state is more often repressive rather than beneficent, and a counter-rhetoric which makes the state 'their' state has grown up over the years. This is one of the many strands of possible interpretation available to the figures in Whitaker's account of an east coast village in the months immediately before the war swept over that area. His celebration of the many possibilities of the past is a timely reminder of the large areas of life in Sri Lanka which go on despite the fighting. Whitaker starts his argument with the observation that other countries may also seem trapped inside a mythologized past; his example is American but it would not be difficult to find British parallels in this era of 'Victorian values'.[21]

But it would be foolish to pretend that any of this local evidence suggests that the popular hold of rival Sinhala and Tamil nationalisms is anything less than it is. What the evidence does show is the sheer quantity of the public argument for these two ideologies within Sri Lanka. This is the over-production I alluded to earlier, which may be either quantitative, as in the case of those Sri Lankan newspapers which seem to carry almost nothing except verbatim texts of politicians' speeches invoking the glories of the past, or qualitative, as in the moment in Woost's village when the construction of a few compost heaps and the presence of the Minister is hyperbolically likened to the first arrival of the founder-king Vijaya and his men on Lankan soil. In both cases the disproportion between rhetorical means and rhetorical ends can be taken as a symptom of the desperation which accompanies the telling of the national past in Sri Lanka. Given the facts of population growth, economic upheaval, and cultural change in post-Independence Sri Lanka, the need for some unifying ideology is apparently overwhelming. Critics of existing divisive strains of nationalism will never succeed unless they can find some alternative ideal of unity to which they can attach their criticisms.

Where might such an alternative be found? The village evidence points to one area – the sentimental appeal to village unity couched in terms of kinship (however remote this may be from the local facts) – which can be opposed to outsiders' versions of unity; but it is hard to see a way to extrapolate this sentimental appeal without staying trapped within the bounds of fictive kinship which ideologically demarcate existing ethnic groups. But relatively unexplored areas of the past also offer possibilities. The old kingdoms were largely indifferent to internal cultural difference, and this fact needs to be brought out and elaborated by concerned historians.[22] Early anti-colonial struggle, as exemplified by the pretender movements of the nineteenth-century Kandyan countryside, was also largely indifferent to internal ethnic divisions among the colonized. Again, these movements, alluded to by one of Woost's local politicians but largely ignored on the national stage, require more detailed historical study and greater public attention.[23]

But the thrust of my argument throughout this introduction has been that the history of the conflict has been essentially a political history, in which particular cultural resources have been deployed to suit the interests of key political actors. This collection concludes with a return to national politics, and the problems of the past in the 1980s. Kemper's paper deals with the circumstances in which J.R. Jayewardene commissioned the updating of the Mahavamsa in the 1980s, including some detailed discussion of Jayewardene's use of Buddhism throughout his political career. The fact that the new Mahavamsa could not be written in the manner of the old is further evidence of the changes that are concealed behind the appeals to the past. The committee which oversaw the project abandoned the old chronological structure in favour of a thematic approach, and combined the Pali verse of the original with sections in demotic Sinhala. The history book, commissioned by a government seeking to bolster its own Buddhist legitimacy but forced to adjust to the ideals of impersonal academic scholarship, is in some ways an ideal symbol of the cultural contradictions of post-colonial politics.

Chapter ten, by Serena Tennekoon, describes a different attempt to rewrite the national past after the traumatic events of 1983. In his recent survey of the ethnic crisis, the distinguished Tamil anthropologist

Stanley Tambiah has called for a new breed of 'imaginative and liberated non-sectarian historians' who will 'deconstruct' the histories which legitimate the present conflict.[24] Tennekoon describes just such an attempt by the small group of left-wing intellectuals in Sri Lanka associated with organizations like the Committee for Rational Development (CRD), Social Scientists' Association (SSA), and Movement for Inter-racial Justice and Equality (MIRJE). Since the late 1970s these groups have sponsored seminars and meetings and published a number of important critiques of dominant nationalist arguments.[25] Unusually for the Sri Lankan intelligentsia, they have been at pains to make sure their analyses are available in Sinhala and Tamil, as well as English. As a result, their work came under sustained attack in the letters columns of the most popular Sinhala newspaper, the *Divayina*, in 1984. The arguments used by their critics should be familiar enough to readers of the earlier papers in this collection, although the hostility they aroused is depressingly predictable. Even so, the very fact that an argument of this sort could be aired in the Sinhala press represents a significant fissure in the public façade of nationalist ideology, unimaginable even a few years earlier.

Criticism, however brave and laudatory, will only remain at the level of gesture unless accompanied by political action. The same intellectuals involved with groups like the SSA and MIRJE have also in many cases identified themselves with the 1987 Peace Agreement. This has subjected them to the possibility of a very different kind of attack. Since the agreement the zealots of the JVP have assassinated both government supporters and figures from those parties of the left which have supported it; alleged supporters of the JVP have been detained, and, in some cases, killed in return. By late 1988 ideology and argument had been eclipsed by brute terror as the JVP sought to keep alive the dream of Sinhala nationalism even as the realities of geo-politics, in the unanswerable form of Indian power, closed in around it. Meanwhile the Tigers fought on in the north, subjecting the Indian troops to intermittent harassment. In 1989 they joined the new government in Colombo in talks and a joint call for Indian withdrawal. Beneath the ethnic divide lies a different, long-simmering, divide – between the political class, which still clings to national power, and many of the country's youth, whose demand for a share in the spoils of government is couched in a language which mixes apocalyptic Marxism with ethnic chauvinism. The most pressing political need is for the reintegration of disaffected youth on both sides of the ethnic divide. But that requires resources, education, and employment. Meanwhile it seems that Sinhala nationalists and Tamil nationalists have finally found a common enemy in the Indian interloper.

One of the best-known stories of the Buddha describes how one day he was visited by a woman troubled by a death. He told her to go around the city and ask for a grain of mustard seed from any household which had not been visited by death. She returned empty-handed and the Buddha had made his point about the ubiquity of suffering and loss in this world. In recent years it has seemed as if anyone who were to go from house to house in Sri Lanka might also expect to return empty-handed. Amid all the suffering of recent events there is a reluctance to single out particular losses. But Serena Tennekoon, who wrote the penultimate chapter of this book, and Newton Gunasinghe, one of whose characteristically brave and imaginative public interventions is discussed in that chapter, both embodied a spirit of rational criticism and humane scholarship which has otherwise been one of the major casualties of the Sri Lankan conflict. Their early deaths, a few months apart, have saddened us all.

Notes and references

1 I am grateful to the contributors to this volume, especially Steven Kemper, for comments on an earlier version of this introduction.

2 P. Levi, *If this is a Man*, London, 1987, p. 15. The 'Lager' to which Levi refers is, of course, the Nazi death-camp.

3 Of a total 1981 population of 14,850,001, 74 per cent (10,985,666) were Sinhala (Sinhalese), 12.6 per cent (1,871,535) Sri Lanka Tamil, 5.6 per cent (825,233) Indian Tamil, and 7.1 per cent (1,056,972) Moors (Muslims). The last three categories are all predominantly speakers of Tamil, but are differentiated by religion (Muslim) and/or putative origin: Sri Lanka Tamils are descendants of the settled Tamil population of the north and east; Indian Tamils are the descendants of estate labourers imported from south India in the British period. Separatist sentiment has been almost entirely confined to the Sri Lanka Tamil population, although this has not prevented rioters from attacking Indian Tamils in recent years.

4 See W.H. Wriggins, *Ceylon: Dilemmas of a New Nation*, Princeton, 1960; R. Kearney, *Communalism and Language in the Politics of Ceylon*, Durham, NC, 1967.

5 D. Hellmann-Rajanayagam, 'The Tamil "Tigers" in northern Sri Lanka: origins, factions, programmes', *Internationales Asienforum*, 1986, vol. 17, pp. 63–85; B. Pfaffenberger 'Fourth world colonialism, indigenous minorities and Tamil separatism in Sri Lanka', *Bulletin of Concerned Asian Scholars* 1984, vol. 16, pp. 15–22.

6 On the 1983 violence see J. Manor (ed.) *Sri Lanka in Change and Crisis*, London, 1984; S.J. Tambiah, *Sri Lanka. Ethnic Fratricide and the Dismantling of Democracy*, London, 1986; H.A.I. Goonetileke, 'July 1983 and the national question in Sri Lanka: a bibliographic guide', *Race and Class* vol. 26, 1984, pp. 159–193.

7 Wriggins, *Ceylon*; Kearney, *Communalism and Language*; Manor, *Sri Lanka*; Tambiah, *Sri Lanka*; K.M. de Silva, *Managing Ethnic Tensions in Multiethnic Societies: Sri Lanka 1880–1985*, Lanham, 1986; A.J. Wilson, *The Break-up of Sri Lanka*, London, 1988; see also Nissan and Stirrat, this volume.

8 E. Said, *Orientalism*, London, 1978; R. Inden, 'Orientalist constructions of India', *MAS*, 1986, vol. 20, pp. 401–446.

9 Cf. L. Perera, 'The Pali chronicle of Ceylon', in C.H. Phillips (ed.) *Historians of India, Pakistan, and Ceylon*, London, 1961; H. Bechert, 'The beginnings of Buddhist historiography; *Mahavamsa* and political thinking', in B.L. Smith (ed.) *Religion and the Legitimation of Power in Sri Lanka*, Chambersburg, 1978.

10 For examples of 'popular historical consciousness' see, e.g. P.E.P. Deraniyagala (ed.) *Sinhala Verse (Kavi)*, Colombo, 1955, vol. 3, pp. 211–12; E.R. Leach, *Pul Eliya – A Village in Ceylon*, Cambridge, 1961, p. 21; M.S. Robinson, 'The house of the mighty hero or the house of enough paddy? Some implications of a Sinhalese myth', in E.R. Leach (ed.) *Dialectic in Practical Religion*, Cambridge, 1968. More general discussions can be found in R. Gombrich and G. Obeyesekere, *Buddhism Transformed. Religious Change in Sri Lanka*, Princeton, 1988, pp. 440–443; E. Nissan, *The Sacred City of Anuradhapura: Aspects of Sinhalese Buddhism and Nationalism* Ph.D. thesis, London, 1985, pp. 322–356; *idem*, 'History in the making: Anuradhapura and the Sinhala Buddhist nation', *Social Analysis* (forthcoming). The argument presented here owes a great deal to Nissan's approach.

11 K. Malalgoda, 'Millennialism in relation to Buddhism', *CSSH*, 1970, vol 12, p. 436.

12 R.L. Stirrat, 'The riots and the Roman Catholic church in historical perspective', in Manor, *Sri Lanka*.

13 V. Samaraweera, 'The Muslim revivalist movement, 1880–1915', in M. Roberts (ed.) *Collective Identities, Nationalisms and Protest in Modern Sri Lanka*, Colombo, 1979; cf. Rogers, this volume.

14 The term 'political class', while vague, has proved useful in recent discussions of Sri Lankan politics; e.g. E. Meyer, 'Seeking the roots of the tragedy', in Manor, *Sri Lanka*; M.P. Moore, 'The ideological history of the Sri Lankan "peasantry"', *MAS*, 1989, vol 23, pp. 179–207.

15 T. Nairn, 'The modern Janus', in *The Break-up of Britain*, London, 1981, p. 340.

16 J. Russell, *Communal Politics under the Donoughmore Constitution, 1931–1947*, Dehiwela, 1982.

17 Wriggins, *Ceylon*; D. Peiris, *1956 and After. Background to Parties and Politics in Ceylon Today*, Colombo, 1958; Nissan and Stirrat, this volume.

18 Moore, 'Ideological history'; Brow and Woost, this volume.

19 On the importance of 'place' as an aspect of belonging in Tamil culture elsewhere see E.V. Daniel, *Fluid Signs. Being a Person the Tamil Way*, Berkeley and Los Angeles, 1984.

20 E. Gellner, *Nations and Nationalism*, Oxford, 1983, p. 56.

21 P. Wright, *On Living in an Old Country. The National Past in Contemporary Britain*, London, 1985; T. Nairn, *The Enchanted Glass. Britain and its Monarchy*, London, 1988.
22 Tambiah, *Sri Lanka*, p. 140.
23 Malalgoda, 'Millennialism'.
24 Tambiah, *Sri Lanka*, p. 140.
25 Social Scientists' Association, *Ethnicity and Social Change in Sri Lanka*, Colombo, 1984 [hereafter *ESC*]; Committee for Rational Development, *Sri Lanka: the Ethnic Crisis*, Delhi, 1984.

PART I

Colonialism, history and racism

Chapter two

The generation of communal identities[1]

Elizabeth Nissan and R.L. Stirrat

Introduction

Communal violence in Sri Lanka often appears to have an ancient history. Sinhala and Tamil communities in Sri Lanka both tend to view their relationship in terms of histories which stretch back for at least 2,500 years. These histories buttress the opposing territorial claims of the two communities, and make conflict between them seem inevitable. For Sinhala, history justifies their claim to impose their rule over the whole island of Lanka. For Tamils, too, history is used to justify demands, in the past for a degree of autonomy for Tamil-dominated areas, and today for total separation from the Sinhala-dominated parts of the country. Yet when we look at the shorter historical term at least, we find that during the colonial period violent clashes erupted between groups defining themselves in terms of religious affiliation but not between groups defining themselves as Sinhala and Tamil.[2] How, and why, did these different understandings of the past come into being?

Our primary contention is that different state forms depend upon, and generate, different senses of collective identity. Nationalist identities in Sri Lanka have only recently begun to be considered in their wider historical context even though such an approach is familiar to students of nationalism more generally. Understanding of communal conflict in Sri Lanka has been hindered by the unwarranted and anachronistic imposition of the dominant political identities of the present day on to the past. It is necessary to examine changing state formations if we are to begin to understand why it is that political conflict now takes the form that it does. Broadly, we need to examine the processes by which a nation-state was created in Sri Lanka out of the kingdoms of the past in order to understand the nature of present-day political identities. Too often kingdoms and nation-states are conflated in both popular and academic literature on this subject.

Views of the past

Let us first briefly outline dominant Sinhala and Tamil representations of the past. In general, Sinhala people claim that even if they were not the first inhabitants of the island, a status they allow to the 'primitive' Veddas, they were at least the first 'civilized' settlers of Lanka. They claim to be descended from north Indian Aryan ancestors who spoke an Indo-European language which developed into Sinhala. Prince Vijaya, the mythical ancestor of the Sinhala people, and his followers are said to have arrived on the shores of Lanka on the day of the Buddha's death; but even before Vijaya's arrival, Lanka had a close relationship with the Buddha. According to the island's ancient chronicle histories, the Buddha had visited the island on a number of occasions and had announced that in Lanka his 'doctrine should ... shine in glory'.[3] However, the Sinhala were only converted to Buddhism in the third century BC by Mahinda, son of the great Indian emperor Asoka, during the reign of King Devanampiyatissa. Since then, so it is claimed, they have with few exceptions always been Buddhist. During the Anuradhapura period (circa third century BC – ninth century AD), a great Sinhala-Buddhist civilization flourished in Sri Lanka. This state was continually under pressure from South Indian Tamil-speaking Hindus; one in particular, Elara, ruled Anuradhapura for over forty years in the second century BC until he was defeated by the heroic Sinhala-Buddhist, King Dutugämunu. Eventually, pressure from the Tamil invaders forced the Sinhala to retreat southwards, first to Polonnaruwa, then to various other capitals until the last phase of Sinhala independence, which centred on Kandy. The Kandyan kingdom was eventually ceded to the British in 1815. Some of the Tamil invaders of earlier times stayed in Lanka and their descendants form the communities of Tamils in northern and eastern Sri Lanka today. But, the Sinhala claim is that these Tamil communities never, or only rarely, formed separate political entities. Rather, once settled in Lanka they accepted the suzerainty of the Sinhala kings.

Not surprisingly, the Tamil version of the past is somewhat different. In its 'soft' version it is admitted that Sinhala people were settled in Lanka long before the Tamils arrived. But, it is argued, Tamils have lived in Lanka for at least 1,000 years, and formed their own autonomous political units independent of Sinhala control. Satchi Ponnambalam, for example, claims that the original inhabitants of Lanka were really Tamil; that the Sinhala were originally Tamils who converted to Buddhism and adopted Sinhala, a language based on Pali, the language of the Buddhist texts; and that much of what Sinhala people now uphold as monuments of their past greatness was actually produced by Tamil artistry.[4] The historical arguments are endless, but as it is the Sinhala who are politically dominant in the island, so too it is Sinhala history which sets the terms of the debate.

Despite the fact that these two histories are opposed versions of the past, each stressing the claims of the community which generates it, they share many features in common. Both present the past in terms of the interaction of two opposed entities, Sinhala and Tamil, who have always been as separate as they are today. Second, they consist of arguments over events which allegedly occurred between the fourth century BC and the tenth century AD. Third, they present the two communities as historically and continuously opposed through warfare, joining an ancient past to the present with no regard for the hiatus of centuries. Fourth, the histories are both concerned with a 'national people's' claim to its own territory. Finally, each side presents the other as little more than barbarians. Both sides in the present political context back up their respective claims through the selective use of histories and through the selective and competitive use of archaeological evidence. Factions on each side have been willing to destroy, or reinterpret, evidence which would support the other party. Differing maps are produced which purport to show the distribution of Sinhala and Tamils in Lanka during past centuries.

Equally striking is the fact that several assumptions which underlie popular representations of the past are also found in many academic writings on Sri Lanka.[5] Thus political scientists such as Kearney, sociologists such as Moore, anthropologists such as Obeyesekere and Roberts, and historians such as de Silva and Samaraweera all in one way or another accept the essentials of the popular view of the last two millennia of the island's history; in effect they assume that in the past, as today, Sri Lanka has been dominated by two exclusive groups, Sinhala-speaking Buddhists and Tamil-speaking Hindus.[6] Thus Obeyesekere, writing of the period prior to the sixteenth century claims that,

> there were historically two major opposed ethnic identities, Sinhalese and Tamil. The historical conflicts between Sinhalese and South Indian invaders reinforced and stabilized the Sinhala-Buddhist identity ... Sinhalese people could be mobilized by their rulers to fight foreign invaders ... the myths became, on occasion, rallying points for Sinhalese nationalism.[7]

In a more extreme vein, Bechert argues that 'a form of nationalism was developed in ancient Ceylon which was very close to modern nationalism with its conceptions of a united nation with common linguistic, cultural and religious traditions'.[8] Similarly, Rahula sees Dutugämunu's victory over the Tamil king Elara in the second century BC as, 'the beginning of nationalism among the Sinhalese. It was a new race with healthy young blood.'[9]

Whilst many of these writers accept that the boundary between the Sinhala and Tamil groups has not been impermeable historically, with some south Indian immigrants having gradually become Sinhala,[10] the two polar identities are nevertheless assumed to have existed as 'nations' in similar form throughout the centuries, and to have been related through opposition and conflict. In such work, the way in which different state forms depend upon, and in turn generate, different kinds of identity remains unremarked; and because of this theoretical lacuna it has been possible for the dominant political identities of the present day – identities which we argue have been generated in part by the form of the modern Sri Lankan state – to be imposed upon the past without recognition of their historical specificity.

This point can be illustrated with reference to the work of the eminent historian of Sri Lanka, K.M. de Silva, who has attempted to correct many popular biases in his account of the Anuradhapura period. The Anuradhapura kingdom, de Silva argues, was a fairly weak feudal state, in which there was constant tension between centrifugal and centripetal forces. Nevertheless, de Silva takes for granted the existence of two distinct racial groupings on the island – Dravidian Tamils and Indo-Aryan Sinhala. And even if he is careful to argue that 'Sinhala' did not necessarily equate with 'Buddhist' at this early time, nor 'Tamil' with 'Hindu', he still seems to assume that an Indo-Aryan racial grouping, the Sinhala, was in some way opposed to a Dravidian grouping, the Tamils. Thus his first chapter, entitled 'Colonizers and Settlers', contains the following sub-sections: 'the Aryan colonization', 'Buddhism' and 'the Dravidian influence'. Despite his claim that 'ethnicity was not an important point of division in society in Sri Lanka in the [Anuradhapura] period ..., and it would seem that neither the Sinhala nor the Tamils remained racially pure',[11] it remains unclear just what categories were important in the polity if not these, for his account is structured according to precisely these modern-day racial terms. Their applicability is not questioned.[12]

Anomalies in Sri Lankan history: the pre-colonial state

Because much of Sri Lankan history is written from a partisan Sinhala or Tamil point of view, it is often difficult to disentangle the historical evidence from the nationalist framework imposed upon it. But it does seem that prior to the nineteenth century the ideal congruence of race, language, religion and political territory assumed in nationalist discourse was not clear-cut. Indeed, at times the situation was, by today's terms of reference, very muddled. Several examples can be used to show how the imposition of national categories on to the past produces apparent anomalies which are resolved when a different view of the pre-colonial state is adopted.

1 The great historical centres of Sinhala-Buddhist civilization are Anuradhapura and Polonnaruwa. Today these centres are popularly treated by Sinhala people as being purely the result of Sinhala-Buddhist enterprise. Yet there is inscriptional evidence of Tamil-speaking groups living in such centres; Tamil-speaking soldiers were crucial elements in the armies of the Sinhala kings, even acting as guards for the Temple of the Tooth in Polonnaruwa,[13] whilst architectural and sculptural evidence indicates strong linkages with south India and Tamil civilization, and probably the presence of south Indian craftsmen.

2 In Jaffna, which today is the heartland of Sri Lanka Tamils, there are both place names which are undoubtedly Sinhala in origin,[14] and Buddhist remains from the first millennium AD. Both these pieces of evidence are used by the Sinhala to claim that they have rights to control Jaffna, and not surprisingly Tamil activists occasionally destroy new-found archaeological evidence of such Buddhist antecedents. Yet we know that there were sizeable Buddhist-Tamil communities in south India at this period,[15] and if Sinhala place names can be used to claim Jaffna for the Sinhala then Tamil place names could be used to claim parts of what is now Sinhala Sri Lanka for the Tamils.[16]

3 In the coastal zones of south-western Sri Lanka today, the population is almost entirely Sinhala-Buddhist. In the revival of Sinhala-Buddhist culture in the late nineteenth century some of the most important activists were members of the Salagama, Durava and Karava castes.[17] Yet what evidence there is indicates that these groups are the descendants of immigrants from Hindu south India: from Kerala (Malayalam speakers) and Coromandel (Tamil speakers). Contact between the Sri Lankan littoral and south India seems to have been maintained until the nineteenth century, and these immigrant groups were only slowly 'Sinhalized'.[18] Indeed, even today some groups claiming to be Sinhala still use Tamil as their domestic language.

4 The last independent kingdom in Sri Lanka was centred on Kandy in the interior of the island, and only fell to the British in 1815. Although represented in modern Sinhala-Buddhist history as the refuge of indigenous Sinhala culture, Kandy was ruled in its last years by a dynasty of Tamil-speaking kings, the Nayakkars from Madurai in south India.[19] These kings maintained affinal links with south India, and do not seem to have suffered as a result.[20] It was

> under one of these kings that the Buddhist monastic order was revived, and they are said to have had to become Buddhist to be able to rule Sri Lanka. One of these kings, Kirti Sri Rajasinghe, is credited with the restoration of many Buddhist temples in the island, and is often upheld as the great Buddhist revivalist of his age. What is less often mentioned is that he is also credited with the restoration of some major Hindu temples, such as Munneswaram on the west coast. Again, some of the Kandyan chiefs who were signatories to the Kandyan convention (drawn up when the kingdom fell to the British) signed their names in Tamil script rather than Sinhala.[21] Some of the major Sinhala aristocratic families had south Indian immigrant forebears. There was anyway a sizeable Tamil-speaking population in the Kandyan kingdom whose presence is attested in present-day place names (e.g. Bamunugama, 'Brahmin village') and personal names (e.g. Hettiarachige, 'chief of the Chettis', a Tamil trading caste). Yet today people with such personal names living in such villages consider themselves fully Sinhala-Buddhist and would be horrified to be called Tamils.

Other examples could be given but the picture does not change. Pre-colonial and most of colonial Sri Lankan history does not conform to the model of two opposed nations imposed upon it by present-day Tamil and Sinhala rhetoricians.[22] For long periods of time groups which would now be characterized in terms of the Sinhala–Tamil divide lived more or less at peace with one another. There were dynastic wars; but Sinhala–Tamil communal violence dates from after Independence. This is not to say that there were no differences between groups of people living in the island: the point is simply that differences of language, custom and religion were made into something new by the devices of a modern state, as we will elaborate below.

Pre-modern and modern state formations

Models of the pre-modern state developed by theorists such as Anderson, Gellner, Stein and Tambiah help us understand historical material from Sri Lanka which, in terms of the dominant two-nation model of the island's history, often appears anomalous. From such work, the pre-modern states of south and south-east Asia, despite variations in detail, emerge as relatively loosely structured organizations built up on the bases of heterogeneity, relativity, and graduality, and on the ideal of the delegation of power from the centre.

Burton Stein's work on south India exemplifies such an approach. Stein, drawing on Southall's work on Africa, argues that the pre-modern state in South India is best conceptualized in terms of the 'segmentary state':

> The parts of which the state is composed are seen as prior to the formal state; these segments are structurally as well as morally coherent units in themselves. Together, these parts or segments comprise a state in recognition of a sacred ruler whose overlordship is of a moral sort and is expressed in an essentially ritual idiom.[23]

Earlier, he notes that,

> The scope of the constituent units of the state was limited to well defined and ethnic territories: its chiefs were, in most cases, leaders or spokesmen of the dominant groups of the local territory.[24]

Such a picture fits in, in a very general way, with what Gellner has to say in *Nations and Nationalism* about the nature of 'pre-industrial' or 'agrarian' society.[25] Gellner argues that in such societies there was no homogeneity of culture. Rather, society consisted of horizontally stratified ruling, administrative, and commercial classes over 'laterally insulated communities'; there was no ideal of congruence between cultural and political units; the stress was placed on cultural differentiation rather than on homogeneity.

In sum, what both Stein and Gellner, as well as other writers such as Anderson and Tambiah,[26] are describing is a state based on very different principles from those which underlie the modern nation-state. First, the pre-modern state was defined through its centre rather than by its boundaries. Power – often expressed in a ritual idiom – radiated out from the centre. When the centre was strong, its effective power extended further out; when it was weak, units and territories previously under its domination became autonomous or fell under the control of another centre. Boundaries, in Anderson's words, were 'porous and indistinct'; 'sovereignties faded imperceptibly into one another'.[27] By contrast, the modern state is territorially defined through ritualized boundaries which are recognized in international law, and which can only be crossed on the fulfilment of legally defined criteria.

Seen as ideal types, there are a number of significant features of the modern nation-state which can be contrasted with earlier state forms.

1 In contrast to the pre-modern state in which authority was legitimated from above – authority being passed down from the gods, or in Sri Lanka from the Buddha, through the king to lower mortals in a sort of 'great chain of being' – in the modern democratic state authority is ideally legitimated from below. In political theory, at least, the authority of the ruler ostensibly rests on the will of the people.

2 The pre-modern state consists of a series of dissimilar groups articulated about the centre, possibly in dissimilar ways. The modern state ideally consists of like individuals connected to one another and to the state in identical fashion. The space of the pre-modern state can be culturally, politically, and legally heterogeneous; that of the modern state is ideally homogeneous. Whilst in the pre-modern state the centre is stressed and made sacred by being hedged around with taboos, in the modern state boundaries are stressed and made the arena of taboo.

3 The problem of, and for, the modern state in terms of these principles is how 'homogeneous' is 'homogeneity', and what is to be judged significant and insignificant in assessing this homogeneity. This in turn raises the question of just what a 'nation' is, and of the relationship between 'nation' and 'state'.

Despite the claims made by many modern historians and ideologues, and despite the assertions made by various rulers at various times to be rulers of the whole island, it seems that the polity of pre-modern Sri Lanka was, at its most centralized moments, a series of semi-autonomous states owing certain ritual and material obligations to an overlord.

Second, and perhaps of most significance for our present purposes, ethnic, religious, and linguistic differences were not used as the bases for inclusion or exclusion from the polity.[28] At various times groups would speak alternative languages, adhere to alternative religions and claim alternative identities. The quasi-autonomous Vanniyar kingdoms, for example, which stretched in a broad band across north central Sri Lanka between the fourteenth and eighteenth centuries often consisted of Tamil-speaking Hindus; yet at various times they accepted the overlordship of the kings of Kandy.[29]

To sum up: in the pre-modern states of Sri Lanka, there could not have been signs of incipient Sinhala–Tamil conflict as understood today because these categories did not bear the nationalist connotations that they now bear. The 'state' of the past and that of the present are very different; only the latter is associated with the idea of the 'nation', an idea which is too often projected back in time. Our central concern in the remainder of this chapter is to examine why politics in Sri Lanka today has come to be dominated by the violent opposition between two groups – or 'nations' – defined with reference to linguistic and racial criteria, whose identities have emerged and become progressively polarized over the last 150 years or so.

The colonial experience

In 1796 the British took over the coastal regions of the island from the

Dutch. In 1815 they annexed the interior kingdom of the country and its centre, Kandy, uniting the island under one political authority. Great changes followed from this.

British interest in Sri Lanka was first aroused by its strategic significance in the Indian Ocean, but fairly quickly the country became an important arena for British commercial interests. Trade and commerce in the Portuguese and Dutch territories had been administered by the political authorities. The British, however, introduced an independent capitalist sector, particularly in coffee and, later, tea estates. One of the results of the growth of the estate sector was the arrival of large numbers of south Indian Tamil labourers, of whom we shall say more later. Another result was the construction of a system of roads primarily designed to serve European commercial and strategic interests. Other innovations, of equal importance, derived as much from ideological commitment as from capitalist imperatives. The British colonial authorities in Sri Lanka were committed to the liberal values of nineteenth-century Britain and believed themselves to be involved in a civilizing process. The introduction of ideas about the individual, about rights in private property, and about the various aspects of modern society which Weber referred to as bureaucratization and rationalization were all parts of this process.

Yet at the same time, in Sri Lanka as in India, the British recognized that they were dealing with a heterogeneous situation. They were faced with people speaking a variety of languages, wearing a number of costumes, and following different religions. The colonial government recognized customary variations in certain contexts, and allowed differences of practice to continue. Such heterogeneity posed both intellectual and pragmatic problems.

Intellectually, the problem of the social variety found in Sri Lanka in the nineteenth century was simply dealt with by interpreting it in biological terms: different groups in Sri Lanka were, it was argued, different races and different races had different customs. Language, religion, custom and clothes were taken in various combinations as markers of racial variation.[30] The result was that by the end of the nineteenth century a large number of distinct 'races' were recognized by the authorities in colonial Sri Lanka. Besides the Tamils and the Sinhala, who were further divided into 'Up Country' and 'Low Country' Sinhala, and 'Ceylon' and 'Indian' Tamils, there were also 'Moors' (i.e. Muslims, again divided into Ceylon Moors and Coast Moors), Veddas, Burghers (divided into Dutch and Portuguese Burghers), Malays, Eurasians and Europeans. Furthermore, other groups were also considered 'races' at times: the Mukkuvars, the Vagga, the Rodiya and so on.[31]

However many races may have been recognized at various times, only a few racial categories became politically significant. Recognition of difference is one thing, but what is important is the kind of practical significance that these perceptions came to have, the ways in which difference became formally instituted in legal and political procedures, and the effects of such institutionalization on the nature of the groupings themselves. These differences were instituted slightly differently in the colonial legal system than they were in the political system, in that more groupings were given legal recognition at the level of family law (which was to follow each group's customary practice) than were granted the right to political representation. Sir Alexander Johnston, for instance, collected information on the customary laws of the Tamils of Jaffna, the Mukkuvars in different parts of Batticaloa and Trincomalee, the Colombo Chetties, the Tamils of Puttalam, the Parawas and the Parsees. He also collected information on Kandyan Sinhala law, but could not do so for Low-Country Sinhala. The Low Country had been governed under Roman Dutch law, and this was continued under the British (although it did not apply to Hindus or Muslims living in these areas).[32]

The decision to institute customary practice in the legal system, of course, did not mean that in this area there was no change, for each group's 'custom' had now to be codified once and for all in a manner that substantialized and reified custom, making it less responsive to circumstance. Codification also reified the group to which the particular law applied. This involved a radical change. Under British rule Kandyan law, for instance, was first applied on a territorial basis to all those who lived within what was defined as Kandyan territory, whatever group they belonged to. European racial theory, which conflated assumed biological characteristics with customary law, soon gained dominance over this territorial principle, and Kandyan law became a personal law, applicable only to those who were deemed Kandyan Sinhala by biological descent. Thus a 'racial' category was created in a new way.

It is significant that the British again chose to organize political representation on a racial basis. In 1833 a common administration for the whole island was set up, consisting of government by the Governor and Legislative and Executive Councils. Three unofficial members of the Legislative Council were to be natives nominated by the Governor, who chose one Low-Country Sinhala, one Burgher and one Tamil. In 1889 two more unofficial members were added to represent the Kandyan and the Moor communities. Thus from the beginning, political representation at national level was instituted by the British on a communal basis.

The constitution of the Legislative Council was altered several times in the next few decades, but the principle of some degree of communal representation remained. In 1910 provision was made for the election of four unofficial members, two of whom were to be European, one

Burgher, and one 'educated Ceylonese' from whatever community. Six more unofficial members were nominated on a racial basis: two Tamil members, two Low-Country Sinhala, one Kandyan and one Muslim. Wider electoral principles were introduced in 1920, when 16 out of 24 unofficial members were to be elected. In 1923 the Council was again changed, and a territorial principle of representation introduced. Out of 37 unofficial members, 23 were to be elected to represent territorial constituencies, while 11 would be elected to represent specially created communal electorates. Three more would be nominated.

Although communal representation had been supplemented by other kinds of representation in the 1920s, it had remained an important political principle for one hundred years. This changed in 1931, when a new constitution based on the recommendations of the Donoughmore Commissioners was brought into being which abolished communal representation in favour of territorial electorates. Although the commissioners suggested means by which communal interests might be protected, these recommendations were ignored by the colonial authorities.[33]

Of equal importance in the long term was the administrative division of the island according to language. Areas with a predominance of Sinhala speakers were administered in Sinhala whilst areas with a predominance of Tamil speakers were administered in Tamil. Most schools used one or other of the vernacular languages, but a small élite was educated in English. The importance of this administrative distinction is reflected in the fact that the boundaries of 'ancient Tamil Eelam' follow the administrative boundaries of the colonial era with uncanny exactness.[34]

By the end of the nineteenth century there was a major paradox at the heart of the Sri Lankan polity. On the one hand all citizens in Sri Lanka were to be treated equally: the island was subject to one set of rules and one set of governors; in terms of citizenship, all should be equal. Yet at the same time, British rule substantialized heterogeneity, formalizing cultural difference and making it the basis for political representation. This should not be interpreted as the manifestation of a wish to 'divide and rule'; it was done out of misguided 'liberal' sentiments which sought to protect the different customs of different 'races'. British policy was deeply influenced by the racial theory that had developed from the relationship between contemporary studies of language, etymological and historical, and of evolutionary theory. The 'Aryan Myth', as Poliakov has called it, had a particularly strong hold in European thought of the period, and in Indology.[35] In England in particular the myth of Anglo-Saxonism, in which exclusivity was stressed, had developed from the time of the Reformation. It is associated with the rise of England as a nation-state, and its subsequent spread in empire – justified in part by ideas of inherent Anglo-Saxon superiority over other races, and by the idea of the civilizing mission.[36]

European scholarship on Sri Lanka (as on other colonies) was structured by these interests, too, and they conditioned colonial historiography. 'Aryans' (Sinhala) came to be opposed in absolute terms to 'Dravidians' (Tamils) historically. Language and race were conflated, so that eventually the smaller 'races' mentioned earlier as being recognized by the British as separate entities were subsumed into the Tamil–Sinhala divide. By 1922, for example, it was ruled in court that Low-Country Sinhala and Kandyan Sinhala 'did not belong to different races but the same race'.[37]

The generation of identities

British ideas form only part of the story. Of more importance in the long run was how the political identities of the Sinhala and the Tamils came into being, how these groups came to represent the differences between themselves, and how these ideas were used.[38] It is important to remember that there was no moment when all Sinhala or all Tamils finally realized that they were a separate 'race' or a unified 'nation'. Such ideas are always in a state of 'becoming', continually in process. Although the discussion which follows is mainly concerned with the Sinhala side of the story, much the same kind of process took place amongst the Tamils; indeed, part of the process involves the reactions of each side to the other. We may seem only to emphasize the Sinhala side of this story, but it should be remembered that it is paralleled among the Tamil community.[39]

Today, ideas about 'Sinhala-ness' centre around four main themes.

1. That the Sinhala share a certain biological nature; that they are a 'race'. The unity of the Sinhala is now asserted over and above Low Country/Up Country or caste differences. Indeed, the 1981 census was the first to treat the Sinhala as a unity. Although respondents had been classified in separate Up Country and Low Country categories by the enumerators, this division was not maintained in the published records. No such unification of the Tamil population was effected in this census.
2. That one manifestation of this biological community is the sharing of a common language.
3. That 'true Sinhala' also share a common religion: they are Buddhist.
4. That the island of Sri Lanka is in its entirety the land of the Sinhala and of Buddhism: it is the Sinhala-Buddhist nation. The biological

people, its language, religion, culture and territory are all intimately linked.

In their present configuration these elements of Sinhala-ness first developed amongst certain Low Country groups during the course of the nineteenth century. By the early twentieth century they had gained currency within intellectual and radical circles in the country at large, and since then they have spread to become dominant throughout the country.

In the late eighteenth and early nineteenth centuries there was a revival of interest in Buddhism, particularly in the coastal areas south of Colombo.[40] In part, this revival involved matters of caste status. The monastic order was at that time monopolized by members of the Goyigama caste, the highest caste in Sri Lanka; others could not be ordained. In response, members of the Karava, Salagama and Durava castes, all active in trade and commerce, introduced new lines of ordination from south-east Asia, claiming a prestige for their castes equivalent to that of the Goyigama. The new monks were upheld as exemplars of pure practice, whilst their Kandyan Goyigama counterparts were castigated for indolence and corruption.

By the middle of the century, however, new factors were at work. Part of the cultural baggage of British rule included the missionaries, who engaged in increasingly hostile attacks on Buddhism. The Buddhist monks did not counter-attack at first, but in the latter half of the nineteenth century they participated in a series of public debates with missionaries, again in the coastal areas. Between 1883 and 1915 there was also a series of violent clashes between groups of people defined in religious terms in which a few deaths occurred, although the prime objects of attack were 'sacra'.[41] These clashes were usually over ritual precedence and the demarcation of sacred space, but they also expressed tension between the ruled and the rulers; between the indigenous religions of Buddhism and Hinduism, and the imported religions of Islam and Christianity.[42] None of the clashes of the colonial era, however, involved violence between Buddhists and Hindus, and the violence was of a different nature to that found today. The conflict should not be seen as a forerunner of the communal violence between Sinhala and Tamils which has appeared since 1956.[43]

The revival of Buddhism in Low-Country Sri Lanka in this period was not just opposed to the old élite, but became an important form of assertion against the alleged superiority of British civilization. However, the stress placed on Buddhism was only part of a wider front of cultural assertion which also included race and language. If the British saw themselves as members of a superior race, with a superior language and a superior civilization based on Christianity, then the critique of the British focused on these same themes. Indeed, western (and particularly British) categories formed the framework in which these groups worked out their Sinhala-ness and their Buddhist-ness. They used organizational forms borrowed from the western missionaries, such as the Young Men's Buddhist Association, and developed a 'protestant' form of Buddhism, a Buddhism which western intellectuals deemed to be 'proper' and 'original', shorn of syncretic trappings.[44]

Another important area of western influence involved ways of looking at the past, at history. In the latter part of the nineteenth century, the British began to open up the Dry Zone area of Sri Lanka, which had been the seat of the ancient kingdoms of the island. Archaeological interest was kindled in the area with the discovery of the extensive remains of ancient civilization in the jungle. Archaeology proceeded alongside investigation of the written chronicles of the island, chronicles dating back 1,500 years, written by Buddhist monks and telling primarily of royal exploits in relation to Buddhism. The physical remains became a testament to the historicity of the chronicles.[45] Where British archaeology and Orientalist scholarship saw itself as disinterested, as involving pure and scientific scholarship, it also provided grist for the Sinhala activist mill. Sinhala activists could now claim that when the British were dressing in skins and covering themselves in woad their own ancestors were producing a high civilization. The stress on Buddhism found in the chronicles was eagerly taken up by Sinhala activists, but there was also a rediscovery of 'pure' language, of the history of Sinhala, and of its relation to the 'Aryan' race. Such a process was not limited to the Sinhala. It occurred in parallel amongst the Tamils, who also discovered a great national civilization in the past, and stressed a modernized form of Hinduism and their language.[46] But at this time the developing Tamil and Sinhala identities were not in direct competition; they were primarily directed against, and mediated by, the British. It was only later, after Independence, that the British were to be replaced by the Tamil as the 'dangerous other' implied in much of the self-conscious proclamations of Sinhala identity and community.

The growth of conflict

During the first half of the twentieth century, two main political and economic processes interacted with the growing sense of Sinhala and Tamil identity to set the stage for communal violence after Independence: the spread of the franchise and the increasing frequency of major economic problems.

Earlier, we mentioned how the British in the nineteenth century had appointed representatives of the Sri Lankans on a communal basis. In the years between the First World War and Independence in 1948, there were several Commissions of Enquiry concerned with the extension of the franchise. The same problem recurred throughout the discussions of these Commissions: whether or not there should be some sort of communal provision built into a system of universal franchise.[47]

The British by now saw 'communalism' in politics as retrogressive, and preferred a constitution based broadly on the Westminster pattern, which would ignore the issue of sectional representation. Sinhala people tended to support a widening of the franchise on the basis of 'one person, one vote', the system the British now favoured. In such a system, given their numerical majority, Sinhala interests would be secure. Not surprisingly, the minority Tamils saw such a system as necessarily discriminatory, and so they continually demanded an electoral system which would protect the 'rights' of the minorities. Eventually, they asked for some sort of federal system based on communal representation. Communal representation had earlier provided the basis for membership of advisory bodies to the government, firmly establishing 'Tamil-ness' and 'Sinhala-ness' as basic political identities.[48] During negotiations over successive constitutions the Tamils therefore adopted a position which talked in terms of racial and cultural difference because they were in a minority. In contrast, the Sinhala could support a system much more in tune with the 'modern state' with its stress on homogeneity, equality of voting rights, the universal franchise and the rights of the individual irrespective of race or religion.[49] In creating a unitary state which rejected communal representation, the British hoped that the communal consciousness which saw such a constitution as inherently favouring the Sinhala would dissipate.

Yet if wranglings over the franchise forced Tamils into a more extreme communal position, in other spheres communalism was gaining support amongst Sinhala. In the nineteenth century large numbers of Indian Tamils had arrived in Sri Lanka to work on the estates, whilst smaller numbers migrated to Colombo and became important in certain industries, notably in the docks. Large numbers of Ceylon Tamils from the north had also moved south for work, particularly in business and in government service. In the 1920s and 1930s, when an increasing economic crisis brought about high levels of unemployment, sections of the Sinhala population believed that the problem would be resolved by getting rid of the Tamil interlopers, whether they were from India or from the north of Sri Lanka. By 1927 any unity the trade union movement might have had in Colombo, at least, had gone; Sinhala unionists unsuccessfully demanded the repatriation of Indian labour.[50]

Thus from around 1920 onwards communal tension increased. The ideologies generated by Sinhala and Tamil activists in the late nineteenth century gained wider currency. Sometimes total fantasy took over, as in the small Helese movement, which denied that the Sinhala were in any way related to the people of India.[51] What began as a series of claims by both Tamils and Sinhala against the British was transformed into claims directed against each other. While the British were present there was relative calm; but only eight years after Independence communal violence broke out between Sinhala and Tamils for the first time.

Independence and after

Sri Lanka became independent in 1948, and one of the first acts of the new government was to disenfranchise the estate (or Indian) Tamils. It was argued that they did not really belong to Sri Lanka, where they were only temporary residents, but belonged instead to India. This move was in part a response to the fact that in some Kandyan electorates the estate Tamils were numerically dominant, but it was also a matter of restricting the left-wing vote, for the Indian Tamils voted overwhelmingly for left-wing candidates. The Ceylon Tamils, like the Sinhala, saw the estate Tamils as foreigners, different from themselves, and did little to fight against their disenfranchisement.

In general, however, the country was ruled between 1948 and 1956 by a government which continued the policies developed under colonial rule. The official language of government was still English, and parliament was controlled by western-educated, western-orientated members of the élite. Between them and the electoral masses a growing gap developed.

Since the beginning of the century, ideas of the Sinhala nation promulgated by nationalists like Anagarika Dharmapala became increasingly popular throughout Sinhala society. The actual mechanisms by which these ideas were spread remain obscure: as yet there has been no relevant research on the ways that ideas of nation and state became dominant in rural, not to mention urban, Sri Lanka. All we can do is suggest certain channels of dissemination, and certain political conditions, which promoted the spread of such ideas.

First, there was the growth of the vernacular press. Sri Lanka has always had a high literacy rate, and newspapers became popular throughout the island. And as Anderson has argued, 'print capitalism' is of major importance in creating a sense of commonality, of linguistic community.[52] The spread of newspapers was in turn related to the expansion of education, both before and after Independence. Even under British rule the history of the island was presented as a history of conflict between the Sinhala and the Tamil races, dynastic conflicts being converted into communal images. Such a picture continued to be promulgated after Independence in more extreme ways.

Second, there was the widespread improvement of transport. Rail and road transport became cheaply available throughout the island, allowing large numbers of people to visit the historic centres of the island such as Anuradhapura and Polonnaruwa – places which were by now imbued with a sense of the Sinhala national past because of their importance, as royal capitals and Buddhist centres, in the island's chronicle histories.

But aspects of the island's political history were also important in fostering and promoting ideas of the Sinhala nation. There was a growing tension between a ruling élite and what might be called a 'rural élite' or an 'indigenous élite'; between the Colombo-based, English-speaking, westernized class from which the MPs and the top bureaucrats came, and the Sinhala-speaking, non-westernized class of the village teachers, small-time traders, ayurvedic physicians, monks and students. For the latter, the dreams of Dharmapala's nationalism held forth a promise of power and status, yet Independence had meant little more for them than the replacement of the British by British-educated 'brown sahibs'. It was to these groups, especially to younger monks, that the ideals of Sinhala Buddhist nationalism appealed most strongly. They were instrumental in the defeat of the United National Party (UNP) government in 1956.[53]

The UNP was defeated by the MEP ('People's United Front'), a coalition in which the Sri Lanka Freedom Party, led by S.W.R.D. Bandaranaike, was dominant. The MEP's success was broadly the result of its ability to mobilize local-level rural élites around a programme which promised that Buddhism would be restored to its rightful position in Sri Lanka, and that Sinhala would become the official language. Communal identity came to the forefront of the political campaign. The polity would be reclaimed for Sinhala-Buddhists; the official language policy would open access to all levels of the government.

The first riots broke out a few weeks after the election. The new government had quickly introduced a bill to make Sinhala the official language of the country, a bill with obvious repercussions on the position of Tamil speakers. One of the Tamil parties organized a *satyagraha* (non-violent protest) outside parliament which led to a clash with Sinhala-Buddhist extremists. Violence broke out in Colombo, and then spread to the Gal Oya area in the east of the country, where the previous government had moved large numbers of Sinhala settlers into a colonization scheme in a predominantly Tamil area.[54]

The next outbreak of violence, in 1958, was also sparked off by the language issue. Tamil activists in the north refused to incorporate the Sinhala 'sri' character on to vehicle number plates and began to paint it out on both private vehicles and on the vehicles of the Ceylon Transport Board. Sinhala activists retaliated, painting out Tamil language signs in Sinhala-dominated areas. A train carrying Tamils, who were thought to be on their way to a conference to discuss a further *satyagraha*, was ambushed and the passengers beaten up. Sinhala villagers in the vicinity of the ambush attacked local Tamil shopkeepers, and the rioting spread to Colombo and to other urban areas where Tamils were in the minority. In all, up to 400 people were killed and 12,000 made homeless, almost all of them Tamils.[55]

Two points should be noted about the violent outbursts of the 1950s. The clashes of 1956 and 1958 involved Sinhala and Ceylon Tamils; Indian Tamils were not drawn into the conflict. Second, the conflicts erupted over issues of language (the use of Sinhala or Tamil) and access to land.

From that time, for almost nineteen years there were no major outbreaks of violence between Sinhala and Tamils, although tension between the two groups continued to develop. The Sinhala argument was that the island was properly theirs; they formed the majority and their language should be the national language. As for land settlement, two arguments were advanced. First, because everyone was a citizen of Sri Lanka, anyone could settle in any part of the island. There were, according to Sinhala claims, no 'Sinhala' or 'Tamil' areas but just Sri Lanka. Alternatively, and with increasing frequency, the argument was advanced that the Tamils had taken over what were 'really' Sinhala areas of the island. The Tamils, on the other hand, argued that to make Sinhala the only official language of the island was to discriminate against Tamil, and that the settlement of Sinhala in Tamil areas was a deliberate effort to swamp the Tamils and to deprive them of their land.

During the post-Independence period the economy of Sri Lanka faced greater and greater problems. There was a short-lived boom associated with the Korean war, but with a rapidly growing population with increasing material aspirations, successive governments were unable to meet the demands of the voters. The economy became politicized with the nationalization of certain sectors, and more importantly as political parties and MPs began to control access to all sorts of resources: to objects, to finance, and to jobs. The institutions of the state were increasingly subsumed by the political machines and alliances of politicians; access to the resources of the state became a matter of access to politicians. One effect of this was that Tamils were effectively excluded from the channels through which resources were distributed. Particularistic ties between MPs and their followers became of utmost importance, and, in such a situation, for any MP representing a Sinhala area to allocate resources to a Tamil area was madness. Tamils became steadily more and more alienated from the state.

In 1970 a coalition consisting of various left-inclined parties led by the SLFP under Mrs Bandaranaike came into power. The victory of the

United Front (UF) marked a further shift in the nature of the Sri Lankan polity. It nationalized the estate sector early on, and as it did so increasing numbers of Sinhala obtained estate jobs, often through the patronage of MPs, and large numbers of Indian Tamils became redundant. Second, they introduced a complex system of quotas for entry into higher education.[56] These were ostensibly designed to favour rural backward areas of the country, but in practice they favoured Sinhala students over Tamil students. On an open system of entry to higher education, according to Sinhala arguments, Tamils had been disproportionately successful. The government also changed the constitution in 1972 (a move which the UNP repeated in 1978). In both cases, the life of the government in power was prolonged through constitutional change, but this was not the only effect. We would argue that the manipulation of the constitution encouraged those Tamils who were beginning to demand complete autonomy to press their claims; it demonstrated that the constitution was not immutable, that it could be manipulated for party political ends.

In 1976 the Tamil United Liberation Front (TULF) was formed and stood in the 1977 election on the platform of total independence for the Tamil-speaking areas of Sri Lanka.[57] Previously, the Tamil demand had been for some sort of parity with Sinhala, or at least for a system which would protect the rights of Tamils in Tamil areas. With the foundation of the TULF, however, it became clear that sizeable numbers of Tamils, particularly in the north of the country, had lost all hope that such concessions could be obtained.

In the 1977 election the UNP won a huge majority of seats and the TULF became the official opposition. Within a month of the election serious rioting broke out in many Sinhala-dominated areas where Tamils formed a minority. Rumours that Tamils had killed Sinhala in Jaffna appear to have spread in the south; a train running from Jaffna to Colombo was stopped half-way at Anuradhapura, where Tamil passengers were attacked and killed. Rioting then became widespread, almost always involving Sinhala attacks on Tamils.

After 1975 small groups of Tamil terrorists, commonly referred to as the 'Tigers', began to appear in the north of Sri Lanka. They focused their attacks on the representatives of the state in the north: on police, soldiers, government officials and government property. They also attacked those Tamils whom they considered to be collaborators with the Sinhala, such as UNP party men. In response, the government moved larger numbers of troops and police into the north and introduced such judicial measures as the Prevention of Terrorism Act, in part modelled on regulations used in the United Kingdom. By 1983 the army was allowed to shoot, kill and bury without the need for any inquest, although this power was subsequently withdrawn.

The next major outbreak of violence was in 1981. Large numbers of Sinhala police were moved to the north to supervise local government elections. After a shooting incident, the police went on the rampage in Jaffna, setting fire to areas of the town, and killing and looting. Jaffna library – the second largest library in Sri Lanka and the main library for Tamil material in the country – was burnt; its destruction was interpreted by Tamils as a deliberate attack on Tamil learning, culture and history. From Jaffna the rioting spread to the east coast where Indian Tamils, refugees from the events of 1977, were attacked. There was also trouble in the tea estates and surrounding areas, and in the Colombo suburbs. In at least one case a government MP was active in organizing the anti-Tamil attacks.

In 1983 a major outburst of retaliatory violence against Tamils occurred in the south after 13 soldiers had been killed in Jaffna. The armed services, the police and the thugs of the UNP were all involved in attacks against Tamils and Tamil property.[58] The Tamil guerrilla response has become increasingly severe since that time.

If we compare the violence of the 1950s with that of the 1970s and early 1980s we find several differences. The rioting of 1977 differed from that of the 1950s in two important respects. First, Indian Tamils – both in the estate areas and in towns – were subject to attack, particularly around Colombo. Previously only Sri Lankan Tamils had been attacked. Secondly, certain arms of the state were involved in the rioting: the police, for example, were actively involved in attacks on Tamils in various areas. A new situation was emerging in which certain sections of the Sinhala population were identifying Tamils of all varieties as threats to the state. So where there had once been limited violence between Sinhala and Sri Lankan Tamils, there came to be generalized violence between Sinhala and all Tamils no matter what their origin.

Further, the violence on both sides has become increasingly organized. On the Sinhala side the police, army and at least sections of the UNP became involved. On the Tamil side, guerrilla groups proliferated. At first they attacked particular military or state targets. Later they broadened their attacks to include Sinhala civilians more widely. In 1985, for example, a major attack was launched on Anuradhapura, by then the northernmost Sinhala stronghold, in which many Sinhala civilians were killed and the central Buddhist temple of the city – a temple closely associated with the history of the Sinhala-Buddhist nation – was attacked. In 1986 an Air Lanka aircraft was destroyed at Katunayake International Airport. The Tamil demand for a separate state, rather than for some degree of lesser autonomy, has become stronger as the scale and frequency of the violence has increased on both sides.

Prior to 1977 the ruling party – be it the UNP or the SLFP – generally attempted to reach a working compromise with the Tamil leadership, only to be faced with an opposition party which emotively accused it of 'selling out' to the Tamils, to the detriment of Sinhala interests.[59] For as long as the UNP and the SLFP formed the two dominant parties in the house, political wranglings over the issue were played out within the framework of Sinhala party politics. In 1977, however, the UNP victory overwhelmed the SLFP. For the first time a Tamil party confronted the ruling UNP as the official opposition. The SLFP was in no position to deflect attention away from this confrontation.

In recent years, and particularly since 1977, violence has become more common as a political resource – not just in inter-communal affairs but also in intra-Sinhala affairs – a trend which can be directly related to the dismal performance of the Sri Lankan economy over the last thirty years. As 'the Sinhala' and 'the Tamils' have become the dominant political identities within the country, competition for resources has tended to be seen as competition between these two groups. The Tamils of the north and east have tended to lose out in terms of access to economic resources – particularly of access to the fruits of major development projects – and the failure of the electoral and bureaucratic systems to channel resources to these areas has stimulated armed opposition against what is seen as the Sinhala, rather than the Sri Lankan, state.[60]

Summary discussion

We have argued that the kind of confrontation that we see today between Sinhala and Tamils in Sri Lanka is the outcome of processes set in motion during the colonial era. The unification of the island under British rule, the introduction of a unitary bureaucratic structure and the other appurtenances of the modern state, the import of basically western ideas about 'race' and its relation to 'nation', the development of communications, the impact of the mass media and of a state education system – all of these have combined to produce a situation in which two broadly defined 'communities' or 'nations' stand opposed as separate entities. However, we would not argue that nationalism was entirely imposed upon Sri Lanka from the outside. We see the process as one of interaction between colonizers and colonized, each with their own cultural practices, and each also acting on interests that were structured by the overarching relations of power. Thus it was that the British set the terms of reference by which national identity would be worked out without anticipating the consequences.

Very broadly speaking, we have argued that there is a fundamental difference between pre-modern polities such as those of pre-colonial Sri Lanka which were segmentary in nature, and modern nation-states which cannot contain heterogeneity so easily and which are more clearly bounded in both spatial and cultural terms, and that these differences have their effect on the ways in which political identities are constructed. Theorists on nationalism tend to be broadly divided between 'primordialists', who see ethnic identities as basically continuous through time and see nothing particularly new about the way in which nationalism articulates these identities, and 'modernists', for whom everything about national identity is a recent fabrication and illusion.[61] The history of Sri Lanka has generally been written in primordialist terms, with nationalist assumptions anachronistically applied to the past. To argue, as we do here, that a Sinhala national identity is relatively new seems controversial to many, who cite chapter and verse from very ancient chronicles or inscriptions which proclaim that Sri Lanka must be ruled by Buddhists to prove their point. In our view, looking at such material in this way does not constitute proof – this is precisely what nationalist rhetoricians themselves do. To understand this material we need to look at it in its historical context (a task which so far has not been adequately done). It seems unlikely that 'Buddhist' implied 'Sinhala' in its modern sense in earlier times. On the other hand present-day understandings of Sinhala identity and history are not simply totally new inventions designed to serve the interests of the modern state, and which could have been given almost any content. Present-day political identities have developed from old materials used in new ways as circumstances, ideas, and institutions have changed. Given European racial theory, which underpinned the colonial writing of the island's history, and given the kinds of historical material that were available in the island, there were certain parameters limiting the possible content of nationalist history. The use and re-use of old materials – of archaeological remains, of ancient chronicles and inscriptions – does provide some continuity with the past. But we should not allow continuity at this level to blind us to the fact that these materials are used in very different ways today; they have different connotations and meanings today, which we can only understand by looking at changing forms of the state, and the ways in which different communities are articulated into the wider polity.

Notes and references

1 This paper is a revised version of parts of our earlier 'State, Nation, and the Representation of Evil', *Sussex Research Papers in Social Anthropology* 1, 1987. An earlier version was read at the Centre d'Etudes de l'Inde et de l'Asie du Sud, Paris. We would particularly like to thank Eric Meyer and Michael Carrithers for their comments.

2 J.D. Rogers 'Social mobility, popular ideology, and collective violence in modern Sri Lanka', *JAS*, 1987, vol. 46, pp. 583–602; *idem, Crime, Justice and Society in Colonial Sri Lanka*, London, 1987, pp. 157–209.

3 *Mv*. 1. 20.

4 S. Ponnambalam, *Sri Lanka. The National Question and the Tamil Liberation Struggle*, London, 1983, p. 19.

5 A particularly virulent example of how present-day images of the past generate bitter academic conflict can be found in the debate between Gunasinghe and Pathmanathan; see P.A.T. Gunasinghe 'Review article of S. Pathmanathan's *Kingdom of Jaffna*', *Sri Lanka Journal of the Humanities*, 1978, vol. 4, pp. 99–112; S. Pathmanathan, 'The Kingdom of Jaffna – propaganda or history?', *Sri Lanka Journal of the Humanities*, 1979, vol. 5, pp. 101–125.

6 R. Kearney, *Communalism and Language in the Politics of Ceylon*, Durham, NC, 1967; *idem* 'Language and the rise of Tamil separatism in Sri Lanka', *Asian Survey*, 1978, vol. 18, pp. 521–534; M. Moore, *The State and Peasant Politics in Sri Lanka*, Cambridge, 1985; G. Obeyesekere, 'The vicissitudes of the Sinhala-Buddhist identity through time and change', in M. Roberts (ed.) *Collective Identities, Nationalisms and Protest in Modern Sri Lanka*, Colombo, 1979; M. Roberts, 'From southern India to Lanka', *South Asia*, 1980, n.s. vol. 3, pp. 36–47; *idem, Caste Conflict and Elite Formation*, Cambridge, 1982; K.M. de Silva, *A History of Sri Lanka*, Delhi, 1981; V. Samaraweera, 'The evolution of a plural society', in K.M. de Silva (ed.) *Sri Lanka: A Survey*, London, 1977.

7 Obeyesekere, 'The vicissitudes', pp. 282–3.

8 H. Bechert, 'The beginnings of Buddhist historiography: Mahavamsa and political thought', *Ceylon Studies Seminar*, Peradeniya, 1974, p. 7.

9 W. Rahula, *A History of Buddhism in Ceylon*, Colombo, 1956, p. 79.

10 For example, Obeyesekere, 'The vicissitudes'; Roberts, *Caste Conflict*; de Silva, *A History*.

11 Ibid., p.13.

12 The striking exception to these views of the past is the work of R.A.L.H. Gunawardana; see Gunawardana, this volume. Other useful reanalyses may be found in *ESC* and Committee for Rational Development, *Sri Lanka – The Ethnic Confict*, Delhi, 1984.

13 G.W. Spencer, 'The politics of plunder: the Cholas in eleventh century Ceylon', *JAS*, 1976, vol. 35, pp. 410, 416; *idem, The Politics of Expansion: The Chola Empire of Sri Lanka and Sri Vijaya*, Madras, 1983, p. 51.

14 S. Gnanaprakasar, 'Sinhalese place names in the Jaffna peninsula', *Ceylon Antiquary and Literary Register*, 1917, vol. 2, pp. 167–169; B. Horsburgh, 'Sinhalese place names in the Jaffna peninsula' *Ceylon Antiquary and Literary Register*, 1916, vol. 2, pp. 54–58.

15 S. Liyanagamage, 'A forgotten aspect of relations between the Sinhalese and the Tamils', *Ceylon Historical Review*, 1978, vol. 25, pp. 95–142.

16 K. Kularatnam, 'Tamil place names outside the Northern and Eastern Provinces', *Proceedings of the First International Conference of Tamil Studies*, Kuala Lumpur, 1968.

17 K. Malalgoda, *Buddhism in Sinhalese Society 1750–1900*, Berkeley, 1976.

18 Roberts, *Caste Conflict*, pp. 18–34.
19 L.S. Dewaraja, *The Kandyan Kingdom of Ceylon, 1707–1760*, Colombo, 1972.
20 There is some debate as to how far the risings against the Nayakkar kings of Kandy were inspired by anti-Tamil feeling (see Gunawardana, this volume). After the fall of Kandy to the British the pretenders to the throne claimed to be descendants of the royal family, i.e. Tamils, as part of their attempt at legitimation; see K. Malalgoda, 'Milennialism in relation to Buddhism', *CSSH*, 1970, vol. 12, p. 436.
21 S.J. Tambiah, *Sri Lanka. Ethnic Fratricide and the Dismantling of Democracy*, London, 1986, p.98.
22 Thus Obeyesekere's statement that, 'the existence of a Tamil kingdom in the North implied the existence of an ethnically homogeneous Tamil community in the sixteenth century' confuses the notion of a kingdom with that of a nation; Obeyesekere 'The vicissitudes', p. 292.
23 B. Stein, *Peasant, State and Society in Medieval South India*, Delhi, 1983, p. 23.
24 Ibid., p. 8.
25 E. Gellner, *Nations and Nationalism*, Oxford, 1983.
26 B. Anderson, *Imagined Communities*, London, 1983; S.J. Tambiah, *World Conqueror World Renouncer*, Cambridge, 1976; *idem*, 'The galactic polity: the structure of traditional kingdoms in S.E. Asia', in S. Freed (ed.) *Anthropology and the Climate of Opinion*, New York, 1977.
27 Anderson, *Imagined Communities*, p. 26.
28 Cf. C. Bayly, 'The pre-history of "communalism"? Religious conflict in India, 1700–1860', *MAS*, 1985, vol. 19, pp. 177–203.
29 For examples of the role of 'Sinhala' kings in patronage of Hindu temples see M. Whitaker, *Divinity and Legitimacy in a Temple of the Lord Kantan*, Ph.D. thesis, Princeton, 1986; S. Arumugam *Some Ancient Hindu Temples in Sri Lanka*, Colombo, 1980.
30 There was a contrast between how the British approached heterogeneity in Sri Lanka and how they approached it in India. In the latter, faith rather than race or language appears to have been more important; see F. Robinson, *Separatism among Indian Muslims*, Cambridge, 1974, p. 348.
31 The British had particular trouble with groups such as the Karava fishermen north of Colombo who spoke Tamil yet claimed to be Sinhala. Here the solution was to argue that they were originally Tamils who were becoming Sinhala, but it is equally possible to argue that they were 'really' Sinhala who had lost contact and come under Tamil influence. See R.L Stirrat, 'Some preliminary remarks on religious and ethnic identity in Sri Lanka', ms.
32 H.W. Tambiah, *Sinhala Laws and Customs*, Colombo, 1968.
33 T. Barron, 'The Donoughmore Commission and Ceylon's national identity', *Journal of Commonwealth and Comparative Politics*, 1988, vol. 26, pp. 147–157.
34 See for example the map in Ponnambalam, *Sri Lanka*, p. 258.
35 L. Poliakov, *The Aryan Myth*, New York, 1971.

36 H.A. MacDougal, *Racial Myth in English History*, Montreal, 1982; G. Newman, *The Rise of English Nationalism*, London, 1987.
37 Tambiah, *Sinhala Laws*, p. 83.
38 To paraphrase Hardy's comments about the creation of separate electorates for Muslims in India, whilst the British created the roles (of Tamil and Sinhala), they found the writing of the script then taken out of their hands; P. Hardy, *The Muslims of British India*, Cambridge, 1972, p. 167.
39 See Hellmann-Rajanayagam, this volume.
40 K.M. de Silva, *Social Policy and Missionary Organizations in Ceylon 1840–1855*, London 1965; Malalgoda, *Buddhism in Sinhalese Society*.
41 For references see Rogers, 'Social mobility'.
42 These Sri Lankan processes find parallels in India. During the nineteenth century, religious revival amongst both Hindus and Muslims grew apace. Furthermore, clashes centred around sacra, particularly the cow. As in Sri Lanka, the revival became closely associated with 'rising groups'. See Hardy, *Muslims*; K.W. Jones, *Arya Dharm*, Berkeley, 1976; J.R. McLane, *Indian Nationalism and the Early Congress*, Princeton, 1977; R. Tucker, 'Hindu traditionalism and nationalist ideologies in nineteenth century Maharashtra', *MAS*, 1976, vol. 10, pp. 321–348; R.G. Fox, 'Urban class and communal consciousness in colonial Punjab', *MAS*, 1984, vol. 18, pp. 459–489; S.B. Freitag, 'Sacred symbol as mobilising ideology: the North Indian search for a Hindu community', *CSSH*, 1980, vol. 22, pp. 597–625; G. Pandey, 'Rallying around the cow', in R. Guha (ed.) *Subaltern Studies*, Delhi, 1983, vol. 2; A.A. Yang, 'Sacred symbol and sacred space in rural India', *CSSH*, 1980, vol. 22, pp. 576–596.
43 Here we are relying on Bayly's distinction between religious conflicts, 'disputes over symbols, rites and precedents', and 'communal conflicts in which the broader aspects of a group's social, economic and political life were perceived as being unified and marked off from others by religious affiliation'; Bayly 'The pre-history', p. 179.
44 G. Obeyesekere, 'Religious symbolism and political change in Sri Lanka', *Modern Ceylon Studies*, 1970, vol. 1, pp. 43–63.
45 E. Nissan, *The Sacred City of Anuradhapura: Aspects of Sinhalese Buddhism and Nationhood*, unpublished Ph.D. thesis, London, 1985.
46 See K. Kailasapathy, *The Cultural and Linguistic Consciousness of the Tamil Community in Sri Lanka*, Colombo, 1982; K.M. de Silva, 'The religions of the minorities', in K.M. de Silva (ed.) *Sri Lanka. A Survey*, London, 1977; B. Pfaffenberger, 'The cultural dimension of Tamil separatism in Sri Lanka', *Asian Survey*, 1981, vol. 21, pp. 145–157; *idem*, 'Fourth world colonialism, indigenous minorities and Tamil separatism in Sri Lanka', *Bulletin of Concerned Asian Scholars*, 1984, vol. 16, pp. 15–22.
47 W.H. Wriggins, *Ceylon. Dilemmas of a New Nation*, Princeton, 1960; J. Russell, *Constitutional Politics under the Donoughmore Constitution 1931–1947*, Dehiwala, 1982.

48 It should be mentioned that the generation of a common Sinhala identity took time. In the 1920s there was still a sizeable number of Kandyan Sinhala demanding separate representation from Low-Country Sinhala and who also favoured a federal system of government; L.A. Wickremeratne, 'Kandyans and nationalism in Sri Lanka: some reflections', *CJHSS*, 1975, vol. 5, pp. 49–67; Russell, *Constitutional Politics*.
49 Russell, *Constitutional Politics*.
50 K. Jayawardena, *The Rise of the Labor Movement in Ceylon*, Durham, NC, 1972.
51 K.N.O. Dharmadasa, 'Language and Sinhalese nationalism: the career of Munidasa Cumaratunga', *Modern Ceylon Studies*, 1972, vol. 3, pp. 125–143.
52 Anderson, *Imagined Communities*.
53 Wriggins, *Ceylon*; P.T.M. Fernando, 'Elite politics in the new states; the case of post-independence Sri Lanka', *Pacific Affairs*, 1973, vol. 46, pp. 361–385.
54 For details see Kearney, *Communalism and Language*.
55 Ibid.; T. Vittachi, *Emergency '58*, London, 1958.
56 C.R. de Silva, 'Weightage in university admissions: standardization and district quotes in Sri Lanka, 1970–75', *Modern Ceylon Studies*, 1974, vol. 5, pp. 151–178.
57 The TULF was an amalgam of the Federal Party and the Tamil Congress which had previously competed for the Tamil vote.
58 G. Obeyesekere, 'The origins and institutionalisation of political violence', in J. Manor (ed.) *Sri Lanka in Change and Crisis*, London, 1984.
59 J. Manor, 'Sri Lanka: Explaining the Disaster', *The World Today*, 1983.
60 The recent rise of armed opposition to the state in the south cannot be considered here but may be related to similar factors. There was no general election from 1977 to 1989, and the government did not have the resources at its disposal to provide for all. Those outside channels of political patronage had no legitimate means of expressing their alienation and discontent. Since the 1987 peace agreement with India this alienation and discontent has found expression in the violent tactics of the JVP.
61 A.D. Smith, *The Ethnic Origins of Nations*, Oxford, 1986, pp. 7–13.

Chapter three

The people of the lion: the Sinhala identity and ideology in history and historiography

R.A.L.H. Gunawardana

The evolution of group identities and of ideologies associated with social groups represents one of the most fascinating areas of historical research. It is also one of the most exacting fields of study requiring of the historian an inordinate amount of caution. The historian who undertakes an inquiry of this type must constantly keep in mind that group consciousness, like all ideology, is historically determined and historically limited. The Sinhala ideology in its contemporary form, with its associations with language, race and religion, forms an essential part of contemporary Sri Lankan culture and has succeeded in thoroughly permeating such areas of intellectual activity as creative writing, the arts and historical writing. It is not an exaggeration to say that during the last hundred years the Sinhala ideology in its contemporary form has radically refashioned our view of Sri Lanka's past. Since many writers assume that the Sinhala ideology in its current form has a very old history, it may be relevant to point out that even in certain European languages the word race (Fr. *race*, Ital. *razza*) dates only from about the sixteenth century and that the biological definition of the term as denoting a group distinct from other members of the species by specific physiological characteristics is of still more recent origin. In both Sinhala and Tamil, it is difficult to find a satisfactory equivalent to this word. Hence it does not seem likely that racial consciousness can be traced back very far into the past of these two linguistic groups. Thus, when an author of popular historical writings speaks of the mythical Vijaya as having been anxious to find a queen 'of his own Aryan race' and further states that 'his pride of race revolted at the thought of any but a pure Aryan succeeding to the Government which he had striven so laboriously to found'[1] or when academic historians writing about ancient Sri Lanka refer to 'the Sinhala race,'[2] they are all presenting a view of the past moulded by contemporary ideology. These examples have been cited here to emphasize the need to re-examine this dominant and popular historical view, to go back to the original documents and to place the appearance of different types of group consciousness in their historical settings.

I

The Brāhmī inscriptions, which are the earliest historical documents in Sri Lanka,[3] reflect an initial stage in the growth of group consciousness. Perhaps the most important basis of group identity at this time was lineage. Individuals who set up inscriptions generally gave the names of their fathers or of both fathers and grandfathers, while some of them traced their paternal descent back for three or four generations. Some inscriptions, particularly those of the Brāhmaṇas, refer to the *varṇa* status of the authors. Occupations and socio-political status of donors are cited in many inscriptions. It is particularly noteworthy that in a significant number of records the terms *upāsaka* and *upāsikā* are used to describe the donors, reflecting the early beginnings of a religious identity. A few of the records point to other group identities like Kabojha, Milaka and Dameḍa. It is likely that Kabojha and Milaka were tribal groups. Paranavitana has suggested that Dameḍa was the equivalent of Tamil.[4] Whether the term was used in this period to denote a tribal, linguistic or some other group deserves careful investigation. The term Sinhala, on the other hand, is conspicuous by its absence.

The disparate nature of the earliest settlements on the island would not have been conducive to the development of strong group identities which brought together a large number of people into one cohesive unit. While lineage was perhaps the most important criterion from which people derived their social identity, socio-political position, *varṇa* or ritual status, religion and tribal affiliation were other factors which determined group identity at this primary stage of the development of group consciousness.[5] During the period from about the middle of the second century BC to about the second century AD Sri Lanka witnessed the unfolding of a crucial process of social change, bringing about the dissolution of communal property rights and the separation of the primary agricultural producers from elements essential for their livelihood. Parallel and related to this process was the evolution of a state apparatus which brought the whole island under the control of the rulers of Anurādhapura.[6] It is most likely that the emergence of the state brought with it changes in the ideological sphere, paving the way to a new group identity.

The term Sinhala (Pāli Sīhaḷa, Sanskrit Siṃhaḷa) occurs for the first time in Sri Lankan literary sources in the *Dīpavaṃsa*[7] which has been assigned to the fourth–fifth centuries AD. In this chronicle the term occurs only once, and here it is stated in this cryptic verse that the island was known as Sīhaḷa 'on account of the lion (*laṅkādīpo ayaṃ āhu sīhena sīhaḷā iti*). The term Sīhaḷadīpa or 'Sinhala island' occurs in the *Samantapāsādikā*,[8] the commentary on the Vinaya section of the Pāli Canon, written by Buddhaghosa in the fifth century AD. The text states that the earlier commentaries used by Buddhaghosa had been written in the language of Sīhaḷadīpa. Fa-Hian, who also visited the island in the fifth century, refers to it by the name 'the country of the lions.'[9] The term Heḷadivi, the equivalent of the Pāli Sīhaḷadīpa, occurs in one of the graffiti at Sīgiri which have been assigned by Paranavitana to a period extending from the eighth to the tenth century AD.[10] By the eighth century, the name was being used to denote a group of people, as is evident from an inscription found at a ruined monastic site in the Ratubaka Plateau in Central Java, which refers to the Siṃhaḷas.[11]

Though the earliest reference to the term Sinhala in Sri Lanka sources is in the *Dīpavaṃsa* there is evidence in other sources which suggests that the name can be traced back to an earlier date. In the Allahabad inscription of Samudragupta which has been assigned to the fourth century AD, there is a reference to Saiṃhaḷaka, obviously a name derived from Siṃhaḷa, among those who accepted the suzerainty of the Gupta emperor and paid him tribute.[12] Pelliot has drawn attention to the occurrence of a Chinese rendering of the name Sīhaladīpa in the literary works of the second and third centuries AD.[13] Three Brāhmī inscriptions from the far south of the Indian subcontinent, written in a language which has been identified as Tamil in its formative stages, are also relevant to this study. According to the reading presented by Subrahmanya Ayyar,[14] the term Īḻa is found in these three records. Some epigraphists do not accept his readings of the Ariṭṭāpaṭṭi and the Çittaṉṉavāçaḻ records, but they agree that the Tirupparankuṉṟam inscription refers to 'Īḻa householders' and that the term Īḻa should be identified as denoting Sri Lanka.[15] Ayyar suggested an early pre-Christian date for the record. Mahadevan[16] assigns it to the first–second centuries AD. He interprets the term *caiy-aḷan* in an inscription from Muttupaṭṭi assigned to the same period, as a reference to a person from Sri Lanka, but this translation is doubtful. The term Īḻa in all these records has been identified by epigraphists as denoting Sri Lanka. Īḻa denoted Sri Lanka in classical Tamil works.

Robert Caldwell, the nineteenth-century philologist, was one of the earliest scholars to suggest that the term would have been derived from the Pāli Sīhaḷa and the Sanskrit Siṃhaḷa and the suggestion has been accepted by the compilers of the *Tamil Lexicon* published by Madras University.[17] This view seems to be quite plausible since the *Çēntan Tivākaram*, one of the earliest lexicons in the Tamil language, equates Çiṅkalam with Īḻam.[18] If we accept this explanation of the origin of Īḻam, it would imply that the term Siṃhaḷa was also being used by the first or second century of the Christian era to denote a principality and certain types of people from that principality. If indeed the term Īḻam was derived from Sīhaḷa, its current use in politics reminds one of the observation made by Marc Bloch, the great medievalist, about the term 'Frenchman'. It is a historical irony that Gauls bear today a name derived from that of the Franks whom they considered to be their enemies. Bloch pointed out that this inappropriate and unfortunate name gave rise in later times, 'among the more reflective of our thinkers, to feelings of tragic anxiety'.[19]

It seems very likely that the beginnings of the Sinhala consciousness arose as part of the ideology of the period of state formation. It is only to be expected that an ideology which evolved during such a period would emphasize a sense of unity. However, state society in Sri Lanka was a society divided on the bases of class as well as lineage, clan, occupation, ritual status and political position. The chronicles give a fair idea as to how, in such a context, group consciousness developed and what form it assumed. The *Mahāvaṃsa* has been generally assigned to the sixth century AD, but it can be argued that it is a later work. In this chronicle the term Sīhaḷa occurs only twice. However, on closer examination it becomes clear that the sixth and the seventh chapters of the *Mahāvaṃsa* present a myth which forms a central element in the Sinhala ideology.

According to the myth, the daughter of the king of Vaṅga by a princess from Kaliṅga, runs away from home and joins a caravan heading for Magadha. On the way, in the Lāḷa country, the caravan is attacked by a lion who abducts the princess. From the union of the princess with the lion are born a son and a daughter, Sīhabāhu and Sīhasīvalī. When the children grow up, they flee with their mother from the lion's den and reach the frontier regions of their grandfather's kingdom. Here they are befriended by a kinsman who rules the frontier province. In his search for his offspring the lion ravages villages in the vicinity. Sīhabāhu kills the lion. On the death of his grandfather, he is offered the kingdom of Vaṅga, but he prefers to found a kingdom with a new capital city, Sīhapura, where he reigns with his sister as his queen. They have sixteen pairs of twins. Vijaya, the eldest, is of violent disposition. He and his seven hundred followers (*parivāra*) harass the people. When the enraged 'great men' (*mahājana*) of the kingdom demand that Vijaya be put to death, the king exiles his son, together with his followers. Their ship touches at Suppāraka, but as a result of their conduct, they are driven away again and they land in Sri Lanka.

On the day of their arrival in Sri Lanka the Buddha lies dying, but his thoughts are on the safety of Vijaya and his followers. The Buddha assigns Sakka to protect them, and the latter sends the God Uppalavaṇṇa to the island. Uppalavaṇṇa sprinkles charmed water on the men and ties sacralized thread (*parittasutta*) on their hands for their protection.

Kuvaṇṇā, a *yakkhinī*, lures the men to devour them but is foiled by the power of the thread. Vijaya overpowers and espouses Kuvaṇṇā and, with her help, massacres the *yakkhas* in the island to win over the kingdom. He rules from Tambapaṇṇi and his followers establish five other settlements: Anurādhagāma, Upatissagāma, Ujjeni, Uruvela and Vijitapura. The chronicle explains that the region where Vijaya landed and the island itself were known by the name Tambapaṇṇi because the hands of Vijaya and his followers turned red when they touched the earth. The chronicle also gives a definition of the term Sīhaḷa: 'The king Sīhabāhu, since he had slain the lion (was called) Sīhaḷa and, by reason of the ties between him and them, all those (followers of Vijaya) were also (called) Sīhaḷa.'[20] Since it is not possible to hold a consecration ceremony without a queen of *kṣatriya* birth, an envoy is sent to southern Madhurā to ask for the hand of the daughter of the Pāṇḍya king. The Pāṇḍya king sends his daughter, many other maidens and 'a thousand families of the eighteen guilds of workmen (*pessakārake*).'[21] On the arrival of the princess, Vijaya marries her after brusquely dismissing Kuvaṇṇā, and members of his retinue marry the other maidens from Madhurā. Vijaya is consecrated and rules for thirty-eight years at Tambapaṇṇi, and every year he sends pearls and chanks to his father-in-law at Madhurā. Kuvaṇṇā goes to Laṅkāpura, the city of the *yakkhas*, where she is killed by a *yakkha*. Her son and daughter flee to the Malaya region and live there 'with the king's assent' (*rājānuññāya*). The boy takes the girl to wife, and from them are sprung the Pulindas.

The story of Vijaya is found in the *Dīpavaṃsa* and it is evident from the comments in the *Vaṃsatthappakāsinī*, the commentary on the *Mahāvaṃsa*, that there was another version in the chronicle of the Abhayagiri monastery. The Vijaya story was certainly not the only 'colonization myth'[22] about Sri Lanka. The *Divyāvadāna* presents another story while the account of Hiuen Tsang cites two more. One of the stories cited by Hiuen Tsang (Hiuen Tsang I) is similar to the Vijaya myth. However, the earlier episodes take place not in and around Vaṅga but in south India. Further, it is the killer of the lion who is exiled as punishment for his parricide. He founds a kingdom on the island. 'Because the original founder got his name by catching a lion (chih-sse-tseu)', the myth explains, 'they called the country (after his name) Siṃhaḷa (Sang-kia-lo).'[23] In the second story (Hiuen Tsang II), which is basically similar to that in the *Divyāvadāna*,[24] Siṃhaḷa was the son of a great merchant of Jambudvīpa called Siṃha (Sang-kia). Siṃhaḷa comes to the island with five hundred merchants, looking for gems, and stays back to live in the company of *rākṣasīs*. When the merchants discover that they are about to be imprisoned by their paramours, they escape from the island with the help of a flying horse.

Siṃhaḷa is elected king in his own country, but he leads an expedition to the island and founds a new kingdom after vanquishing the *rākṣasīs*. 'Because of the king's name', the story states, 'the country was called Siṃhaḷa.'[25] Some analysts of these myths have drawn attention to similarities between certain elements in them and Buddhist stories like the Padakusalamānava, Sutana, Ghaṭa, Valāhassa and Devadhamma Jātakas, and it has been suggested that either the myths were influenced by the Jātakas or both groups were derived from a common source.[26]

The *Mahāvaṃsa* version of the Vijaya myth contains certain elements which are discordant with the myth of the visit of the Buddha that the same chronicle presents. During the first visit to the island, the Buddha is said to have expelled the *yakkhas* who lived in the island to Giridīpa, but Vijaya and his followers find a flourishing kingdom of the *yakkhas* in the island. However, the *Dīpavaṃsa* version of the Vijaya myth makes no mention of Kuvaṇṇā or of Vijaya's encounters with the *yakkhas* and is, therefore, consistent with the myth of the Buddha's visit. The discrepancy between the two main chronicles raises the problem of whether the *Dīpavaṃsa* deleted part of the Vijaya myth to present a more consistent account or whether those elements in the *Mahāvaṃsa* version relating to the presence of the *yakkhas* represent later accretions. The *Vaṃsatthappakāsinī* provides additional information about the *yakkhas* when it states that the chief of the *yakkhas* at Sirīsavatthu was Mahālālasena and that he married Polamittā, the daughter of the *yakkhinī* called Goṇḍā. The text also tells us that the two children of Kuvaṇṇā were called Jīvahattha and Dipellā.[27] However, it is not possible to consider these statements as indicative of the relative date of this part of the myth since it is not clear from the contexts whether the author of the *Vaṃsatthappakāsinī* is citing, as usual, information from the ancient Sinhala chronicle of the Mahāvihāra or whether he was merely drawing on the extended versions of the myth current in the oral tradition in his own time. The *Divyāvadāna* is more useful in this respect since it shows that a version of the myth which spoke of the presence of *yakkhas* at the time of the arrival of Siṃhaḷa was prevalent at the time *Dīpavaṃsa* was written.[28]

Most of the myths cited above present the view that the island was originally inhabited by the *yakkhas*, and in all these stories the attitude towards the *yakkhas* is one of hostility. In the *Dīpavaṃsa* the Buddha is the hero who vanquishes them, while in the *Divyāvadāna* and the Hiuen Tsang II version, it is Siṃhaḷa, the eponymous hero, who is credited with the achievement. It is likely that the two sets of myths were of independent origin and had a parallel existence. Evidently, the *Mahāvaṃsa* is presenting a combination of these two sets without paying heed to the resultant contradiction. We shall later see that the *yakkhas*, like the element absent from the *Dīpavaṃsa* version, i.e. the arrival of Vijaya's

bride from Madhurā, form an essential comp
message that the *Mahāvaṃsa* version of the n

In the geographical information in the my
seen pointers to the original homes of the imn
settled in the island. Barnett saw in them indicat
migration: one of Dravidians from Bengal and Oris
'mainly Aryan', from the western regions of India.[2
the rejection of the view that the Vijaya story wa
historical fact' but he tended to attach significance to
references.[30] He seems to have considered references
Madhurā as later accretions, but he detected in other in
he thought were allusions to the arrival of the first wave
from the western parts of India and of a second wave of
from the east. It is noteworthy that, though the *Mahāvaṃ*
Lāḷa as a region between Vaṅga and Magadha, several writers
both Barnett and Basham have identified it with Lāṭa on the
coast of India. Paranavitana was inclined to accept the same vie
attempt to trace 'the original home of the Aryan settlers'
north-western parts of India.[31]

However, while all the different versions of the myth reflect
may be called the 'immigrant mentality' of a dominant element of
population of Sri Lanka and their belief that they came from Ind
attempts at locating 'the original homes' on the basis of geographica
references in the myths would amount to confusing ideological statements with accounts of actual events. The discrepancies between different versions of the myths also point to the need for caution. The *Mahāvaṃsa* refers to Vaṅga, Kaliṅga, Lāḷa, Magadha, Suppāraka and Madhurā. The *Dīpavaṃsa* does not refer to Madhurā and gives Bharukaccha as a place visited by Vijaya on his way to Sri Lanka. On the other hand, Hiuen Tsang I locates the home of Siṃhaḷa in south India, whilst the *Divyāvadāna* presents Siṃhaḷa as a merchant from a kingdom called Siṃhakalpa and implies it was in Jambudvīpa. The Hiuen Tsang II version of the myth does not refer to any specific part of India, but merely states that Siṃhaḷa was from Jambudvīpa. As Mendis correctly detected, one of the main functions of the different versions of these 'colonization myths' seems to be to explain the origin of the name Sinhala (Siṃhaḷa). Some versions attempt to explain how the island came to be called by this name, while the *Mahāvaṃsa* version seeks to explain how the island came to be called Tambapaṇṇi and how a certain group of people came to be called the Sinhala. Mendis believed that 'Siṃhaḷa was originally the name of the island and the people got their names from it many centuries later.'[32] However, it has to be pointed out that such a sequence is not evident from the source material examined above, and, in fact, the information in the south Indian Brāhmī

ptions seems to preclude such an assertion. The writings of icritos, who accompanied Alexander to India, testify to the fact that obane or Tambapaṇṇi was the earliest historical name of the d.[33] Even in the second century AD Ptolemy referred to the island as probane, though he noted that it was also called Salike.[34] The *ahāvaṃsa* version of the Vijaya myth, it would thus appear, originally volved at a time when the island was still known as Tambapaṇṇi and a roup of people living there were called the Sinhala.

Evidently there were two distinct connotations of the term Sinhala. The long and detailed description of the origin of the ruling family presented by the myth carries the implication that it was the members of this lineage who were the real People of the Lion. This association of the term is also found in the later chronicle, *Cūlavaṃsa*. After describing the matrimonial alliance that Mahinda IV formed with Kaliṅga and his elevation of members of his lineage to high positions in the kingdom, the *Cūlavaṃsa* states that he thereby strengthened the Sinhala lineage (*Sīhaḷavaṃsaṃ*).[35] Obviously, the term is being used here to denote the ruling dynasty.

Basham and Obeyesekere have drawn attention to the elements of bestiality, parricide and incest in the myth.[36] While in certain versions of the myth there is no reference to an animal and Siṃha is merely the name of a man, in those versions where Siṃha is in fact a lion the relationship between the lion and the eponymous ancestor assumes a dual character. The latter is both 'the progeny of the lion' as well as 'the slayer of the lion'. It is noteworthy that the *Mahāvaṃsa* uses the term *ādinnava*, a very rare word, to describe this relationship. The word can be associated with *ādi*, meaning 'beginning,' as well as with *ādiyati*, 'to seize.' It is most likely that this word was deliberately chosen to convey the dual character of this relationship. This element of the myth endowed the ruling dynasty with a marvellous origin which marked it out from the populace. The depiction of the hero as lion-slayer is comparable with that of Gilgamesh whose prowess in combat with lions is highlighted in a large number of Sumerian seals.[37] It is also possible to suggest that, as a structural element in the myth, parricide represents the negation and abnegation of animal origins. In later times the lion-slaying aspect of the myth is found to be given greater emphasis. As noted earlier, according to the Hiuen Tsang I version of the myth, the founder of the kingdom received his name on account of his having 'caught' a lion. The *Vaṃsatthappakāsinī*, too, states that Sīhabāhu was called Sīhaḷa because he had 'caught the lion' (*sīhaṃ gahitvā iti*).[38] These sources probably reflect the fact that by about the seventh century the People of the Lion preferred to be known as lion-slayers rather than the progeny of the lion. It is this later interpretation of the term *ādinnava* which influenced Geiger to translate the relevant verse of the

Mahāvaṃsa as cited above. The Hiuen Tsang I version of the myth does not refer to the sibling incest that is found in the *Mahāvaṃsa*. As Romila Thapar has pointed out,[39] while incest of this type explains how two siblings can found a lineage, it also stresses purity of descent. Sibling marriage finds mention in the Dasaratha Jātaka, and, with reference to the Sākyas, in the Pāli Suttas. The story of the sixteen pairs of twins in the Vijaya myth also finds parallels in the Indian myths cited by Thapar.

Information on dynastic emblems of south Indian ruling houses is most useful in enabling us to understand the significance of the term Siṃhaḷa. The Pāṇḍyas had the fish as their emblem, the Cōḻas and the Sinda branch of the Nāga lineage had the tiger, and the Cālukyas had the boar. It is also evident that certain south Indian ruling families had the lion on their crests. Though the bull was the most widely used emblem of the Pallavas of the Siṃhaviṣṇu line, the figure of the lion is found on some of their coins, seals, and on certain early copper plates.[40] The animal figures on the Ūruvapalli grant[41] and the Pikira copper-plate[42] have been identified as lions. It has been suggested on the basis of this evidence that the early Pallavas bore the lion emblem. The lion emblem was also used by some minor Cōḻa ruling houses. The Malēpaḍu plates of Puṇyakumāra, dated in the eighth century,[43] and a record from the Bastar region,[44] issued by a chieftain called Candrāditya, bear the lion crest. Both Puṇyakumāra and Candrāditya claim descent from Karikāla Cōḻa. It is very likely that, similarly, the lion was the emblem of the ruling house of Sri Lanka and that the dynasty got its name from the emblem. As in Sri Lanka, in south India, too, there were myths which sought to explain these emblems. For instance, the myths of the Sinda dynasty explain how their eponymous ancestor had been brought up by a tiger.[45]

There was evidently a second, wider meaning of the term Sinhala. The *Mahāvaṃsa* states that on account of their association with Sīhabāhu (*tena sambandhā*) 'all these' were also called Sīhaḷa (*ete sabbe pi sīhaḷā*).[46] It is not clear from this cryptic verse who 'all these' were, but the preceding verses speak of the followers of Vijaya. In its explanation of the passage, the *Vaṃsatthappakāsinī* states that the seven hundred members of Vijaya's retinue and all their descendants 'up to the present day' are called Sīhaḷas because of their association with the prince called Sīhaḷa (*tena sīhaḷanāmikena rājakumārena sambandhā ete sattapurisasatā ca tesaṃ puttanattapanattā yāvajjakāla manussā ca sabbe pi sīhaḷā nāma ahesunti attho*).[47] Thus it is clear that, at least by the time the *Vaṃsatthappakāsinī* came to be written, a wider meaning of the term Sinhala was gaining currency.

Hypothetically, it is possible to postulate a

dynasty → kingdom → people of the kingdom

sequence in the development of the Sinhala identity. However, there appear to have been certain factors operative at this time that prevented the development of a Sinhala consciousness which embraced all the people in the kingdom. It is particularly noteworthy that both the *Māhavaṃsa* and its commentary specifically exclude a substantial section of the population of the island from the social group denoted by the term. The Vijaya myth recognizes the existence of three major groups of people in the island. While outlining in detail the origin of the Sīhaḷas, it also seeks to explain the origins of the service castes and the Pulindas. Verses 43–45 in the seventh chapter of the *Mahāvaṃsa* describe the settlements established by the seven hundred followers of Vijaya while verses 56–57 refer to the arrival of the thousand families of the service castes sent by the king of Madhurā. The implication that this later group should not be confused with the Sīhaḷas is emphasized in the *Vaṃsatthappakāsinī* when it specifies that the Sīhaḷas were the descendants of 'the seven hundred' who formed Vijaya's retinue and thereby excludes from this group the descendants of 'the thousand families'. The origin of the third major group, the Pulindas who 'occupied the Malaya region', is traced to the offspring of Vijaya and Kuvaṇṇā. Geiger was right in identifying the Pulindas with the Veddas.[48] Sibling incest in the story of their origin emphasizes the 'purity' of their descent and their distinct status. Thus the Vijaya myth seeks to indicate that the three major groups it identifies are separate categories with distinct origins. If the myth suggests any link at all, it is between the Sinhala ruling house and the Pulindas, but here again it is noteworthy that, according to the myth, Vijaya did not have any children by his marriage with the Pāṇḍya princess. Thus, while the violent Vijaya who suffered exile for his reprehensible ways is presented as the ancestor of the Pulindas, the ancestry of the Sinhalese ruling house is traced to Sumitta, the more sedate younger brother whose youngest son Paṇḍuvāsudeva is said to have succeeded Vijaya. On the other hand, the service castes are presented as the descendants of the thousand families from Madhurā: they are thus unlinked by descent or kinship with the other two major groups.

These distinctions that the myth makes are of crucial importance for understanding the nature of group consciousness that was evolving in the period after the formation of a unified kingdom under the control of Anurādhapura. They enable us to distinguish the Sinhala consciousness of this early period from linguistic nationalism and other types of group consciousness typical of more recent times. Of course, the presence of a common language was a basic prerequisite for the emergence of group consciousness. Buddhaghosa's commentaries speak of a language specific to the island. However, it is significant that language was not conceived as the crucial criterion or the basis of the Sinhala identity at this time. The Sinhala group consciousness did not bring together all speakers of the language but deliberately left out a considerable section of the linguistic group including the craftsmen-agriculturists and others who performed ritually 'low' service functions.

In essence, the Vijaya myth is presenting what may be termed a political definition of the Sinhala identity. The ruling house represented the Sīhaḷas *par excellence*. It may be relevant to note here that the Sīgiri monument, constructed by Kāśyapa I (AD 477–95), gave expression to this identity through some of its architectural features. The dominant feature of this monument was the massive figure of the lion after which it was named. The royal apartments were on the summit of the rock. The architectural arrangements were such that the king, descending from his apartments, would walk out through the mouth of the lion, emerging, as it were, from its bowels, and thereby evoking the mythical origins of the ruling house. The ruling dynasty sought to consolidate its power by utilizing such monuments to propagate the Sinhala myth. On the other hand, by emphasizing their equally mythical relationship with the lineage of the Buddha, they attempted to draw upon the growing religious consciousness of the Buddhists in order to strengthen their position.[49] According to the myth, those other than members of the ruling house acquired the Sinhala identity only through their association with the ruler or through being born in families with such associations. This aspect of the Sinhala identity, emphasized by the author of the *Vaṃsatthappakāsinī* in the comment quoted above, is particularly noteworthy since it cautions us against the view held by some writers that 'almost everyone was a Sinhalese' even as early as pre-Christian times.[50]

The seven hundred settlers are described as Vijaya's retinue (*parivāra*) and some of them are specifically referred to as state functionaries (*amacca*). It has been pointed out elsewhere that in ancient Sri Lanka state functionaries were recruited primarily from families of high rank who owned property in irrigation works and land, and that there was a tendency for political office to be associated, generation after generation, with certain families.[51] Traders were another prominent element in the society and their importance is reflected in certain versions of the myth where Siṃhaḷa is presented as a merchant.

The ideology basic to these myths was not a mass ideology which reflected consciousness at a popular level, but an ideology of the leading elements of society which emphasized their identity, distinguishing their position from the lower orders of society, especially the service castes. At this stage, those brought together by the Sinhala identity did not include all the residents of the island, or all the members of a linguistic group: they were primarily the most influential and powerful families in the kingdom. It is likely that it was these elements who were denoted by the term *mahājana* in the myth. In the ancient texts this term did not carry the meaning that its phonetic equivalent *mahajanayā* conveys today, but denoted 'great men.' Thus, at this stage of its development, the Sinhala consciousness was the consciousness of the ruling class. It probably had a regional tinge, at least initially, since, according to the myth, the original settlements founded by the Sīhaḷas were on the banks of the Kadamba (Malvatu) and Gambhīra (Kaṇadarā?) rivers and in the surrounding region. It is worthy of note that the chronicle attributes a different origin to the settlements in the eastern and south-eastern regions of the island.[52] The Vijaya myth seeks to define the position of the Pulindas and their relationship with the Sinhala dynasty: they live in the Malaya region with the assent of the king, thereby acknowledging his suzerainty.

Certain elements of the myth portray the relationship between the king and the 'great men'. It was the 'great men' of the kingdom who protested about the violent and oppressive behaviour of Vijaya. They demanded that he be put to death and Sīhabāhu was constrained to send him away in exile. In the *Divyāvadāna* and Hiuen Tsang II versions of the myth Siṃhaḷa is a merchant who is selected by the people of his kingdom to be the king of their land. In the *Divyāvadāna* Siṃhaḷa protests that he is only a trader, but the people insist that he accepts kingship because he is the only capable person.[53] In the Hiuen Tsang II version Siṃhaḷa is selected on account of his religious merit, wisdom, skill, virtue, loyalty and prudence.[54] While these versions present the view that personal ability and qualities of character rather than ritual status should be the criteria that determine the suitability of a person for kingship, the *Mahāvaṃsa* version seeks to present a markedly different point of view. It embodies the message that the *kṣatriya* status of the ruling family marks them out from the people of all other ritual categories. The story of the mission sent to Madhurā to fetch a *kṣatriya* princess, and Vijaya's treatment of Kuvaṇṇā, serve to underline the point that only such a king who is a *kṣatriya* and who also has a queen of the same *varṇa* status can be consecrated as king: others do not have a legitimate right to rule. Thus while the 'great men' of non-*kṣatriya* status may force the ruling family to govern justly without harassing them, they may not aspire to kingship. The discrepancies between different versions of the myth, reflecting probably their different social origins, point to the tensions within the dominant social groups and the problems of political power in the country at this time.

It is also possible to see the Vijaya myth as an expression of a corpus of religious beliefs. The *yakkhas* and *rākṣasīs* occupy a prominent position in many versions of the myth. In the words of Vijaya 'men are ever in fear of non-human beings'. Oblations (*bali*) are offered to the *yakkhas* to placate them. The *Mahāvaṃsa* version of the myth highlights the potency of sacralized thread as a charm which affords protection against the *yakkhas:* it saves the lives of Vijaya's men. Uppalavaṇṇa is introduced as a god of the Buddhist pantheon vested with the protection of the island, and it is stated that it was the request of the dying Buddha that Vijaya and the island be protected which led to Uppalavaṇṇa being sent by Sakka, the king of the gods. The myth synchronizes the arrival in the island of Vijaya and his retinue with the death of the Buddha. It also seeks to enunciate certain Buddhist virtues and to point out the 'rewards' accruing to those who practise them: the lion was not harmed by Sīhabāhu's arrows as long as he harboured feelings of loving kindness (*mettacitta*) in his heart, but was killed the moment he was moved by wrath.

At another level the myth reflects the importance of certain places other than Anurādhapura as political centres. All the different versions of the myth seek to explain the name Sinhala, and indeed this was one of its basic functions. While it is possible to understand this myth at several such different levels, it is possible to see in its *Mahāvaṃsa* version what Malinowski termed a 'charter'[55] and, in this sense, it is comparable with the myth of the visit of the Buddha that I have analysed elsewhere.[56] One of the primary social functions of the Vijaya myth was the validation of a particular socio-political order. It identifies certain major social groups in the island and seeks to locate their positions in the social order. The Sinhala consciousness presented in the myth was the product of caste (*jāti*) ideology, for the service castes were excluded from membership of the Sinhala group. The Vijaya myth in the *Mahāvaṃsa* also represents the embodiment of a state ideology which sought to unite the dominant elements in society and to bring them under a common bond of allegiance to the ruling house. When the island came to be called Sīhaḷadīpa, or the island of the Sinhala, this name reflected the claim of the ruling house and this dominant social group to political power over the whole island. By implication, this ideology sought to relegate all other social groups, like the service castes and the Pulindas, to subservient positions. Evidently, chronicles like the *Mahāvaṃsa* served as valuable media for the propagation of this ideology.

Invasions from south India posed a threat to the dominant position occupied by this social group, and when powerful kingdoms of the Pāṇḍyas, the Pallavas and the Cōḻas appeared in the south Indian political scene these invasions were indeed a serious threat to Sinhala political power. The Sinhala ideology presented in the chronicles reflects the tension and antipathy aroused by this threat. It is particularly noteworthy that the chronicles present a version of history which had been moulded to conform to the needs of this ideology. For these chroniclers all kings since the mythical Vijaya were rulers of the island. It is only through a re-examination of the *Mahāvaṃsa* in the light of evidence from the early Brāhmī inscriptions and literary works like the *Dhātuvaṃsa*, the *Sīhaḷavatthuppakaraṇa* and the *Sahassavatthuppakaraṇa* that the process of political development in the island leading to the emergence of a unified kingdom can be reconstructed. Information from inscriptions at sites distributed over a wide area, such as Periya Puliyankulam, Occāppukaḷḷu, Ämbul-ambē, Yaṭahalena, Lenagala, Gōnavatta, Bambaragala, Kandēgamakanda, Kusalānkanda, Olagamgala, Moṭṭayakaḷḷu, Bōvattēgala, Koṭṭadämūhela, Kolladeniya and Kirimakulgolla, when taken together with evidence in the literary sources mentioned above, points to a situation quite different from what the author of the *Mahāvaṃsa* would have us believe. It is evident from information in these sources that at the beginning of historical time there were several petty rulers holding sway over various parts of the island. Of these rulers those at Anurādhapura were the pre-eminent. Dēvanaṃpiyatissa of Anurādhapura sent a delegation to the court of Asoka, held a consecration ceremony with the ritual goods provided by the latter and assumed the titles *dēvanāṃpiya* and *mahārāja*. There is no evidence, however, to show that the other rulers acknowledged his suzerainty or that he was more than a mere aspirant to overlordship over the whole island.[57]

It is against this background that the accounts of the campaigns of Duṭṭhagāmaṇī (Duṭugämuṇu) which form an integral and important element in the Sinhala ideology, particularly in more recent times, have to be examined. The *Mahāvaṃsa* would have us believe that Eḷāra, against whom Duṭṭhagāmaṇī waged his war, was the ruler of the whole of northern Sri Lanka and that members of Duṭṭhagāmaṇī's lineage had been rulers of the entire Rohaṇa kingdom ever since Mahānāga established his power at Mahāgāma. Duṭṭhagāmaṇī is presented as waging war in the interest of Buddhism. His campaigns culminate dramatically with the capture of Anurādhapura after a duel fought in accordance with the *kṣatriya* rules of chivalry. Thus a Buddhist prince of the Sinhala dynasty who ruled over the southern principality conquers the northern principality which was ruled by a Tamil who, though known for his just rule, was yet a man of 'false beliefs'. This view of events given by the chroniclers has influenced modern historical writings, and the chauvinist Sinhala writings have picked on these campaigns as representing the exemplary victorious war waged by the Sinhala against the Tamils. However, even the author of the *Mahāvaṃsa*, who was obviously transposing to an earlier period conditions more typical of his own times, found it difficult to reconcile material available in his sources with the anachronistic picture he was trying to present. Some information in the *Mahāvaṃsa* itself suggests that not all the people who fought against Duṭṭhagāmaṇī were Tamils. For instance, Nandhimitta, a general in Duṭṭhagāmaṇī's army, is said to have had an uncle who was a general serving Eḷāra.[58] Though the *Mahāvaṃsa* tried to present Duṭṭhagāmaṇī as ruler of a unified Rohaṇa fighting against the sole ruler of the northern plains, it is evident that the sources used by the chronicler carried accounts of Duṭṭhagāmaṇī fighting against not one but thirty-two different rulers. As I have pointed out previously,[59] the most plausible explanation of the available evidence is that Duṭṭhagāmaṇī was a powerful military leader who unified the island for the first time after fighting against several independent principalities. His campaigns do not appear to represent a Sinhala–Tamil confrontation and, as noted already, the development of Sinhala consciousness is a phenomenon observable after the formation of a unified kingdom ruled by the kings of Anurādhapura.

The Sinhala ideology elaborated in the account of the campaigns of Duṭṭhagāmaṇī clearly reflects the influence of the religious identity which evolved with the expansion and consolidation of Buddhism in the island. Both the *Mahāvaṃsa* and the *Cūlavaṃsa* present the view that support for the Sinhala dynasty against the Damiḷas is conducive to the glory of Buddhism. Duṭṭhagāmaṇī in the *Mahāvaṃsa* and Dhātusena in the *Cūlavaṃsa* are both presented as waging war against the Damiḷas to restore Buddhism to its proper position. Describing the south Indian invasions in the fifth century, the *Cūlavaṃsa* states that all men of good birth (*janā kulīnā sabbe*) left the area occupied by the invaders to go and live in Rohaṇa.[60] And, after describing the victory of Dhātusena, the chronicle says that he 'restored to its former place the *sāsana* destroyed by the foe'.[61] The chronicle seeks to create the impression that there was a strong anti-south Indian feeling among the dominant elements in Sri Lankan society, but it is less than convincing. A few strophes after the statements cited above it admits that some men of 'good birth' did opt to serve the Tamil rulers. After capturing power Dhātusena is said to have taken punitive action against those 'men of good birth who had attached themselves to the Damiḷas and protected neither himself nor the *sāsana*'.[62] The claim that the Buddhist order was destroyed by the invaders is also refuted by the inscriptional records of this period. These records indicate that there were Buddhists among the invaders. Some of them were generous patrons of the Buddhist clergy and one of their kings bore the title Buddhadāsa which meant 'the servant of the Buddha'.[63]

It is only after the development in south India of a militant form of Hinduism, which adopted a pronounced hostile stance against both Buddhism and Jainism, that Tamils would have been considered foes of the faith by the Buddhists of Sri Lanka. The Sanskrit literary works composed by the Pallava king Mahendravarman I (AD 600–30) and such Tamil writings as the *Tiruvātavūrar Purāṇam* and the *Periya Purāṇam* reflect the intensity of the hostility that the devotees of the Saiva faith harboured against the Buddhists and the Jainas. Tiruñānaçampantar is said to have defeated the Buddhist inhabitants of the Potimankai settlement at debate and converted them to Saivism. It is also said that another Saiva saint, Māṇikkavāçakar, participated in a similar debate at Çitamparam where he humiliated a Buddhist monk from Sri Lanka.[64] It has been suggested that Tiruñānaçampantar lived in the seventh century, and Māṇikkavāçakar has been assigned to the ninth century.[65] However, in the earlier periods there is no evidence of such antipathy toward the Buddhists. Thus, while the Buddhist identity was one which linked the Buddhists of Sri Lanka with coreligionists in south India and other parts of the Asian continent, it is only after about the seventh century that prerequisite conditions matured making it possible to link the Sinhala identity with Buddhism and to present Tamils as opponents of Buddhism.

In the second instance where the term Sinhala occurs in the *Mahāvaṃsa* Vaṭṭagāmaṇī is described as *mahākāḷasīhaḷa*.[66] Though Paranavitana preferred to see in this phrase an allusion to Yama,[67] its literal meaning is 'the great black Sinhala'. It is also noteworthy that the father of Duṭṭhagāmaṇī was called Kākavaṇṇatissa which means 'Tissa the crow-coloured'. Both the father and son of King Mahāsena bore the title Meghavaṇṇa which means 'one with the colour of the rain cloud.' The paintings and graffiti from Sīgiri also provide valuable information on physical features of the upper rungs of Sri Lankan society at the time. The complexions of the ladies depicted in the paintings vary from a light yellow-brown to a deep blue or black colour. These ladies are richly adorned with jewellery including tiaras, earrings, necklaces and bangles. The paintings certainly depict members of the highest social strata. The variety of physical types that they represent clearly indicates that the dominant social group at the time was not physically homogeneous. The 'amateur poets' who scribbled verses on the Mirror Wall at Sīgiri were mostly giving expression to their admiration of the damsels in the paintings. These verses reveal a certain preference for ladies with a lighter complexion, described as the 'golden-hued' (*ranvaṇ*) ones, although some of the poets considered those with dark complexions beautiful and desirable. There were several admirers who wrote verses expressing their desire for the darker maidens, whose complexions were poetically compared with the hue of the blue lily *mahanel* (*Nymphaea stellata*). In a verse that has been often quoted, one damsel is compared to a blue *kaṭroḷa* (*Clitoria ternatea*) flower.[68] 'When I remember the blue lily-hued ones there is no sleep for me, O friend, I have become like unto an ass', another visitor to Sīgiri laments in a poem scribbled on the wall.[69] The fact that some Sri Lankans did indeed prefer to be dark rather than light in complexion is evident from the *Saddharamālaṅkāra*, a literary work datable to about the beginning of the fifteenth century. In this work there is a story about a lady who performed several actions which she thought would bring her rewards in future births. She then wished that, through the effects of the 'merit' (*puñña*) thus accumulated, she should be born with the complexion of a blue lily in every successive birth.[70]

The *Dharmapradīpikā*, which has been assigned by most scholars to the end of the twelfth century, also provides information on the ideas of physical beauty in early medieval Sri Lanka. This work presents a discussion on the five characteristics of female beauty. In its description of the skin characteristics of the ideal beauty, it refers to both the dark (*käḷiya*) and the golden-hued (*heḷilla*) maiden, in that order. The ideal beauty had to have a clear and uniform complexion, 'untainted by other colours', and it could be either the colour of the blue lily or that of the *kiṇihiri* (*Cochlospermum religiosum*) flower.[71] In literary works, objects of golden colour were compared with the *kiṇihiri* flower. The *Vesaturudā Sanne*, an exegetical work written in the period of the Polonnaruva kingdom, compares people clad in gold-coloured clothes and wearing golden ornaments to *kiṇihiri* trees in full bloom. It also states that *kiṇihiri* trees in bloom looked as if they were covered with golden nets.[72] Thus, preferences about skin pigmentation appear to have varied as would be expected in a physically heterogeneous society. The sources examined above reflect the rather unusual aesthetic values of a society in which there were not one but two alternate ideals of physical type: black is beautiful, the *Dharmapradīpikā* asserts, and so is the 'golden' hue. The *Buddhavaṃsa* reveals that these aesthetic values influenced even the Buddhist tradition. That the *Buddhavaṃsa* contains 'the word of the Buddha' is the popular view, but the fact that it refers to the death of the Buddha, the distribution of his relics and even to relics venerated in Sri Lanka clearly shows that it is a late work composed probably in Sri Lanka. In its description of the chief disciples of the Buddha, this work states that Sāriputta was of the colour of the *koraṇḍa* flower which, according to the *Vesaturudā Sanne*,[73] was golden in colour, and that Moggallāna's complexion was comparable to the black rain cloud and the blue lily.[74] Evidently, here the 'black' rain cloud and the 'blue' lily are supposed to denote the same complexion. It is particularly interesting to note that, in this text, the two chief disciples of the Buddha are representatives of the two main physical types. Thus these two physical types came to be not only idealized but also 'enshrined': the figures of two chief disciples are to be found up to the present day in Buddhist shrines scattered over many different parts of the island. It seems reasonable to suggest that this emphasis on these two physical types reflects the heterogeneous composition of the dominant social stratum.

It will have been evident from the preceding discussion that the social group brought together by the Sinhala consciousness does not appear to have coincided with the linguistic grouping in the island or to have represented a single physical type, and that it is only after about the seventh century that it could have been linked with a religious grouping. It is the political and social criteria which clearly stand out in an examination of the factors that united the Sīhaḷas. At the time Dhātusena ascended the throne in the fifth century, the Sinhala consciousness was evidently not strong enough to unite the leading elements in society in opposition to the south Indian invaders. At the end of the seventh century, Mānavamma, a Sinhala contender for the throne, captured power with aid from the Pallavas, but the dynasty he founded soon proved to be capable of maintaining their independence and successfully resisted intervention by powerful south Indian kingdoms for more than two centuries. This long period of political rivalry between the Sinhala and the South Indian kingdoms witnessed the rise and expansion of a militant and vigorous form of Hinduism in south India, which displaced both Buddhism and Jainism. On the other hand, Buddhism maintained its dominant position in the religious life of the people of Sri Lanka. These developments provided the prerequisite conditions for the growth of a tendency towards the convergence of the Buddhist and the Sinhala identities. From the time of Kāśyapa V (AD 914–23) kings began to actively propagate the idea, implicit in the chronicles, that they belonged to the same lineage as the Buddha.[75] An inscription issued by Mahinda IV (956–72) claims that the Buddha had given the assurance that none but Bodhisattvas would become kings of Sri Lanka[76] – thus kings of Sri Lanka had to be not only Buddhists but also men destined to be Buddhas. Such ideas would have had considerable political potency at a time when the Sinhala kingdom was confronted with the threat from the Hindu kingdoms of south India. The success of the Sinhala rulers in defending their independence until the time of Mahinda V would have been due primarily to their achievement in utilizing these ideas to mobilize the leading elements in their kingdom, particularly those who traditionally bore arms, in support of their dynasty. However, even at this stage, it is doubtful whether the Sinhala grouping and the Buddhist grouping in the island were identical. While nearly all the Sinhala were Buddhists, there is still no evidence to suggest that the service castes were now being considered members of the Sinhala group.

The long period of Cōḻa occupation in the island, spanning the tenth and eleventh centuries, and the intense rivalry between the south Indian and the Sinhala kingdoms would have been conducive to the extension of the Sinhala identity to cover a wider social group. However, there were still impediments to such a development. Inscriptions from the period immediately after the Cōḻa occupation reveal that caste (*jāti*) distinctions had become so rigid that they even affected the organization of Buddhist ritual. According to a lithic record set up by Vijayabāhu I (1017–70), he constructed two terraces on the summit of Sumanakūṭa. The upper terrace was reserved for men of 'good caste', and was enclosed by a wall which had gates fitted with locks. He had a second terrace built on a lower elevation for those of 'inferior caste' (*adhama jātīn*) who came to worship the footprint of the Buddha.[77] Such arrangements for the performance of ritual at this important centre of pilgrimage reveal how sharply the differences between these two status groups were being emphasized.

Evidently, the intense political rivalry between the Cōḻa and the Sinhala kingdoms in the time of Parākramabāhu I (1153–86) affected even the *religieux*. Up to this time it was the *nikāya* (monastic fraternity) affiliation which divided them, and these *nikāya* divisions had cut across political boundaries. Several monks from south India had produced commentarial works on Buddhist texts in which they professed to follow the traditions of canonical interpretation of the Mahāvihāra *nikāya* at Anurādhapura. In the reign of Parākramabāhu I, various Buddhist fraternities were unified under the leadership of Sāriputta.[78] Thus, for the first time, the *saṅgha* in Sri Lanka gave precedence to unity on the basis of political and regional grounds, rather than to unity on the basis of sectarian affiliation. Sāriputta's writings were severely criticized by Kassapa, a monk who lived at the Nāgānana monastery situated 'in the heart of the Cōḻa kingdom', at Cōḻādhināthapura. Sāriputta's interpretations, he claimed, encouraged lapses in discipline in the Cōḻa land and, as such, they had been rejected by the leading monks of that land who cleansed the *saṅgha* of monks who supported such views.[79] The tenor of this criticism implies that there was something more than mere disagreement on doctrinal matters. That a certain element of regional rivalry had come into these disputes is more clearly shown in the *Sīmālaṅkāra*, a work from the same period, which was devoted to the problem of demarcating ceremonial boundaries. In this work the author declares his intention to vindicate the position of the Sinhala monks. All those who know the Vinaya rules and wish for the perpetuation of the *sāsana*, he maintains, should accept the opinions of the Sinhala monks which are in accordance with the scriptures and their commentaries. They should certainly reject the views of the Coḷiyans which are false and contrary to these. It was a Sinhala monk, he declares with obvious pride, who wrote the *Sīmālaṅkāra* and its commentary.[80] It is evident from these polemical writings that, while the Buddhist identity transcended political boundaries, attempts were being made during this period to mark out within this larger identity the separate positions of the Cōḻa and the Sinhala monks.

The political conditions of this period were favourable for the extension of the Sinhala identity, and, by the time Guruḷugomi wrote the

Dharmapradīpikā, the term Sinhala had acquired a wider meaning. While reiterating the earlier view that the kings of the dynasty, who were descended from Sinhala (i.e. Sīhabāhu), the father of Vijaya, constituted the primary group denoted by the term Sinhala, Guruḷugomi also gives three other connotations of the term. The island ruled by the dynasty received the name of the dynasty; the inhabitants of the island received the name of the island; and their language was called *siṃhaḷabhāṣā*.[81] Guruḷugomi's view of a

dynasty → island → inhabitants of the island → their language

sequence in the extension of the meaning of the term Sinhala reflects an important stage in the evolution of the Sinhala identity. Unlike previous writers, he does not refer or allude to the separate position of the service castes. He further differs from his predecessors by stating that it was by being inhabitants of the island ruled by the Sinhala dynasty rather than by being descendants of a particular social group that those other than the members of the ruling house acquired the Sinhala identity. Thus, it is evident that by this time the term Sinhala had come to acquire a wider connotation. However, it is also noteworthy that in this context the phrase 'the inhabitants of the island' apparently denoted the Sinhala-speaking population who were the preponderant element among the residents in the island and did not include within its meaning other linguistic groups, especially the Tamil-speaking group who had established extensive settlements during the preceding period of Cōḻa rule.

While the Sinhala identity was thus being extended to cover a wider group than in the previous period, there are indications that not all the members of the group within this period were Buddhists. The influence of Saivism lingered on during the period which followed Cōḻa rule. This faith received the patronage of three successive rulers: Vijayabāhu I, Vikramabāhu and Gajabāhu II. The *Cūlavaṃsa* claims that Gajabāhu brought nobles of 'heretical faith' from abroad and had his kingdom filled with 'briers of heresy'.[82] The Tamil tradition claims that he was converted to Saivism.[83] It has been suggested that both Vikramabāhu and Gajabāhu were Hindus.[84] In its description of the invasion of Māgha (1215), the *Pūjāvaliya* states that this invader compelled 'the great men' to adopt false faiths.[85] Liyanagamage has suggested that this is a reference to people being converted to the Vīrasaiva sect of Saivism.[86] The vehemence with which Vīdāgama Maitreya attacks Saivism and other faiths in his *Buduguṇālaṅkāraya*,[87] written in the fifteenth century, also points to the influence of these faiths amongst the Sinhala-speaking population at the time. It is evident from the preceding discussion that, while it is possible to speak of a Sri Lankan variety of Buddhism during this period, as distinct from the Cōḻa and other varieties of the Theravāda, this does not imply that the terms Buddhist and Sinhala denoted the very same group. These terms denoted two intersecting groupings, and, though there was a substantial population which came within both, there were people who belonged to one group, but not the other.

This period did not witness the growth of a Sinhala consciousness which could prevent the rise to power of kings who were not members of the Sinhala group. And, during the six centuries which followed, there are several instances of Kaliṅga and Tamil princes assuming royal power in Sri Lanka. The position of the kings of the Kaliṅga dynasty which came to power at the end of the twelfth century, appears to have been challenged by Tamil as well as Sinhala contenders to the throne. Nissaṅka Malla, the first king of this dynasty, was a clever propagandist who used lithic records to propagate the view that *kṣatriya* status and adherence to the Buddhist faith were essential prerequisites for kingship. He argued that non-Buddhists such as princes of Cōḻa and Keraḷa origin were unsuited to rule the island which 'belonged to the *sāsana*' and that it would be as ludicrous for a man of the Govi caste to aspire to kingship as for a firefly to try to emulate the sun.[88] It is noteworthy that, to a certain extent, Nissaṅka Malla was seeking to counter the Sinhala ideology by emphasizing that it was not the Sinhala identity but criteria related to religious affiliation and ritual status which determined the suitability of a person to be the king of the island.

II

The period of political disintegration which followed the collapse of the Polonnaruva kingdom witnessed significant changes in the composition of the population of the island. The chronicles contain several references to these developments, but it is in works like the *Vittipot* (which have not received adequate attention from historians) that these events are described in detail.[89] That there were several waves of immigration which brought not only linguistic groups like Demaḷa, Malala, Kaṇṇaḍa and Doḷuvara (Tulu) from south India but also the Jāvakas from south-east Asia. Myths of this period reflect the distribution of the immigrant population over different parts of the island, especially in the northern, western and southern coastal regions.[90] These groups of immigrants who originally spoke different languages came to be absorbed into the two main linguistic groups in the island. Their incorporation and assimilation seems to have been slow and long-drawn; but it was a relentless process in that few retained their original languages or group identities for any considerable length of time. Nevertheless, this very process of incorporation did leave its impact on the polity and on what came to be perceived as Sinhala culture.

There were two kingdoms which were clearly the most prominent among the multitude of diminutive polities which arose during this period. At most times there were several polities in the Sinhala-speaking areas. Swept by political winds, the political centre of the main kingdom shifted hastily from place to place until finally it came to rest in the central highlands. The other noteworthy kingdom was in Jaffna where immigrants would have added to existing populations to form the heaviest concentration of Tamil-speaking peoples. Though the establishment of a unified realm covering the whole island would have been the dream of many a potentate, this objective was achieved only in the reign of Parākramabāhu VI (1412–67) who is said to have vanquished Sinhala, Demaḷa, Malala, Kaṇṇaḍa and Doḷuvara foes.[91]

Evidently, this was a period of cosmopolitan culture when fluency in six languages was considered to be a desirable accomplishment by Sinhala scholars. The hierarch of the Galaturumula fraternity who lived at the end of the thirteenth century or the beginning of the fourteenth century was the first person to be referred to by the title *ṣaḍbhāṣā parameśvara*, 'the lord of six languages.'[92] The reign of Parākramabāhu VI marks a high point in the development of cultural contact between the Sinhala and Tamil linguistic communities. Nannūrutun Miṇisannas, a Tamil prince who was married to the king's daughter, composed the Sinhala lexicon *Nāmāvaliya*.[93] It is clear from this scholarly work that the author had attained a high level of proficiency in the Sinhala language. The author of the *Kokila Sandesa* spoke proudly of his ability to preach in both Sinhala and Tamil.[94] It was also a period when Tamil poems and songs were popular among the Sinhala community. According to the *Kokila Sandesa*, poems composed in Sinhala, Tamil, Pāli and Sanskrit were recited at the court of Parākramabāhu VI.[95] Maha Väligama was described by the same poet as a place where Tamil songs were sung, and his description clearly reveals an appreciation for this genre of music.[96] The popularity of the cults of Gaṇapati (Gaṇeśa) and Pattini was a factor conducive to the expansion of Tamil cultural influences among the Sinhala. The *Parevi Sandesa*, written in the middle of the fifteenth century by Toṭagamuvē Rāhula, refers appreciatively to Tamil songs being sung at the temple of Gaṇapati in southern Sri Lanka.[97] The *Vayantimālaya*, a poetical work on the goddess Pattini which has been assigned to the period of the Kōṭṭe kingdom, was a translation of a Tamil work.[98]

The interest of the Sinhala literati in Tamil literature persisted during the period of the Kandyan kingdom, when a significant number of Tamil works were translated into Sinhala. Some of these, like the *Mahāpadaraṅga Jātaka*, were Buddhist works[99] and point to the prevalence of Tamil literary works of Buddhist inspiration even at this late date. Kirimäṭiyāvē, the scholar responsible for some of the translations made during this period, speaks of his knowledge of the Tamil and Grantha scripts.[100] South Indian scripts were used at times even to write the Sinhala language.[101] It is particularly interesting to note that some leading Sinhala officials in the Kandyan kingdom used the Grantha and the Tamil scripts in their signatures.[102]

The Sinhala consciousness persisted during this period, particularly among certain sections of the literati, as is evident from works like the *Pūjāvaliya* and the *Cūlavaṃsa*. However, unlike in certain earlier periods, this ideology does not appear to have been propagated by the state, and it does not seem even to have received persistent support from kings. Some instances have been cited by certain scholars as pointing to the influence of the Sinhala consciousness. The death of Parākramabāhu VI was followed by a struggle for power, and when Prince Sapumal, the governor of the northern regions, captured power and ascended the throne, he faced an uprising in the southern part of the kingdom. Paranavitana has suggested that this uprising, which is referred to as *Siṃhalasaṃge* in the Dädigama inscription,[103] and as *Siṃhalaperaḷi* in the *Rājāvaliya*,[104] was 'an upsurge of national sentiment' amongst the Sinhala against a ruler of Malayali extraction.[105] However, this appears to be too sweeping a conclusion to draw simply from the name given to the uprising. In his study of the Kōṭṭe kingdom, Somaratne has suggested that the incident was a rebellion organized by the supporters of Vīraparākramabāhu, whom Sapumal deposed.[106] Vīraparākramabāhu was himself a prince of Tamil descent, being the son of Prince Miṇisannas, but he had been chosen by Parākramabāhu VI to be his successor.

More recently, while commenting on an earlier version of this chapter, C.R. de Silva has cited two texts from the period of the Kandyan kingdom as providing 'evidence that the Sinhala-Buddhist identity was used to mobilize the whole ethnic group against external threats.'[107] If this were indeed the case, the seventeenth century would mark a significant stage in the development of Sinhala consciousness, but it would be very difficult to be convinced that the passages cited by de Silva support his conclusion.[108] While religion appears to have been an important factor in the wars of the times, it is also noteworthy that, according to the *Paraṃgi Haṭana*, the leading men serving in the army of Rājasiṃha II (1635–87) were trying to demonstrate their loyalty to the king as well as their valour and ability as fighting men. The text goes on to relate how these men were rewarded by the king with high office, honours and wealth.[109] On the other hand, the Sinhala linguistic group was divided on grounds of religion as well as political affiliation. A considerable proportion of the group was now living under European rule and some of them had been converted to the Christian faith. Under these conditions, the connotations of the term Sinhala had begun to change. While the use of the term *Trisiṃhaḷa* to connote a wider region in the island persisted, the term Sinhalē, in its territorial sense, appears to have been used primarily to denote the Kandyan kingdom,[110] rather than the area occupied by the entire linguistic group. As Pieris has observed, Kaḍavata, with its tamarind tree which served as a landmark, was recognized as the boundary between the Sinhalē and the maritime regions under European rule.[111] Though there were at times desertions from among the Sinhala militia who served under the Portuguese and the Dutch – especially when the invading armies had been reduced to severe straits through the able use of guerilla tactics by the defenders of the Kandyan kingdom – it is noteworthy that the European powers did despatch armies with large numbers of Sinhala from territories under their rule to fight against the Sinhala of the Kandyan kingdom. Of particular significance is the fact that there were no instances of 'the whole ethnic group' being united in an uprising against the foreign occupation of the maritime provinces.

Clearer evidence of expression of Sinhala consciousness and antipathy towards the Nāyakkar rulers of Kandy is to be found in the *Kiraḷa Sandesa* and the *Vaḍuga Haṭana* cited by Sannasgala and Dharmadasa.[112] These two works were written by a supporter of Ähälēpola, a contender to the throne, after the last Nāyakkar king had been captured by the British. In these works the author attacks the last king for his false beliefs and calls him a 'villainous, wicked and heretical eunuch of a Tamil'. Obviously, this attack on the king was designed to justify Ähälēpola's betrayal of the king and his treasonable dealings with the British. On the other hand, some authors of Sinhala texts in the nineteenth century refer to the last Nāyakkar king as the *siṃhaḷa maharajatumā*, i.e. 'the great Siṃhaḷa king' or 'the great king of the Siṃhaḷa'.[113] It would appear that the term Sinhala in this context was not being used in an ethnic sense, but rather in a political sense, to denote the kingdom and not the dynasty as in earlier times. Dharmadasa has argued that the expression of 'Sinhala Buddhist' sentiments in the two texts cited earlier did not constitute isolated incidents and that there was similar 'ideological motivation' behind previous instances of opposition to Nāyakkar rule. However, it is difficult to agree that his evidence is adequate for such a conclusion. Dharmadasa cites two previous instances of opposition to Nāyakkar rulers. The first was when the last king of Sinhala descent decided to designate his brother-in-law, a Nāyakkar prince, as his successor. Some nobles supported the claims of Prince Unambuve, a son of the king by a Sinhala lady who was not of *kṣatriya* status. However, under conditions of intense rivalry among the Sinhala nobility, ritual status turned out to be the decisive criterion, and even the leading courtier who had supported Unambuve's claims later accepted office under the Nāyakkar king.[114] In the second instance, a section of the nobility plotted to kill Kīrtti Śrī Rājasiṃha, who is described in one source as 'a Tamil heretic'. This description, however, occurs in the *Vaḍuga Haṭana* which was written not during the period of Nāyakkar rule but in the reign of Queen Victoria when, as will be seen later, an altogether different intellectual milieu had come into being. It is also significant that the leaders of the plot could not decide on a Sinhala noble to replace the Nāyakkar king, and were attempting to win the throne for a Thai prince.

Rebellions led by sections of the nobility were not uncommon occurrences even when Sinhala kings were on the throne. On the other hand, it is significant that a small band of Nāyakkars from south India did manage to remain on the throne of Kandy for almost a century and that the Sinhala consciousness could not unite the nobility to depose them. During this epoch the Sinhala consciousness did not possess the class character of an earlier epoch. It may be also suggested that cultural cosmopolitanism would have contributed to the weakening of the Sinhala consciousness and that the feudal ethos would have further diminished its influence. Unlike the ruling class of the Anurādhapura kingdom, the Kandyan nobility did not possess a powerful unifying ideology strengthened by myths. The feudal ideology of the Kandyan kingdom emphasized 'noble' (*radala*) status to such an extent that in effect the *radala* constituted a sub-caste. However, the *radala* nobility was a group whose unity was severely undermined by factional rivalry. In such an atmosphere only a person whose ritual status placed him well above the *radala* could be king. The failure of Unambuve and the support given to the Thai prince by the rebels highlight this situation. The success of the Nāyakkars in maintaining their position was due as much to the divisions among the nobility as to the fact that none among them could claim *kṣatriya* status. Even though the social origins of the Nāyakkars may appear to be a matter of dispute today,[115] at that time they were the only group in the island who were accepted as *kṣatriyas* and, therefore, as men who were qualified to wear the crown. Apart from the ideology of status, the other major ideological influence was Buddhism. All Nāyakkars had to, at least overtly, declare adherence to the Buddhist faith. Thus it is evident that the decisive criteria of the legitimacy of power had been derived from principles related to ritual status and religious affiliation rather than membership of the Sinhala group. Owing to a combination of factors, the ideology of ritual status gained such an influential position in the last century of the period of the Kandyan kingdom that in effect it disqualified members of the Sinhala group from ascending the throne.

III

It was during the period of colonial rule that the Sinhala consciousness underwent a radical transformation and began to assume its current form. In developing their group consciousness the social classes created by colonial rule drew as much on European thought as on their own past traditions. The period during which the modern Sinhala consciousness evolved witnessed the rise into prominence of racialist theories in Europe. These theories were particularly influential in the study of Asian languages and history. William Jones' lecture on the structural affinities between Indian and European languages, published in 1788, marked the beginning of a new trend of thought in both Asia and Europe. Racial theories followed closely on the heels of theories of linguistic affinity, and the relationship between languages was explained as reflecting the common ancestry and common blood of the speakers of those languages. In 1819 Friedrich Schlegel used the term 'Aryan' to designate the group of people whose languages were thus structurally related.[116] The new racial theory which spoke of a common origin of the non-Semitic peoples of Europe and India had many enthusiastic supporters. Hegel was one of them. He hailed the theory of the affinity of the European languages with Sanskrit, referring to it as 'the great discovery (*die grosse Entdeckung*) in history', comparable to the discovery of a continent. It revealed, he stated, the historic relationship between the German and Indian peoples. For Hegel, 'the dispersion of these peoples, starting from Asia, and their distinct evolution beginning with the same ancestry', were 'irrefutable facts (*unwidersprechliches Faktum*).'[117]

If the Aryan theory found an influential supporter in Hegel, it found its most effective propagandist in Max Müller. In his writings Müller very often used the term 'Aryan race', and some of his research efforts were directed towards locating 'the cradle of our race' and the identification of languages classifiable within the Aryan group. His career spanned more than half a century, and his standing as one of the foremost scholars in Oriental languages added authority to his views. Müller considered the affinity between languages to be indicative of the origin of the speakers of those languages from a common racial 'stock'. It was his view that the same blood flowed in the veins of both Englishmen and Bengalis,[118] and in his later writings he described himself as 'the person mainly responsible for the use of the term Aryan in the sense of Indo-European'.[119] Racialist thought owed as much to ethnology as it did to comparative philology, and contemporaries of Müller like Knox and Gobineau were propounding a theory of 'the white races'.[120] By about 1875, as Maine observed in his Rede Lecture, a new theory of race, derived primarily from the researches on philology, had come into being. Maine questioned the assumptions basic to this theory. 'There seems to be no doubt', he nevertheless observed, 'that modern philology has suggested a grouping of peoples quite unlike anything that had been thought of before'.[121]

In the later years of his career Müller did have some misgivings about the use of the term 'Aryan race'. 'To me an ethnologist who speaks of Aryan race, Aryan blood, Aryan eyes and Aryan hair, is as great a sinner as a linguist who speaks of a dolichocephalic dictionary or a brachycephalic grammar', he wrote in his *Biography of Words* published in 1888. 'Aryan, in scientific language, is utterly inapplicable to race', he further stated. 'It means language and nothing but language, and if we speak of Aryan race at all, we should know that it means no more than x + Aryan speech'.[122] While this passage reveals Müller's strong reaction to the confusion resulting from the use of common terms by philologists and ethnologists, it is worth noting that the last conditional clause somewhat diminishes the emphatic ring of the preceding statement. In fact, Müller continued to use the term race, and the very essay in which these passages occur was devoted to a search for what he termed 'the cradle of our race'.[123] He was not very precise about the use of the term and he did not specify exactly what he meant when he said that race was 'x + speech'. Those who had been influenced by Müller's earlier views were even less inclined to avoid confusion between race and language. The theory of the Aryan race was by this time too well established to be shaken by such a statement. Müller's later work did not undermine the race theory, but contributed to the popularity of the mystical search for 'the original home of the Aryans', and the 'study' of their expansion which seems to have been conceived in terms evocative of the expansion of the political power and the languages of European states in more recent times.[124]

No traces of the influence of the Aryan theory are to be found in William Knighton's *The History of Ceylon*, published in 1845, or in Charles Pridham's *An Historical, Political and Statistical Account of Ceylon and its Dependencies*, published in 1849. Knighton referred to the similarities between the inhabitants of India and Sri Lanka which he thought pointed to immigrations from the neighbouring subcontinent.[125] It was Pridham's conjecture that the population of the island represented a fusion of immigrants from India and from China or Siam.[126]

B.C. Clough, who compiled the first Sinhala–English dictionary, published in parts in 1821 and 1830, was the first writer to present the view that the Sinhala language was derived from Sanskrit.[127] It is interesting to note that this view was not easily accepted by some exponents of the Aryan theory. Christian Lassen, whose influential work *Indisches Alterthumskunde* was published in 1847, distinguished Sinhala from the Aryan languages of the north Indian people (*die*

Arischen Inder) and listed it with the south Indian languages.[128] James de Alwis used the introduction to his edition of the *Sidath Sangarawa*, published in 1852, to present a view which, though basically similar to Clough's, took a different position on the nature of the relationship between Sanskrit and Sinhala. De Alwis was aware of the researches of William Jones and Franz Bopp. He argued that Sinhala shared a common origin with Sanskrit: it was not, however, a dialect of Sanskrit. De Alwis's hesitant presentation of his argument reveals that his views were not clearly formed at this time.

> To trace therefore the Singhalese to one of the Northern family of languages, and to call it a dialect of Sanskrit, is apparently far more difficult than to assign to it an origin common with the Telingu, Tamil, and Malayalim in the Southern family ... the Singhalese appears to us either a kindred language of Sanskrit, or one of the tongues ... which falls under the head of the Southern class. Yet upon the whole we incline to the opinion that it is the former.[129]

In his work published in 1859, James Emerson Tennent was more inclined to agree with Lassen, and spoke of 'unequivocal proof' of the affinity of Sinhala with 'the group of languages still in use in the Deccan; Tamil, Telingu and Malayalim', adding, however, that Sinhala appeared to have borrowed terms pertaining to religion from Pāli and those pertaining to science and art from Sanskrit.[130]

The years that followed saw the publication of two major works, both of which wielded a deep influence on the evolution of the Sinhala consciousness. In 1861 Müller published his *Lectures on the Science of Language* in which he declared that 'careful and minute comparison' had enabled him 'to class the idioms spoken in Iceland and Ceylon as cognate dialects of the Aryan family of languages'.[131] Müller's pronouncement was to wield a decisive influence over the Sri Lankan literati. On the other hand, Robert Caldwell's study of the comparative grammar of south Indian languages was certainly another major factor behind the hardening of opinion around the Aryan theory. In his work published in 1856 Caldwell presented a theory which was both a counter and a complement to the Aryan theory. Caldwell used the term Dravidian to designate what he termed 'a family of languages', and this was the first time that the south Indian languages had been categorized in this manner. According to Caldwell, the Dravidian 'family' included six 'cultivated dialects' (Tamil, Malayalam, Telugu, Canarese, Tulu and Kadagu) and six 'uncultivated dialects' (Tuda, Kota, Gond, Khond or Ku, Oraon and Rajmahal).[132] It was also Caldwell's opinion that there was 'no direct affinity' between Sinhala and Tamil.[133]

De Alwis's essay of 1866 on the origin of the Sinhala language reflects the new climate of opinion that had set in. Not only does he refer to 'the Aryan invasions' in this essay, thereby presenting what was to become a popular interpretation of the Vijaya myth, but also he seeks to prove, citing both Müller and Caldwell, that Sinhala belonged to 'the Arian or Northern family, as contradistinguished from Dravidian, or the Southern class of languages'.[134] Like many who were influenced by Müller's theories, he was not very careful about making distinctions between race and language. 'Though the complexion of the Sinhalese presents different shades', he wrote, 'the "copper colour" is that which prevails over the rest, and this it would seem is the colour of the Aryan race, so much honoured by Manu (ch.iv, *sūtra* 130) when he declared it an offence to pass over even the shadow of the copper-coloured man'.[135] The *Manudharmaśāstra*, which de Alwis quoted, does not easily lend support to his assertion. The term *babhru* in the *sūtra* quoted and translated by him was considered to be a difficult term by many a commentator. Medhatithi interpreted it as denoting 'a brown cow' or 'the Soma creeper'. Nandana accepted this first meaning, while Nārada rendered it as 'a brown creature'.[136] In his authoritative translation of the text, Müller preferred to render it into English as 'a reddish-brown animal'.[137] However, what is most interesting about de Alwis's statement is that, at a time when the Aryan theory was gaining general acceptance in Europe and south Asia, he was claiming Aryan status not only for the Sinhala language, but also for the speakers of that language. Following Müller and Caldwell, de Alwis was trying to apply the Aryan/Dravidian dichotomy to the Sri Lankan context. Though in Indian writings, as Thapar has pointed out, 'the upper castes were the Aryans and the lower castes were the non-Aryans',[138] de Alwis was attempting to place within the Aryan category 'the copper-coloured' Sinhalese without such caste limitations.

The Aryan theory provided a section of the colonial peoples of south Asia with a prestigious 'pedigree': it elevated them to the rank of the kinsmen of their rulers, even though the relationship was a distant and tenuous one. The term Ārya also had greater appeal because of its previous religious associations. In Sinhala the term *caturāryasatyaya* denoted 'the four noble truths' of Buddhism; *Ārya-aṣṭāṅgikamārga* denoted 'the noble eightfold path' of spiritual advancement and *ariyapuggalā* were individuals known for spiritual attainments. In the *Cūlavaṃsa* the term Ariya had been used to denote a group of people, but it is remarkable that, in this instance, it denoted people who were clearly distinguished from the Sinhala. In its description of the reign of Bhuvanekabāhu I (1272–1284), the chronicle distinguishes the Ariya mercenaries from the Sinhala soldiers.[139] Kulasuriya has pointed out that some of the south Indian migrants who arrived in the thirteenth and fourteenth centuries were described in certain Sinhala texts as people of 'Ariya descent'.[140] No Sinhala kings have been referred to as Ariya and, interestingly enough, it was the dynasty which ruled over the Tamil kingdom in Jaffna who called themselves *Ārya Cakravarti* or 'Ārya emperors'. It is an irony of history that in later times it was the Sinhala who came to be associated with the term Ārya and were, as such, distinguished from the Tamil speakers.

The classification of the Sinhala language in the Aryan group received the support of several influential writers including Childers, Goldschmidt, and Kuhn.[141] Meanwhile, as in Europe, in Sri Lanka, too, the exponents of racial theories received strong support from physical anthropology. M.M. Kunte's lecture on Ceylon, delivered in 1879, was one of the most important sources of support. 'There are, properly speaking, representatives of only two races in Ceylon – Aryans and Tamilians, the former being divided into descendants of Indian and Western Aryans', Kunte declared, adding that he had discovered that 'the formation of the forehead, the cheek-bones, the chin, the mouth and the lips of the Tamilians are [*sic*] distinctly different from those of the Ceylonese Aryans'.[142] C.F. and P.B. Sarasin identified three principal 'well distinguishable' races in Sri Lanka: the Sinhala, the Tamil and the Veddas, and they believed that the Tamils were more closely related to the Veddas than the Sinhala.[143] Rudolph Virchow, too, tended to agree that there were three races in Sri Lanka. He considered 'the Sinhalese race' to be the result of a mixture of Vedda elements and immigrants from India. There were resemblances between these two groups, but they were both distinct from the Tamils. Though the Sinhala were 'a mixed race', there was no doubt that 'the Sinhalese face' was 'an importation from the Aryan provinces of the Indian continent'.[144] These theorists disagreed on the position of the Vedda group and its relationship with the other two groups they had identified, but the views of Kunte and Virchow added strength to the opinion that the Sinhala were either Aryans or 'a mixed race' derived from the fusion of the Aryans and the aboriginal inhabitants in the island. Thus, by the end of the nineteenth century, linguistic groups were being given new definitions in terms of physical characteristics which were supposed to be specific to those groups. The Sinhala and Tamil identities thereby acquired a racial dimension.

These new theories were not easily admitted into the history books. A.E. Blazé's *A History of Ceylon for Schools*, published in 1900, does not show their influence. However, there is evidence even from about the end of the nineteenth century that these theories were gaining wide popularity. In December 1897, a magazine called *Buddhist* carried an article entitled 'The Aryan Sinhalese'. A booklet called *Aryan Sinhalese Names* was published in 1899. In 1910 A.E.R. Ratnaweera founded the magazine named *The Aryan*. If history books had reservations about the Aryan theory at the beginning of the century, they had begun to overcome these reservations by the 1920s. Blazé's book was revised, though with obvious hesitation, to accommodate the new theory, and the mythical founder of the Sinhala kingdom was introduced as 'believed to be of Aryan race'.[145] H.W. Codrington, whose *Short History of Ceylon*, was published in 1926, accepted the theory of the Aryan origin of the Sinhala, but ventured to suggest that their 'original Aryan blood' had been very much diluted through intermarriage:

> Vijaya's followers espoused Pandyan women and it seems probable that in course of time their descendants married with the people of the country on whom they imposed their language. Further dilution of the original Aryan blood has undoubtedly taken place in later ages, with the result that, though the Sinhalese language is of North Indian origin, the social system is that of the south.[146]

A few writers expressed their reservations about this trend of thought. 'Whether the Sinhalese language is a language with an Aryan structure and an Aryan glossary, or a language with a Dravidian structure with an Aryan glossary has divided scholars, and must await a thorough philological investigation', Ponnambalam Arunachalam observed in 1907.[147] W.F. Gunawardhana was more forthright in his criticism. In a lecture delivered at Ananda College on 28 September 1918, he presented the view that in grammatical structure Sinhala was Dravidian, though its vocabulary was mainly Aryan.[148] In a paper entitled 'The Aryan question in relation to India', published in 1921, he further developed this view. He pointed out that it was under Max Müller's influence that the Sinhala claims to membership of the Aryan race had been put forward. While reiterating his earlier views about the affinity between Sinhala and Dravidian languages, he tried to argue that the Sinhala were 'a Dravidian race slightly modified by a Mongoloid strain and an Aryan wash'.[149] It is noteworthy that, while Gunawardhana questioned the classification of the Sinhala as Aryans, his arguments were based on the concept of the Aryan and Dravidian racial categories. His views provoked a lengthy 'refutation' by C.A. Wijesinha who quoted Müller, Kunte and Havell to conclude that the Sinhala 'have hitherto been classified as an Aryan race, and will therefore continue to be classified as Aryan'.[150] In *The Early History of Ceylon* published in 1932, G.C. Mendis also made an attempt to correct this line of thinking by pointing out that Aryan and Dravidian were not racial categories but merely 'large groups of people who speak languages that had a common origin'.[151] His definition deserves comparison with those put forward by more recent students of south Asian history;[152] it was indeed a remarkable contribution as it came from a person who had studied in Germany in the period of the rise of Nazism. Unfortunately, his views lacked clarity: Mendis himself confused language with race, speaking of 'the Sinhalese race' on the same page and of 'Tamil blood' in the second edition of his book.[153] From about the 1920s racialist writings in Sinhala take a vehemently anti-Tamil stance, and they select the Duṭṭhagāmaṇī–Eḷāra episode for special treatment. V.B. Vatthuhamy's *Duṭugämuṇu–Eḷāra Mahāyuddha Kathālaṅkāraya* was one of the first works of this genre. This poem, published in 1923, reveals an intense antipathy towards the Tamils. This was to become a prominent ingredient in the Sinhala ideology of the following period.[154]

If in earlier historical epochs the Buddhist identity reflected a cosmopolitan outlook and extended beyond political boundaries to include coreligionists in different kingdoms, in the twentieth century a new term, 'Sinhala-Buddhist', comes into use to denote a group of people who are distinguished from the Sinhala of the other faiths and also from the Buddhists of other ethnic groups. Anagarika Dharmapala was probably the first person to use the term. He inaugurated the publication of the newspaper *Siṃhaḷa Bauddhayā* in 1906. One of the points emphasized by Dharmapala was the need for a leadership, both among the *religieux* and the laity, to direct 'the ignorant, helpless Sinhalese Buddhists'.[155] The portrayal of 'the Sinhalese Buddhists' as an underprivileged group had a certain basis in fact in that, under British rule, governmental patronage had favoured Christians, particularly those converted to the Anglican faith. The need to struggle for 'the legitimate rights of the Sinhala Buddhists' was to become an essential element of the Sinhalese-Buddhist ideology. And, since this group was numerically dominant in the island, the leadership that Dharmapala looked for was not hard to find, particularly after universal suffrage was introduced to Sri Lanka in 1931.

In the context of the socio-economic transformations taking place under colonial rule, the Sinhala consciousness found it possible to overcome some of the limitations which had prevented its development and expansion in its previous historical forms. Though the Sinhala identity had been 'extended' earlier to cover 'the inhabitants of the island', it was during the post-nineteenth century period that it entered the consciousness of the masses, drawing together that section of the population which belonged to the Sinhala linguistic group through a consciousness overarching their local, regional and caste identities. This consciousness developed among this group of people an appreciation of their common culture. It infused the nationalist movement with certain anti-imperialist potentialities. However, in its varied aspects the Sinhala ideology does not lend itself to being categorized simply as anti-imperialist. In fact, it was also used to serve a contradictory purpose. Dharmapala extolled the past greatness of the Sinhala Aryans 'who had never been conquered', but what he demanded was 'self-government under British protection'.[156] On the other hand, there were certain propagandists of the Sinhala ideology like Ratnaweera, the editor of *The Aryan*, who took great pains to dissociate the Sinhala from the militant nationalists of Bengal and stated: 'It is a consolation to see ... that we are governed by an Aryan nation'.[157] It is not surprising that such an ideology did not produce an anti-imperialist movement of mass proportions.

However, it must be emphasized that the weakness of the nationalist movement cannot be explained only in terms of the ideology, and that the character of the ideology was itself to a considerable extent conditioned by the nature and limitations of the socio-economic changes that had taken place. While British rule undermined certain aspects of pre-colonial social relations, it had not set in motion that process observable in European history which swept aside pre-capitalist institutions and 'lumped together into one nation' different social groups, subordinating all other identities to the unifying national ideology of the bourgeoisie. As Engels noted, the European process derived its motive power from a particular combination of an industry, an industrial bourgeoisie and a centralizing market.[158] The nascent bourgeoisie of the period of colonial rule in Sri Lanka was weak, nurtured by and dependent on foreign capital. Its weakness was reflected in the poverty of its culture, especially in its failure to develop a unifying national ideology, overarching the ethnic identities derived from previous historical epochs. The dominant concepts in the culture of this class represented a combination of ideas borrowed from contemporary Europe and from earlier epochs of the island's history. Several ideas borrowed from contemporary Europe came from the ideological armoury of racialism rather than from the rich stocks of humanism. Even Buddhist leaders like Dharmapala used the phraseology of anti-Semitism which was then becoming increasingly evident in a certain genre of European writing. In his contribution to the *Twentieth Century Impressions of Ceylon*, published in 1907, Dharmapala speaks of 'the glorious inheritance of Aryan ancestors, uncontaminated by Semitic and savage ideas'.[159] In this new intellectual milieu the Sinhala ideology inherited from the past came to be refashioned and infused with racialism.

The Sinhala ideology has reflected the interests and aspirations of those who have served as its main propagandists, i.e the Sinhala-educated literati, and this has made it difficult for others to recognize its primary social function of mobilizing the Sinhala masses under the leadership of the Sinhala bourgeoisie. In addition to this 'unifying' role, the Sinhala ideology has also played a 'divisive' role. While this ideology has been antithetical to the development of a broad nationalist movement and has thereby contributed to its weakness, in its present form, the Sinhala ideology is a factor which divides the bourgeoisie. It has confronted the bourgeoisie with the critical problem of maintaining their class unity while resorting, for the purpose of mass mobilization, to the propagation of an ideology which hampers the unity of that very class and is disintegrative in its effect on its state. However, the crisis represented by the conflict of identities is not limited to the bourgeoisie; it has also affected other classes. The Sinhala ideology and other similar group ideologies have left a deep and debilitating impact particularly on the working class by dividing it sharply and by hampering the development of its class consciousness.

IV

It will have been evident from the preceding survey that the nature of the Sinhala identity as well as the relationship between the group brought together by this identity and the other groupings based on religion, ritual status and language varied in different periods of history. Thus all these groupings represented historically variable, intersecting social divisions. Identities based on ritual status and religion can be traced back to the most ancient historical documents available in Sri Lanka. The Sinhala identity in its earliest historical form bears the imprint of its origin in the period of state formation, in association with the ruling dynasty and its immediate socio-political base. It is only by about the twelfth century that the Sinhala grouping could have been considered to be identical with the linguistic grouping. The relationship between the Sinhala and the Buddhist identities is even more complex. There is a close association between the two identities, but at no period do they appear to have coincided exactly to denote the self-same group of people.[160] As Jacobson observed with reference to Sumerian history, religion and language provided the bases for distinct identities, but it is difficult to group these distinct features within one convenient 'bundle'.[161]

Our survey highlights the role that the literati, the group which occupies the misty regions on the boundaries of class divisions, played in identity formation in ancient as well as modern times. In selecting and reformulating myths and in giving them literary form, the literati played a significant role in the development of Sinhala ideology in ancient society. They fashioned a version of history to conform with the dominant ideology of their society. This intellectual role was not one that was independent of, or unrelated to, the structure of power. Though it may be rash to generalize about the entire literati on the basis of the evidence in the Pāli chronicles, it can be confidently asserted that these chronicles reveal the important role played by at least a section of the literati in the formulation and propagation of a state ideology in ancient and early medieval society.

The history of the development of the Sinhala ideology since the nineteenth century reveals the formidable role that the study of 'dead languages' and 'the remote past' has played in shaping mass consciousness and thereby in the moulding of the present. It was the study of ancient Oriental languages, particularly Sanskrit, and of comparative philology that initiated in the nineteenth century a trend which came to wield such a decisive influence on contemporary mass consciousness. In Sri Lanka the discipline of history was initially a reluctant draftee, but it is now firmly entrenched within this ideological framework. The depth of the impact of this ideological current becomes evident even from a cursory review of recent research on Sri Lanka in those disciplines categorized as the humanities and the social sciences which perform a crucial social function in either validating or refashioning current ideology. The ability of these disciplines to grow out of the deformations derived from the impact of racialism and communalism will depend on the extent to which those engaged in research and teaching recognize the social function of their disciplines, and develop an awareness of the ideological underpinnings of research and other academic work.[162]

Notes and references

1 John M. Senaveratne, *The Story of the Sinhalese*, Colombo, 1930, p. 16.
2 L.D. Barnett, 'The Early History of Ceylon', in *The Cambridge History of India*, 1921, vol. I, London, reprinted in Delhi, 1955, p. 548; G.C. Mendis, *Our Heritage*, Colombo, 1943, p. 20.
3 See S. Paranavitana, *Inscriptions of Ceylon*, 1970, vol. I, Colombo.
4 S. Paranavitana, 'The Aryan settlements: the Sinhalese', Chapter VI, in *The University of Ceylon History of Ceylon*, Colombo, 1959, vol. I, pt. 1, pp. 87–8.
5 This is evident from the titles borne by people who inscribed the earliest Brāhmī records. See Paranavitana, *Inscriptions of Ceylon*, vol. I.
6 For a discussion on the process of state formation in Sri Lanka, see R.A.L.H. Gunawardana, 'Social function and political power: a case study of state formation in irrigation society', *Indian Historical Review*, 1978, vol. IV, no. 2, pp. 259–73.
7 *Dv*., 9.1
8 *Samantapāsādikā*, the Bāhiranidāna section, edited and translated by N.A. Jayawickrama as *The Inception of Discipline and the Vinayanidāna*, London, 1962, pp. 2, 136.
9 See Samuel Beal, 'Travels of Fa-Hian or Fo-kwo-ki', in *Travels of Hiuen Tsang*, Calcutta, 1957, vol. 1, p. 45.
10 S. Paranavitana, *Sigiri Graffiti, being Sinhalese Verse of the Eighth, Ninth and Tenth Centuries*, London, 1956, vol. II, p. 179.

11 J.G. de Casparis, 'New evidence on cultural relations between Java and Ceylon in ancient times', *Artibus Asiae*, 1962, vol. XXIV, pp. 241–8.
12 J.F. Fleet, *Inscriptions of Early Gupta Kings and their Successors, Corpus Inscriptionum Indicarum*, 1963, vol. III, Varanasi, p. 8.
13 Paul Pelliot, 'Review of Chu-fan-chih, tr. by F. Hirth and W.W. Rockhill', *T'oung Pao*, 1921, vol. XIII, pp. 462–3. The term Sīhaḷa also occurs in an inscription of similar date as the name of a monastery at Nāgarjuṇikoṇḍa in south India. Presumably, this monastery was a residence for monks who came there from the Sīhaḷa kingdom. 'Prakrit inscriptions from a Buddhist site at Nāgarjuṇakoṇḍa,' (ed.) J. Ph. Vogel, *Epigraphia Indica* vol. xx, p. 22.
14 K.V. Subrahmanya Ayyar, 'The Earliest Monuments of the Pandya Country and their Inscrptions', *Proceedings of the Third All-India Oriental Conference*, Madras, 1924, pp. 275–300.
15 T.V. Mahalingam, *Early South Indian Palaeography*, Madras, 1967, pp. 201–11, 245–50, 251–7.
16 Iravatham Mahadevan, *Corpus of the Brahmi Inscriptions*, Madras, 1966, pp. 8–9.
17 Robert Caldwell, *A Comparative Grammar of the Dravidian or South Indian Family of Languages*, 1856, 6th edition, Madras, 1956, p. 109; *Tamil Lexicon*, Madras, 1924, vol. I, p. 382.
18 *Çēntan Tivākaram*, ed. Lōkanāta Mutaliyar, Madras, 1917, p.62.
19 Marc Bloch, 'Sur les grandes invasions: quelques positions de problèmes', *Revue de Synthèse*, quoted in Paul Poliakov, *The Aryan Myth: A History of Racist and Nationalist Ideas in Europe*, London, 1974, p. 19.
20 This is Geiger's translation of the relevant strophe from the *Mahāvaṃsa*. See *Mahāvaṃsa*, tr. W. Geiger, Colombo, 1950, p. 58.
21 The eighteen groups of *pessakārakā* are comparable with the *aṣṭādaśajāti* in south Indian records. See J.F. Fleet, 'Sanskrit and Old Canarese inscriptions', *Indian Antiquary*, 1876, vol. V, pp. 50–3. The Pāli chronicles of Sri Lanka record instances of kings assigning *pessakārakā* (var. *pessiyā*) to serve in monasteries. The groups of people denoted by this term included craftsmen as well as those who performed service functions with a 'low' ritual ranking. See R.A.L.H. Gunawardana, *Robe and Plough: Monasticism and Economic Interest in Early Medieval Sri Lanka*, AAS monograph series no. 35, Tucson, Arizona, 1979, pp. 119–20.
22 I have borrowed this term from Gananath Obeyesekere. See 'Gajabāhu and the Gajabāhu synchronism: an inquiry into the relationship between myth and history', *The Ceylon Journal of the Humanities*, 1970, vol. I, no. 1, pp. 25–36.
23 S. Beal, *Travels of Hiuen Tsang*, Calcutta, 1958, vol. IV, pp. 435–7.
24 *Divyāvadāna*, ed. E.B. Cowell and R.A. Neil, Cambridge, 1886, pp. 523–9.
25 Beal, *Travels of Hiuen Tsang*, vol. IV, pp. 438–42.

26 See L.S. Perera, 'The Early Kings of Ceylon', Chapter VII, in *University of Ceylon History of Ceylon*, vol. I, pt. 1, pp. 98–111; G.C. Mendis, 'The Vijaya Legend', *Paranavitana Felicitation Volume*, ed. N.A. Jayawickrama, Colombo, 1965, pp. 263–92.
27 *Vaṃsatthappakāsinī (Vap.)*, ed. G.P. Malalasekera, London, 1935, vol I, pp. 259–60, 264.
28 While noting that some of the tales in the *Divyāvadāna* had been translated into Chinese in the third century AD, M. Winternitz (*A History of Indian Literature*, Calcutta, 1953, vol. II, pp. 285–6) has assigned this work to the fourth century AD.
29 Barnett, op. cit., p. 548.
30 A.L. Basham, 'Prince Vijaya and the Aryanization in Ceylon', *Ceylon Historical Journal*, 1952, vol. I, no. 3, pp. 163–71.
31 *University of Ceylon History of Ceylon*, vol. I, pt. 1, pp. 82–97.
32 See *Paranavitana Felicitation Volume*, p. 268.
33 J.W. McCrindle, *Ancient India as Described in Classical Literature*, London, 1901, p. 102.
34 J.W. McCrindle, *Ancient India as Described by Ptolemy*, London, 1885, pp. 247–59.
35 *Cv*. 54.10.
36 Basham op. cit.; G. Obeyesekere, 'Religious symbolism and political change in Ceylon', *Modern Ceylon Studies*, 1970, vol. I, no. 1, pp. 43–63.
37 *The Epic of Gilgamesh*, tr. with an introduction by N.K. Sandars, Middlesex, 1980, pp. 36, 94.
38 *Vap*., vol. I, p. 261.
39 Romila Thapar, 'Origin myths and the early historical tradition', in *Ancient Indian Social History*, Delhi, 1978, pp. 294–325.
40 C. Minakshi, *Administration and Social Life under the Pallavas*, Madras, 1938, p. 82.
41 *Indian Antiquary*, 1881, vol. V, pp. 50–3.
42 E. Hultzsch, 'Pikira grant of Siṃhavarman', *Epigraphia Indica* (*EI*), 1905/6, vol. VIII, pp. 159–63.
43 H. Krishna Sastri, 'Malēpaḍu plates of Puṇyakumāra', *EI*, 1911/12, vol. XI, pp. 337–8.
44 *Madras Epigraphical Reports*, Archaeological Survey, Madras, 1908/9, p. 5.
45 K.A. Nilakanta Sastri, *The Cōḻas*, Madras, 1935, vol. I, pp. 24–6.
46 *Mv*. 7.42.
47 *Vap*., vol. I, p. 261.
48 *Mv*., trans. Geiger p. 60.
49 See R.A.L.H. Gunawardana, 'The kinsmen of the Buddha: myth as political charter in the ancient and early medieval kingdoms of Sri Lanka', *The Sri Lanka Journal of the Humanities*, 1976, vol. II, no. 1, pp. 53–62.
50 See Paranavitana, *Inscriptions of Ceylon*, vol. I, p. lxxxix and also Sirima Kiribamune, 'Tamils in ancient and medieval Sri Lanka: the historical roots of ethnicity', *Ethnic Studies Report*, 1986, vol. IV, no.1, p. 10. It

was Paranavitana's contention that the term Siṃhaḷa does *not* occur in a single inscription in the Brāhmī script because the Sinhala identity covered almost the entire population and had ceased to be a distinctive designation. While this *argumentum ex silentio* is unusually weak, the information from the chronicles goes against his supposition and points to a situation persisting even several centuries later when not everyone but only those associated with the royal family were known as the Sinhala.

51 R.A.L.H. Gunawardana, 'Social function and political power'.
52 *Mv*. 9.7–10.
53 *Divyāvadāna*, p. 527.
54 Beal, *Travels of Hiuen Tsang*, vol. IV, p. 441.
55 Bronislaw Malinowski, *Magic, Science and Religion and Other Essays*, Boston, 1948, p. 145.
56 *The Sri Lanka Journal of the Humanities*, vol. II, no. 1, 1976, pp. 53–62.
57 R.A.L.H. Gunawardana, 'The rise of a united kingdom', synopsis of a chapter for the proposed revised edition of the *University of Ceylon History of Ceylon*, vol. I, pt. 1. See also R.A.L.H. Gunawardana, 'Prelude to the state: an early phase in the evolution of political institutions in Sri Lanka', *The Sri Lanka Journal of the Humanities*, 1985, vol. VIII, pp. 1–39.
58 *Mv*. 23. 4–5.
59 See note 56.
60 *Cv*. 38. 11.2.
61 *Cv*. 38. 37.
62 *Cv*. 38. 38–9.
63 See *EZ*, vol. IV, p. 114.
64 See H.W. Schomerus, *Sivaitische Heiligenlegenden (Periyapurāṇa and Tiruvātavūrarpurāṇa)*, Jena, pp. 153, 264–80.
65 K.A. Nilakanta Sastri, *A History of South India*, Delhi 1955, pp. 405–7.
66 *Mv*. 33. 43.
67 S. Paranavitana, *The God of Adam's Peak*, Ascona, 1955, pp. 405–7.
68 Paranavitana, *Sigiri Graffiti*, v. 334.
69 Ibid., v. 449.
70 *Saddharmālaṅkāra*, ed. Bentara Saddhātissa, 1934, p. 176.
71 *Dharmapradīpikā*, ed. R.D.s. Dharmārāma, Pāliyagoḍa, 1951, p. 254.
72 *Vesaturudā Sanne*, ed. D.E. Hettiaratchi, Colombo, 1950, pp. 19, 67.
73 Ibid., p. 67.
74 *Buddhavaṃsa*, ed. R. Morris, London, p. 5.
75 Gunawardana, *Robe and Plough*, pp. 173–4.
76 *EZ*, vol. I, p. 237.
77 *EZ*, vol. II, pp. 202–18.
78 Gunawardana, *Robe and Plough*, pp. 313–37.
79 *Vimativinodanī*, ed. Boratuḍāvē Dhammādhāra Tissa, Colombo, 1935, pp. 96–100.
80 *Sīmālaṅkāra*, ed. Buddhasiri Tissa, Colombo, 1904, pp. 42–3.
81 *Dharmapradīpikā*, p. 55.

82 *Cv.* 70. 53–4.
83 *Çrī Takçina Kaliāça Purāṇam*, (ed.) Vaittiyaliṅka Tēçihar, 1916, pt. 2, p. 20.
84 See Sirima Kiribamune, 'Buddhism and royal prerogative in medieval Sri Lanka', *Religion and Legitimation of Power in Sri Lanka*, (ed.) Bardwell L. Smith, Chambersburg, 1978, pp. 107–18.
85 *Pūjāvaliya*, (ed.) A.V. Suravīra, Colombo, 1961, pp. 108–9.
86 Amaradasa Liyanagamage, *The Decline of Polonnaruva and the Rise of Dambadeniya*, Colombo, 1968, p. 128.
87 *Buduguṇālaṅkāraya*, ed. K. Ñānavimala, Colombo, 1953, vv. 121–83.
88 *EZ*, vol. II, p. 114.
89 See *Trisiṃhalē Kaḍa-im saha Vitti*, ed. A.J.W. Marambe, Kandy, 1926. Ananda S. Kulasuriya cites some material from the *Vittipot* in his 'Regional independence and elite change in the politics of 14th century Sri Lanka', *Journal of the Royal Asiatic Society*, 1976, pp. 136–55.
90 See Gananath Obeyesekere, 'Gajabāhu and the Gajabāhu synchronism: an inquiry into the relationship between myth and history', *The Ceylon Journal of the Humanities*, 1970, vol. I, no. 1, pp. 25–36. It is very likely that there were settlements along the eastern coast as well.
91 *Kokila Sandesa*, ed. W.F. Gunawardhana, Colombo, 1945, v. 251.
92 *Sūryaśataka Sannaya*, ed. M. Piyaratana, in *Vilgammuḷa Pabaňda*, Colombo, 1956, p. 567.
93 *Nāmāvaḷiya*, ed. H. Jayatilaka, Colombo, 1888, vv. 285–6.
94 *Kokila Sandesa*, v. 286.
95 Ibid., v. 155.
96 *Savan purā pavasana demaḷa gī rasin*. Ibid., v. 55.
97 *Parevi Sandesa*, ed. Tangalle Siri Sunandāsabha, Colombo, 1902, v. 140.
98 Puñcibaṇḍāra Sannasgala, *Siṃhaḷa Sāhitya Vaṃśaya*, Colombo, 1964, p. 286.
99 Ibid., pp. 382 ff.
100 Ibid., p. 347.
101 See A.H. Sunder Raman, 'Four Telugu manuscripts in the Colombo Museum Library', *Ceylon Literary Register*, 1933, vol III, no. 5, pp. 193–8.
102 There are several instances of members of the nobility and the gentry using the Grantha and Tamil scripts or a combination of these and the Sinhala script in their signatures. See, for instance, the signature of Dumbara Rājakaruṇā Mudiyansē in documents dated in the years 1688 and 1714 of the Śaka era (Sri Lanka National Archives Documents Nos. 5/63/67/-3 and 12).
103 *EZ*, vol. III, p. 280.
104 *Rājāvaliya*, ed. B. Gunasekara, Colombo, 1953, p. 49.
105 S. Paranavitana, 'The Kotte Kingdom up to 1505', *University of Ceylon History of Ceylon*, 1960, vol. I, pt. 2, p. 679.
106 G.P.V. Somaratne, *The Political History of the Kingdom of Kotte*, Nugegoda, 1975, pp. 142–8.
107 C.R. de Silva, 'Ethnicity, prejudice and the writing of history', *G.C. Mendis Memorial Lecture*, Colombo, 1984, p.4.

108 The sources cited are *Mandārampurapuvata* (ed. Labugama Laṅkānanda, n.p., 1958, pp. 9–10 vv. 72–8; pp. 40–1 vv. 316–7) and *Paraṃgi Haṭana* (tr. P.E. Pieris, *Ribeiro's History of Ceilao*, Colombo, 1909, p. 347 vv. 28–31).
109 *Paraṃgi Haṭana* in P.E. Pieris, *Ribeiro's History of Ceilao* pp. 361–4, vv. 264–374; p. 268, vv. 419–31. See also *Mandārampurapuvata*, pp. 47–51, vv. 352–81.
110 See, for instance, the *Mandārampurapuvata*, p. 9 v. 76.
111 P.E. Pieris, *Sinhalē and the Patriots, 1815–1818*, Colombo, 1950, p. 1.
112 Sannasgala, op. cit., pp. 466–8, 529–31; K.N.O. Dharmadasa, 'The Sinhala Buddhist identity and the Nāyakkar dynasty in the politics of the Kandyan kingdom', *Collective Identities, Nationalisms and Protest in Modern Sri Lanka*, ed. M. Roberts, Colombo, 1979, pp. 99–128.
113 See, for instance, the colophon of the *Narendra-caritāvalōkana-pradīpikā* in Jinadasa Liyanaratne, *Catalogue des Manuscrits Singhalais*, Paris, 1983, p. 119.
114 L.S. Dewaraja, *A Study of the Political, Administrative and Social Structure of the Kandyan Kingdom of Ceylon, 1707–1760* 2nd edition, Colombo, 1988, pp. 84–5, 94.
115 Dewaraja, op. cit., pp. 35–8
116 Poliakov, op. cit., p. 193.
117 G.W.F. Hegel, *Die Vernunft in der Geschichte*, ed. J. Hoffmeister, in *Sämtliche Werke*, Band XVIIIa, Hamburg, 1955, p. 163.
118 Quoted by T.H. Huxley, 'The Aryan question', in *Man's Place in Nature and Other Essays*, London, 1901, p. 281, n. 1.
119 Max Müller, *Essays*, Leipzig, vol. II, 1879, p. 333.
120 Poliakov, op. cit., pp. 232–8.
121 See Henry Sumner Maine, *Village Communities in the East and West*, London, 1881, p. 209.
122 Max Müller, *Biography of Words and the Home of the Aryans*, London, 1888, pp. 120–1.
123 Ibid., p. 91.
124 See ibid., pp. 91–3.
125 William Knighton, *The History of Ceylon*, London, 1845, pp. 2–4.
126 C. Pridham, *A Historical and Statistical Account of Ceylon and its Dependencies*, London, 1849, pp. 20–2.
127 B.C. Clough, *A Dictionary of the English and Sinhalese, and Sinhalese and English Languages*, republished as *Sinhalese–English Dictionary*, Colombo, 1892, p. viii.
128 Christian Lassen, *Indisches Alterthumskunde*, London, 1847, pp. 362–3.
129 James de Alwis, *Sidath Sangarawa, A Grammar of the Sinhalese Language*, Colombo, 1852, p. xlvi.
130 James Emerson Tennent, *Ceylon, an Account of the Island: Physical, Historical and Topographical*, London, 1859, p. 328.
131 Max Müller, *The Science of Language*, London, 1861, republished in 1890, p. 60.
132 R. Caldwell, *A Comparative Grammar of the Dravidian or South Indian Family of Languages*, pp. 3–6.

133 Ibid., p. 109.
134 James de Alwis, 'On the origin of the Sinhalese language ', *Journal of the Ceylon Branch of the Royal Asiatic Society* (*JCBRAS*), 1865/6, vol. IV, no. 13, p. 143.
135 Ibid., pp. 150–1.
136 *Manudharmaśāstra*, ed. Max Müller, *Sacred Books of the East*, vol. XXV, Oxford, 1886, pp. 149–50, note 130.
137 op. cit., p. 149.
138 Romila Thapar, 'Ideology and the interpretation of early Indian history', *Review*, 1982 vol. 5, no. 3 (reprinted by the Social Scientists', Association, Colombo, n.d.), p. 392.
139 *Cv.* 90. 16–30.
140 Kulasuriya, op. cit., pp. 139–40.
141 R.C. Childers, 'Notes on the Sinhalese language: No. 1: on the formation of the plural of neuter nouns; No. 2: proofs of the Sanskritic origin of Sinhalese', *Journal of the Royal Asiatic Society*, 1874/5, vol. VII, pp. 35–48; 1875/6, vol. VIII, pp. 131–55; Paul Goldschmidt, *Report on the Inscriptions Found in the North-Central Province and the Hambantota District, Sessional Paper* No. 24, Colombo, 1875; Ernst Kuhn, 'Origin and language of the inhabitants of Ceylon', *Orientalist*, 1865/6, vol. II, pp. 112–7, republished in *Ceylon Literary Register*, 1932, vol. II, pp. 489–96.
142 M.M. Kunte, *Lecture on Ceylon*, Bombay, 1880, p. 9.
143 C.F. and P.B. Sarasin, 'Outline of two years' scientific researches in Ceylon', *JCBRAS*, 1886, vol. IX, pp. 289–305.
144 R. Virchow, 'The Veddas of Ceylon, and their relation to the neighbouring tribes', *JCBRAS*, 1886, vol. IX, p. 490. See also Virchow's 'Ethnological studies on the Sinhalese race', translated by W.R. Kynsey and J.D. Macdonald as 'Professor Virchow's ethnological studies on the Sinhalese race', *JCBRAS*, 1886, vol. IX, pp. 267–88.
145 L.E. Blazé, *A History of Ceylon for Schools*, 6th edition, Colombo, 1931, p. 9.
146 H.W. Codrington, *A Short History of Ceylon*, London, 1926, p. 10.
147 Ponnambalam Arunachalam, 'Population: the island's races, religions, castes and customs', in *Twentieth Century Impressions of Ceylon*, ed. Arnold Wright, Colombo, 1907, p. 333.
148 W.F. Gunawardhana, *The Origin of the Sinhalese Language*, text of lecture delivered at the Ananda College, Colombo, 1918.
149 W.F. Gunawardhana, 'The Aryan question in relation to India', *JCBRAS*, 1921, vol. XXVIII, pp. 12–60.
150 C.A. Wijesinha, *The Sinhalese Aryans*, Colombo, 1922, p. 110.
151 G.C. Mendis, *The Early History of Ceylon*, Calcutta, 1932, pp. 15–16; 2nd edition, Calcutta, 1935, pp. 6, 9.
152 Cf. Romila Thapar, 'Communalism and the writing of ancient Indian history', in R. Thapar, Harbans Mukhia & Bipan Chandra, *Communalism and the Writing of Indian History*, New Delhi, 1969, p. 10 and Romila Thapar, 'The image of the barbarian in early India', in *Ancient Indian Social History*, New Delhi, 1978, p. 181 n.2.

153 Mendis, *The Early History of Ceylon*, 2nd edition, p. 10.
154 V.B. Vatthuhamy, *Duṭugāmuṇu–Eḷāra Mahāyuddha Kathālaṅkāraya*, Colombo, 1923.
155 See Anagarika Dharmapala, *Return to Righteousness, A Collection of Speeches, Essays and Letters of Anagarika Dharmapala*, ed. A. Guruge, Colombo, 1965, pp. 519–21.
156 Dharmapala, op. cit., p. 517.
157 The editorial, *The Aryan*, 1910, vol. I. no. 2.
158 See Karl Marx and Frederick Engels, *Selected Works*, Moscow, vol. I. 1958, p. 38.
159 Dharmapala, op. cit., p. 487.
160 Gananath Obeyesekere presents a different view about the relationship between the Sinhala and the Buddhist identities. See 'The vicissitudes of the Sinhala–Buddhist identity through time and change', in *Collective Identities, Nationalisms and Protest in Modern Sri Lanka*, ed. M. Roberts, Colombo, 1979, pp. 279–313.
161 T. Jacobsen, 'Political institutions, literature and religion', *City Invincible*, ed. C.H. Kraeling and R. McC.Adams, Chicago, 1960, pp. 64–5.
162 This is a revised version of a paper originally presented to the Seminar on Nationality Problems in Sri Lanka, organized by the Social Scientists' Association and held on 22 December 1979. It was published first in *The Sri Lanka Journal of the Humanities* for 1979 and subsequently in *Ethnicity and Social Change in Sri Lanka*, Colombo, 1984. The author is grateful to the participants in this Seminar and to the late Professor Ralph Pieris for comments.

Chapter four

Historical images in the British period[1]

John D. Rogers

The content and appeal of the histories of Sri Lanka created when the island was under British rule were subject to many influences, including the types of sources available, the broader trends in European historical writing, and the ideological and social positions of the authors and their intended audiences. In the early and middle nineteenth century British writers developed an historical framework that included two assumptions: that in ancient times there was a great Sinhala civilization, which later went into decline; and that distinct and often antagonistic ethnic groups existed throughout the island's long history. Sri Lankan writers in the late nineteenth and early twentieth centuries failed to question either of these assumptions. Instead, they addressed issues such as the precise level of civilization achieved in various eras and the relative contribution of different ethnic groups to the island's welfare. By the early twentieth century these histories exerted a strong influence on popular images of the past, especially among Sinhala people who lived in the Low Country and the towns. In particular, the idea that there was a great and unbroken Sinhala past was widespread, even among uneducated persons. But some of the other themes that came to dominate historical images after Independence, including the portrayal of Tamils as inevitable enemies of Sinhala people, were either absent or not thought relevant to contemporary affairs.

The early nineteenth century: the construction of an ancient past

When the British took control of the coastal areas of Sri Lanka in 1796, they had little understanding of the history and customs of the island. As in India, they soon began to create a body of knowledge that would provide information for both the practical needs of government and a general assessment of indigenous civilization on a universal scale of progress.[2] Later in the nineteenth century this knowledge exerted a strong influence on the way Sri Lankans conceived their own past.

In the early years of British rule a small number of officials and military men wrote general books about their country's new possession. At first Sri Lanka's proper history was seen as having begun in the sixteenth century. Robert Percival, whose book was published in 1803, stated that 'the wild stories current among the natives, throw no light whatever on the ancient history of the island. The earliest period at which we can look for an authentic information, is the arrival of the Portuguese under Almeyda, in the year 1505'.[3] Percival's 'wild stories' were probably fragments of the Mahavamsa and other historical chronicles, which were communicated to him verbally, through interpreters. It was the later 'discovery' of these chronicles, and their treatment as texts, that was to shape the historical images of Sri Lanka that were generated later in the colonial period.

Anthony Bertolacci's book, published in 1817, referred to the tradition that the island had had a higher state of civilization and had supported a larger population in ancient times than it did upon the assumption of British rule, and cited the ruined irrigation works in the Dry Zone to support this claim.[4] Bertolacci, like Percival, probably relied on oral accounts from a small number of informants for his knowledge of 'tradition'. John Davy's work, published in 1821, included a section on the island's history that was drawn from his conversations with Millave, a senior Kandyan headman: 'Part of the information which he communicated was given from a very retentive memory, and part drawn from an old chronicle, or rather historical romance of Ceylon, which he had by him, and to which he referred when his memory failed him'.[5] It is clear from Davy's account that the 'historical romance' in question was a compendium of historical chronicles, including the Mahavamsa and Culavamsa. Davy viewed this section of his book as legend, not history: 'The Singalese possess no accurate records of events, are ignorant of genuine history, and are not sufficiently advanced to relish it'.[6]

In the 1820s a few officials with antiquarian interests began to take the chronicles more seriously, and set out to discover 'authentic' and 'original' texts. Sir Alexander Johnston, a Supreme Court judge, collected historical manuscripts, including some based on the Mahavamsa and Culavamsa, and arranged for their translation and publication in a work edited by Edward Upham.[7] Johnston hoped that an accurate history would enable colonial lawmakers to frame legislation in keeping with the island's customs.[8] In 1833, the same year that Upham's work appeared, George Turnour, an official who was stationed in the Kandyan region, published a letter in the Ceylon Almanac, which stated that earlier writers had been wrong in denying the existence of indigenous historical sources. Turnour, who unlike Johnston was able to read Pali and Sinhala, appended an 'Epitome of Ceylon History', which included the names and regal dates of Sri Lankan kings over a period of 2,358 years, from 543 BC, when Vijaya arrived from Bengal, to 1815, when the last Kandyan king was deposed and the British took control of the entire island.[9] Four years later, in 1837, Turnour published Pali and English versions of the Mahavamsa, which covered the period up to 301 AD.[10] He also demonstrated that Upham's volume was an abridgement and summary of the texts concerned.[11] Turnour planned to publish the Culavamsa, but died before he could complete this work. His findings quickly became standard orthodoxy among British officials.[12] Those parts of Upham's volumes not translated by Turnour continued to be used widely until they were superseded by other editions in the late nineteenth century.

More research needs to be done before it will be possible to assess how far the Mahavamsa and other historical chronicles were known or thought relevant among Sinhala people in the late eighteenth and early nineteenth centuries. Their publication was not a matter of taking widely-known indigenous texts and making them available to an English-speaking audience. Turnour wrote in his preface that he had never met a Sri Lankan who had 'critically' read through the Mahavamsa, and that since it was an 'historical' rather than 'religious' work it was 'seldom consulted by the priesthood, and consequently rarely found in the temples; and I have never yet met with, or heard of, any abridged copy of the work'.[13] As an aid in translating the Mahavamsa from Pali to English, Turnour used a Sinhala version of the commentary on the Mahavamsa, the Mahavamsa Tika, which he found in a Southern Province temple. When he brought this commentary to Kandy and showed it to the monks there, they told him that they had never seen it before, but this may only have been because the Sinhala translation of this Pali text was unfamiliar. Other evidence suggests that awareness of the Mahavamsa may have been more widespread than Turnour's preface indicates. The chronicle was extended and brought up to date in the mid-eighteenth century at the behest of a Kandyan monarch who wanted to portray the Kandyan Kingdom as the successor to earlier Buddhist kingdoms, and it was translated into Thai at some point between 1782 and 1809.[14] Furthermore, the historical references by Bertolacci and Davy suggest that much of its content circulated orally. On the other hand, the publication in the nineteenth century of the Mahavamsa and other indigenous works that included historical narratives undoubtedly contributed to increased awareness of the island's past.[15]

While the 'discovery' of the chronicles was the single most important influence on the development of Sri Lankan historiography, the presence of physical remains of the ancient civilization was essential for establishing the credibility of the texts. Major Jonathan Forbes, who was stationed at Matale in the 1830s, knew of Turnour's work and spent a good deal of time searching for places mentioned in the Mahavamsa. His book *Eleven Years in Ceylon*, which was published in 1840, included detailed accounts of the ruins of irrigation works and cities, and supported the veracity of the chronicles.[16]

The publications of Turnour, Forbes, and Upham served as essential sources for the two principal mid-nineteenth-century syntheses of Sri Lanka's history, William Knighton's *History of Ceylon from the Earliest Period to the Present Time* (1845), and James Tennent's *Ceylon* (1859).[17] Both of these books, like most historical writing in the Western world during this period, sought to place the events they described in the context of human progress.[18] As a result, they not only judged the island's history according to Victorian standards, but they imposed modern social categories, such as nationality, on the Sri Lankan sources. These works had a lasting influence on the island's historiography. Although later Sri Lankan writers challenged particular assessments made by Knighton and Tennent, they did so within the ideological framework put forward by these authors.

Knighton took the secular narratives of the chronicles at face value, and portrayed a glorious past, when the island was 'great and flourishing, prosperous and happy'.[19] He admitted that manufacturing and commerce never progressed far, but argued that these activities were unnecessary in a warm and fertile land. He declared that ancient Sri Lankan agriculture, philosophy, art, medicine, and statecraft all showed that the island had attained a high level of civilization.

Knighton made frequent comparisons with other parts of the world. He accepted James Mill's portrayal of ancient Indian civilization as impractical and dreary, but argued that it did not apply to Buddhist Sri Lanka: 'Gotamo's [Buddha's] discourses . . . exhibit the reflections of a powerful, equable and cultivated mind, and appear as far removed above the absurd tales and precepts of Brahminism, as the simple tenets of Socrates above the mysticism of the priests of Egypt.'[20] Sri Lanka, he admitted, never quite reached the level of ancient Greece or Rome, but the process of the rise and fall of its civilization was similar: 'Some will perhaps smile at such comparisons, and tell us, that Ceylon is, and ever was, too debased and low to be compared with Greece and Rome. Such, however, we boldly assert, is not the case.'[21] Another statement of Knighton's, that Asian nations were civilized 'long before Europe had shaken off the ignorance and degradation of barbarism' was to be repeated and embellished by Sri Lankan writers in future decades.[22]

The image of ancient Sri Lanka as an advanced and prosperous land could hardly remain unqualified in mid-nineteenth-century English-language histories, given British self-confidence in their own civilization and religion. Knighton had a universal but not linear view of progress, and he saw Sri Lanka's development as following a path broadly similar to the three stages he saw for Europe: classical civilization to the Dark Ages to modern advances. In Sri Lanka, invasions from southern India began the long process of classical decline, which was hastened by the 'blighting influence' of Portuguese and Dutch 'rapacity'. Faulty social organization was also to blame; caste was useful in the early years after the arrival of Vijaya, but it led to a lack of initiative and enterprise once the ancient civilization and its irrigation works were in place.[23] In Knighton's scheme, the British role was to initiate the third stage of development, that of modern progress. Just as modern Britain had departed from the path of ancient Greece and Rome, so Sri Lanka needed to leave behind its own past glories, including Buddhism.

Tennent's *Ceylon* portrayed Sri Lanka's past in a somewhat less favourable light, but its comprehensiveness and literary merit ensured that its popularity surpassed Knighton's work.[24] Tennent's historical sections follow Knighton's framework of three stages of development, but he expresses more scepticism about both the accuracy of the chronicles and the accomplishments of the ancient civilization. The tone that runs through Tennent's work is captured in his preface: 'In the *historical sections* of the work, I have been reluctantly compelled to devote a considerable space to a narrative deduced from the ancient Singhalese chronicles; into which I found it most difficult to infuse any popular interest.'[25]

Tennent accepted that the chronicles were accurate on such things as the names of kings, but dismissed some of the other stories found in them. For instance, unlike Knighton he refused to accept that earthquakes had inundated vast extents of land and reduced greatly the size of the island.[26] He also took a less positive view of life in ancient Sri Lanka. Although he called the irrigation works of the Dry Zone 'one of the wonders of the island,' and estimated that they had supported ten times more people than lived in Sri Lanka in the mid-nineteenth century, his book is also full of more tepid praise, as when he states that a series of kings did little but found temples, repair relic chambers, construct irrigation works, and endow land for the support of monks.[27] Tennent attributed the long decline from the modest level of civilization achieved in ancient times to internal as well as external causes: 'Civil dissensions, religious schisms, royal intrigues and assassinations, contributed equally with foreign invasions to diminish the influence of the monarchy and exhaust the strength of the kingdom.'[28]

Ethnic and religious categories play an important role in both narratives. Knighton and Tennent applied nineteenth-century notions of nationality to the peoples described in the ancient texts. They pictured Sinhala-Buddhists as possessing an inherent identity separate from both Veddas, whom they believed were the pre-Vijayan inhabitants, and

Malabars, who spoke Tamil and various other southern Indian languages. According to Knighton, it was the continuous wars between the Sinhala people, the 'proper inhabitants of the island', and the Malabars, invaders from southern India, that led to the decline of Sri Lankan civilization between the ninth and fourteenth centuries. Ethnic categories are even more prominent in Tennent's work. He draws a distinction between the early immigrants from Bengal, including Vijaya, whose contribution he saw as positive, and the later arrivals from southern India, whose influence was 'entirely negative'.[29] Although his account is full of references to the lack of sharp ethnic divisions, such as the taking of queens from southern India and the promotion of 'Brahmanical rites' by Sinhala monarchs, these practices are seen as indicative of Sinhala weakness. Writing about the period between the seventh and eleventh centuries, Tennent notes disapprovingly that 'the exploits and escapes of the Malabars occupy a more prominent portion of the Singhalese annals than that which treats of the policy of the native sovereigns'.[30]

The histories produced by Knighton and Tennent were the culmination of early efforts by the British to create an authoritative body of knowledge about Sri Lanka. This project was motivated by both the needs of government and intellectual curiosity. Tennent was a former Colonial Secretary who felt that officials needed a reliable reference book about the colony. Knighton, on the other hand, sought to tell a story that would be of 'interest to a cultivated mind'.[31] In practice, these goals were not exclusive. Knowledge gathered for administrative purposes helped shape intellectual constructs, such as schemes of progress, which in turn influenced the definition of what knowledge was deemed important.

Elite images of history in the age of mature colonialism

The late nineteenth and early twentieth centuries constitute the age of mature colonialism, when the British administration was established, secure, and confident. During this period many élite Sri Lankans put forward their own versions of the island's history. They wrote in English, and saw their work as a continuation of the tradition established by Knighton and Tennent. Not only did they make frequent references to the accounts of these and other British writers, but they also accepted their general methodological framework. For instance, they assumed that the best and most useful text was the one that was most authentic, or the closest to the original version.

These writers were part of a social class that was the product of changes that had taken place under colonial rule.[32] Its economic base lay in the plantation economy that prospered after the 1840s. Although most of the large plantations were British-owned, they relied on services supplied by a growing indigenous middle class. Businessmen, traders, contractors, white-collar government employees, chief headmen, lawyers, and doctors were prominent in the new élite. Many families also had an important stake in plantation agriculture. English-language education quickly became a mark of the upper reaches of this class, although there were many successful traders and local notables without a good knowledge of English. At the apex of the élite was a small group of Protestant families that had been powerful since Dutch times, but in the late nineteenth century they were challenged by families with less exalted ancestors. Sinhala people from the Low Country and Tamils from the Jaffna peninsula were over-represented in the élite.

Like Knighton and Tennent, whose belief that British rule was ushering in a new era of progress served to justify colonialism, Sri Lankan writers often made arguments that reflected contemporary concerns. One of these was to portray aspects of the pre-colonial past in a favourable light, in order to show that the colonial status of the island was the product of specific historical circumstances, and not inherent in Sri Lanka's people. History written in this vein had the potential to promote a unified Sri Lankan identity in opposition to the British, but the possibility of such an outcome was undermined by a second concern, which was to define the origins and historical worth of the diverse social categories found in nineteenth-century Sri Lanka. Ethnicity and religion, two overlapping but distinct forms of identity, were social categories important to the élites of this period, and Sri Lankan writers, like Knighton and Tennent before them, wrote histories that assumed their past social and political primacy.[33]

The first Sri Lankan to engage in historical scholarship in the European tradition was James d'Alwis (1823–78), a member of a wealthy Sinhala Protestant family that had held many high government positions under the Dutch and the British. D'Alwis, a lawyer who twice sat on the Legislative Council, received an English-language education, but learnt both Sinhala and Pali as an adult.[34] His lectures and publications combined Sinhala cultural pride and a love of linguistic scholarship with an early Victorian world view that included unquestioned adherence to Christianity and the merits of British rule.

D'Alwis read and translated texts and used his findings to challenge specific points made by earlier British writers. He tried to show that ancient Sinhala civilization was closer to Victorian ideas of progress than had been admitted previously. He argued, for instance, that the Pali word *vajira* meant 'diamond', and that fifth-century Sinhala people placed a diamond at the apex of a relic chamber as protection against lightning, thus indicating that they were aware of electricity, and of the non-conducting properties of some substances.[35] He also found ancient equivalents of modern ideas of public opinion, the rule of law, and freedom of religion.[36] Like British writers, he emphasized the continuity of Sinhala civilization: 'It is a remarkable fact that no country in the East possesses so correct a history of its own affairs, and those of Asia generally, as Ceylon.'[37]

Tennent, relying on earlier European writers, had claimed that Sinhala was closely related to the languages of southern India, including Tamil. D'Alwis challenged this assertion, declaring that Sinhala, in common with the languages of northern India, had Indo-Aryan origins. This view was soon accepted generally, as it still is today, although many scholars now believe that Dravidian languages exerted an important influence on Sinhala. D'Alwis's argument was made primarily on philological grounds, but it had broad implications for the perception of ethnicity in the ancient past. The Indo-Aryan purity of Sinhala, d'Alwis argued, was a product not only of its physical isolation from north Indian languages, but of 'the implacable hatred of our forefathers towards their Dravidian neighbours which induced her [the Sinhala language] to repel their advances'.[38] He assumed that language, ethnicity, and political identity were congruent throughout the long history of the island.

D'Alwis was untroubled by any contradiction between the glorification of the Sinhala past and his own Christian faith; like Knighton and Tennent he separated the religious and secular spheres, and within the religious sphere praised Buddhism as more advanced than Hinduism or Islam. The Sri Lankan writers who followed d'Alwis were unable to take such a detached view. One consequence of the late nineteenth-century Buddhist revival was to place religion in the forefront of most social debates and public activities. Faced with the apparent political, economic, and scientific superiority of Christianity, many Buddhists looked to the past for evidence that their faith provided an effective base for action in the modern world. Moreover, upwardly-mobile Buddhist élites used religion to challenge indirectly both the authority of the British and the power and influence of more traditional élite families, many of whom were Christian. Sri Lankan writers, whatever their religious or ethnic background, were influenced strongly by this atmosphere. None were professional historians – many were lawyers who held government appointments at various points in their careers; others were involved in religious or educational associations. These men were national figures, and the histories that they wrote reflected their immediate political and social concerns. Since they did not seek an immediate end to British rule, the anti-colonial aspects of a national history remained muted. Instead, their narratives served equally to place particular ethnic and religious identities in an historical context.

The influence from the West of the increasingly popular racial theories of progress also contributed to the emphasis on 'primordial' identities in the histories of the mature colonial period. Knighton and Tennent often equated race and culture, but they judged the past against a social and cultural ideal that was in theory attainable by people everywhere. The late nineteenth-century racial theories, in contrast, argued that race determined culture. They drew on philological scholarship which showed that most European and north Indian languages had a common 'Indo-Aryan' origin, and argued that there had been an 'Aryan race' that was the parent stock for all cultures, such as the Greek, Roman, and Germanic, that had developed a high level of civilization.[39] The more extreme forms of such theories had little influence on the British in Sri Lanka, but some officials did assume that cultural distinctions were the product of racial or biological facts. As early as 1871 the belief that Sinhala people were a branch of the Aryan race played a role in the formation of the Village Communities Ordinance, which sought to restore a traditional form of local government in rural areas.[40] In this intellectual climate the classification of Sinhala as an Indo-Aryan tongue took on added significance. The north Indian origin of Vijaya was contrasted with the south Indian origin of Tamils, and some writers began calling Vijaya and his followers Aryans. It was then only a short step to call all Sinhala-speaking people Aryans, and to argue that these people, but not other Sri Lankans, shared a common racial origin with the British, their colonial masters.[41]

I will not attempt a comprehensive survey of the histories propagated by élites in the mature colonial period; instead I will discuss several representative authors and then make some reference to the extent that the images they presented reflected popular perceptions. My starting points are four writers who contributed articles to Arnold Wright's *Twentieth Century Impressions of Ceylon*, a 'coffee table' book published in 1907, which contains family biographies of the national élite and includes a series of general articles about the history, religion, administration, and economy of the colony, all of which are illustrated lavishly.[42]

The historical contributions are those by C. M. Fernando, E. W. Perera, Ponnambalam Arunachalam, and the Anagarika Dharmapala. All were firmly ensconced in the national élite, but they had differing points of view that depended in part on their ethnic and religious identities. Fernando was a Sinhala Roman Catholic barrister whose family had a long tradition of government service. He was educated at Cambridge and served on the Kandy and Colombo municipal councils, and he often represented the government in major civil and criminal cases. His contribution to Wright's volume was the explicitly historical piece, 'History of Ceylon', which was divided into twelve parts, beginning with the pre-Vijayan period and ending in 1796. Perera was a Sinhala Protestant advocate who wrote the section 'Ceylon under British rule, 1796–1906'. Like Fernando, he belonged to the Ceylon branch of the Royal Asiatic Society. Perera is best known for his four-year stay in London after the 1915 riots, to lobby for a royal commission to inquire into the repressive measures taken by the government in response to the disturbances. He was also a president of the Ceylon National Congress in the 1920s. Arunachalam, a Tamil barrister, was a member of the Ceylon Civil Service and the Legislative Council. His article, 'Population: the island's races, religions, languages, castes, and customs', offers a different perspective on some historical issues from those presented by the two Sinhala-Christian writers. A fuller exposition of his views is also available through his short book *Sketches of Ceylon History*.[43] Arunachalam, a man with a broad liberal outlook, was the leading figure behind the formation of the Ceylon National Congress in 1919, but he soon fell out with his Sinhala colleagues. Dharmapala was the famous Buddhist lay preacher who devoted much of his life to getting sacred Buddhist sites in India put under Buddhist control.[44] Although he spent a great deal of time outside Sri Lanka, his ideas attained a good deal of exposure through publications and lecture tours. A member of a family that had prospered in the furniture business in the nineteenth century, Dharmapala's views were more radical than those of most other Buddhist élite leaders. He wrote the section on 'Buddhism, past and present' that appeared in Wright's book. Dharmapala was a prolific writer, and his views are also available in a host of other publications.[45]

The continuity of Sinhala history demonstrated by the chronicles was celebrated by all historians, and some equated it with racial continuity. In a 1902 pamphlet Dharmapala claimed that 'the Sinhalese are a unique race, inasmuch as they can boast that they have no slave blood in them, and never were conquered by either the pagan Tamils or European vandals'.[46] At the turn of the century this emphasis on racial purity was unusual, but many writers left the notion of the Sinhala people as an ancient race implicit. Fernando, for instance, believed that the pre-Vijayan and non-Aryan inhabitants were absorbed into Sinhala society, but he also declared that the Aryan Vijaya was 'the first king known to history of united Lanka; and, as such, the Sinhalese race ever revere and honour his memory'.[47] Arunachalam put forward a different view about race. He accepted that linguistic and racial divisions between Aryans and Dravidians existed, but he cited a European scholar to support the view that language and race did not necessarily develop in parallel. He argued that the fact that the Sinhala people spoke an Aryan language did not necessarily mean that they were also racially Aryan. Arunachalam speculated that the Sinhala people were a mixed race of Aryan, Dravidian, Vedda, Mongolian, and Malay origins. The Tamils, according to Arunachalam, were 'an old Dravidian race'.[48]

There were also differences concerning the accomplishments of the ancient civilization and the social groups responsible for them. Arunachalam glorified the past, but he laid stress on the role of Tamils. He argued that Vijaya and his successors 'were forced to depend on the Tamil alliance and employ Tamil colonists in developing the resources of the island. There were continuous alliances by marriage, employment of Tamil soldiers and civilians, and commerce.'[49] Although Arunachalam argued that there was a good deal of co-operation between Sinhala and Tamil peoples, he accepted the validity of these categories for even the earliest historical periods. Arunachalam, like his Sri Lankan contemporaries, but unlike Knighton and Tennent, used the term 'Tamils' rather than 'Malabars' to describe the invaders from southern India, even though many of them spoke languages other than Tamil. This shift was a product of the need to identify directly the Ceylon Tamil population of the north and east of the island with a distinct group found in ancient history.

Sinhala writers, including Christians, were even less inclined to question the applicability of ethnic labels to the distant past. Fernando made a distinction between those parts of the chronicles that were written to glorify Buddhism, and those parts that presented facts. For many Buddhist writers, on the other hand, the Sinhala nation was defined by congruent religious, racial, and linguistic characteristics. The second century BC conflict between Dutugämunu and Elara was portrayed in this way by D. Gunawardene at a meeting of the Colombo Liberal Association in 1893. Gunawardene argued that the 'infidel' Elara's ascension to the throne was 'the beginning of national troubles. . . . The national institutions of the Sinhalese were soon overthrown, the manners and customs were changed and their language made impure.'[50] Dharmapala also identified strongly with a past from which both Buddhism and the Sinhala race were inseparable. In his writings Tamil and Sinhala societies are pictured as completely distinct. Hindu cultural influences on Sinhala people are ignored; in ancient times all aspects of life were dominated by the Buddhist faith. There was no crime, no alcohol, no unhappiness, and no unpleasantness. Sri Lanka was an idyllic land: 'Free from foreign influences, untainted by alien customs, with the word of Buddha as their guiding light, the Sinhalese people lived a joyously cheerful life in those bygone times.'[51] Ancient greatness extended beyond culture and social relations to politics and economic organization. Buddhist kings were elected by the people, who could depose them at will; and trade was in the hands of the Sinhala people, not foreigners.

Most explanations for the decline of the ancient civilization were similar to those put forward by Knighton and Tennent, who cited foreign invasions, internal strife, and the decay of the irrigation system of the Dry Zone. Sinhala writers generally put the primary blame on external forces, principally the Tamils, Portuguese, and Dutch. Arunachalam, on the other hand, argued that the abandonment of the Dry Zone was a result of failures in irrigation and the arrival of the European powers; he ignored the invasions from southern India.[52]

The Portuguese and Dutch generally fared poorly in historical accounts, but there was a Roman Catholic version of history that passed a favourable verdict on the Portuguese.[53] Fernando claimed that Portugal was 'due the credit of opening up the East to the beneficent influences of Western civilisation'. Catholic writers tended to blame violence between the Portuguese and Sinhala people on the machinations of Muslim traders; a 1913 history, written by a missionary, went even further, stating that 'the Singhalese owe to the Portuguese their national existence. Had not the Portuguese landed then in Ceylon, there would be no Singhalese to-day, they would have all become Moormen.'[54]

The Moors, although forming a significant minority of the island's nineteenth-century population, received little attention from most writers, probably because they were rarely mentioned in the chronicles. One exception to this historical neglect was a controversy that erupted in the 1880s, when the government was re-evaluating representation in the Legislative Council, which had since 1833 drawn its three Sri Lankan members from the Burgher, Sinhala, and Tamil 'communities'. A leading Tamil figure, Ponnambalam Ramanathan, argued that the Moors were emigrants from southern India and were in reality Tamils who had adopted Islam.[55] Elite Muslims responded that while there had been much inter-marriage with Tamil women, their ancestors had originally come from Arabia. They maintained that they were a separate racial entity, and denied that Tamils had a right to represent them. The government accepted their argument, and a seat on the expanded Legislative Council was reserved for the Moors.[56]

The place of the British period in the island's history generated disputes that reflected more general historical perspectives. Perera expressed openly the assumption of many authors: 'The modern history of Ceylon might be written in one word – progress.'[57] By progress Perera meant railways, the increase in exports, greater prosperity, the rule of law, and Western education. But even Perera believed that more needed to be done. He concluded his survey with a list of government measures that were necessary to promote additional progress: a more representative political system, better flood relief works, the abolition of the poll tax, systematic colonization of the Dry Zone with peasants from the crowded south-western region, more education, and better access for

Sri Lankans to high civil service positions. Arunachalam also saw the British period as one of progress, but he too had some reservations, pointing out that the island was dependent on Europeans and Indians for its plantation-based prosperity. Arunachalam accepted that benefits filtered down to Sri Lankans, but he called for new sources of wealth with Sri Lankan control.

Dharmapala was the most vigorous advocate of the negative view concerning the British period. He declared that 'no nation in the world has had a more brilliant history than ourselves'.[58] But in recent times the Sinhala people had followed the path of stagnation: 'Crime is increasing year by year, the ignorance of the people is appalling, without local industries the peasant proprietor is on the verge of starvation, cattle are dying for want of fodder, for the pasture lands and village forests have been ruthlessly taken away from him and made crown property, and sold to the European to plant rubber and tea.'[59] In some of Dharmapala's later writings the long decline of ancient Sri Lankan civilization is overlooked, and instead the emphasis is exclusively on the continuity of Sinhala civilization up to 1815, followed by social decline under British rule. By paying little attention to the centuries of war, European penetration, and economic disruption that preceded the fall of the Kandyan Kingdom, Dharmapala was able to abandon the three-stage developmental theory – from ancient glory to decline to modern progress – implicit in the work of most other writers, and substitute a simpler framework that saw a return to the cultural glories of the pre-colonial past as essential for modern progress. The desire to blame the British for breaking the political continuity of Sinhala civilization led Dharmapala to the curious position of glorifying the later Kandyan kings, who were Tamils from southern India. In contrast, writers with a more favourable view of the British period emphasized the depravity of these monarchs. Perera, for instance, referred to the last Kandyan king as 'the Tamil despot, whom treason, despair, and intemperance had developed into a maniac.'[60]

Popular images of history in the age of mature colonialism

How far did the views of English-educated élite writers reflect wider attitudes, especially among Sinhala people? The research necessary to answer this question fully has not yet been done, but there is substantial evidence that certain assumptions present in the historical writing had widespread currency among ordinary people at the turn of the century. The continuity of Sinhala history, as shown through the unbroken narrative of the chronicles, was the most pervasive of these ideas, but the pride felt in it was marred by an awareness that the present condition of the Sinhala people was inferior to what it had been in the past. Many, including most of the Sinhala-educated intelligentsia, believed that Sinhala people needed to unite in order to recapture their past glory. This world view was especially strong among Buddhists, who often presented it in religious rather than ethnic or racial terms, although distinctions between religion, culture, ethnicity, and race were often unclear.

This Sinhala view of history could have been employed to undermine the British, but it was not perceived as inherently anti-colonial, and the government continued to play an important role in promoting it. Most editions of the chronicles that were published in the late nineteenth and early twentieth century were financed by the colonial state, and funds were also spent on the excavation of the ancient cities, which became important tourist attractions. In 1889 the *Buddhist* suggested that its readers use the guide book written by S. M. Burrows, a British civil servant, when they visited Anuradhapura.[61]

It was at Anuradhapura that two conflicting images of history, one held by many Buddhists, and the other by the government, erupted in a riot in 1903. The number of pilgrims visiting Anuradhapura had increased in the second half of the nineteenth century, and popular images of the city were influenced increasingly by the chronicles.[62] There was special pride in the survival of the bo-tree, which had been sent to Sri Lanka by the Indian king Asoka in the third century BC. The immediate provocation of the riot, which involved mainly pilgrims from the maritime districts, was outrage in response to the use by the Public Works Department of stones taken from ancient sites.[63] From the British viewpoint these stones were 'rubbish'; the Archaeological Commissioner had declared that they had no value. But many Buddhists saw the stones as inherently sacred, and their anger stemmed from a sense of close identification with the civilization that had existed over a millennium earlier.

The agitation at the town of Kalutara in the 1890s sprang from similar historical feeling.[64] Petitions cited the Mahavamsa to support a widely-accepted oral tradition that there had been a Buddhist temple at the site of the Kalutara Fort prior to the Portuguese occupation. Many residents wanted the government to allow the temple to be rebuilt, or failing that at least to protect the bo-trees that grew on the site. The villagers saw themselves as descendants of Buddhists described in the chronicles, and they identified 'progress' not only in Western terms, but also as the restoration of some aspects of ancient civilization.

An incident at Tangalla is also representative of popular identification with the past.[65] Around 1898 the jailer, a Buddhist named Kotalawala, planted a bo-tree shoot near a place that was said by oral tradition to be the site of an ancient relic chamber. The site, like that at Kalutara, was on Crown land, and was used for government buildings, including the jail, police station, rest house, court house, and district judge's bungalow. Benjamin Horsburgh, the assistant government agent for the district, pulled up the tree himself and warned Kotalawala against encroaching on Crown land. But in 1901, when on a visit to Tangalla, Horsburgh found that circular and approach paths had been cut on the grass round the site of the relic chamber, and that a large Buddhist procession had been held around it. When Horsburgh told Kotalawala that he would not tolerate any religious veneration of the site, a petition was sent to the Colonial Office in London asking that the government grant local Buddhists four acres of land to restore the temple 'in conformity with the practice of ancient Kings.' The government responded by transferring Kotalawala, who was thought to be behind the petition.

Historical images played a role in the many procession disputes that took place in the two decades after the Kotahena riot of 1883, when Roman Catholics broke up a Buddhist procession. In 1892, when the authorities at Galle wanted to restrict processions on the ground that they spread cholera, Dharmapala wrote an article stating that the Mahavamsa was 'full of the most beautiful accounts of gorgeous processions'.[66] For Dharmapala and many other Buddhists, late nineteenth-century processions were joyful and simple occasions, which were one of the few survivals of what life in general had been like in the ancient past.

The temperance movements of the early twentieth century also provide evidence of popular acceptance of a history that emphasized the continuity of the present-day Sinhala people with ancient Sinhala glories.[67] D. B. Jayatilaka, a Buddhist educationalist, claimed that if Sinhala people stopped drinking they could be as great as their ancestors who built Anuradhapura.[68] John de Silva, a leading intellectual, asserted at a temperance rally that Sinhala people were weak because they lacked unity, 'but if we look back into the ancient history of our Island when the Mahawamsa Kings were ruling, we can see the Sinhalese as a united and powerful nation.'[69]

The existence of a strong sense of historical continuity, coupled with the assumption that the Sinhala people had a great past, did not, however, mean that other aspects of what is now referred to as the ideology of Sinhala-Buddhist cultural nationalism, including the explicit racialism found in some of Dharmapala's writing, were widely adhered to at this time. Images of ethnic conflict in the past had little direct influence on ethnic relations among ordinary people around the turn of the century. Neither the Ceylon Tamils nor the Indian Tamils were identified with the invaders from southern India who had fought Sinhala kings. Although there were a good many small riots along ethnic, religious, and caste lines, Sinhala–Tamil clashes were very rare.[70] Tamils were the largest single ethnic group living in Anuradhapura, but

Buddhist propaganda against the modern town that had grown up near the ruins focused on the colonial government, the Christians, and the Moors as culprits; the Tamils were ignored. In 1915, when Sinhala people rioted against Moors, no Tamils were attacked. In other ethnic or religious conflicts, such as those between Buddhists and Catholics, the distant past did not play an important role in generating passions. History promoted and built up Sinhala identity, but it was not used to identify the contemporary enemies of the Sinhala people.

Conclusions

The images of the past that developed in the British period were produced by the use of nineteenth-century Western historical ideas and methods. The central idea of the historiography, the rise and decline of an ancient civilization, was almost universally accepted after 1840 both because it was plausible – it was confirmed by both the Mahavamsa and the ruined irrigation tanks and cities – and because it was consistent with the pattern of European historiography, which looked to the classical civilization of Greece and Rome. From the viewpoint of British writers, ancient Sri Lanka might be one of the wonders of the world, and its achievements celebrated, but it was none the less a dead end. Further progress depended on the successful introduction of European ways. But in the mature colonial period some Sri Lankan writers questioned this conclusion. They pointed out that the classical civilizations of southern Europe and the Middle East had died out. In contrast, Sri Lankan civilization, although weakened, had maintained its cultural continuity. This continuity was worth maintaining because it gave Sri Lankans, or at least the Sinhala people, a direct link with a great civilization. Here was proof that the present weakness of the Sinhala people was the product of specific historical circumstances that could be reversed. Under the influence of nineteenth-century Western thought, including Oriental studies, modern notions of nationality were increasingly imposed on the past. Thus the evidence that in ancient Sri Lanka religious, linguistic, and ethnic identities were often fluid and not always congruent was either denied or portrayed as an indication of decay. The sharpest version of history, promoted by Dharmapala in the early twentieth century, equated race, religion, culture, and language as unchanging components of the Sinhala nation throughout the ages.

The contemporary identification with the ancient past created difficulties when interpreting the history of more modern times. The British view that the ancient civilization had run its course had to be rejected, but neither was it feasible to call for an unconditional return to classical civilization. The Sri Lankan élites, even Dharmapala, recognized the advantages that capitalism and modern technology had brought them. Instead, many Buddhists focused on religion, the weakest link in the colonial chain. As late as 1909 Dharmapala wrote that the 'Sinhalese people do not want political self government, their most noble religion is a spiritual self government transcending the political principles of selfish statesmen and adventurous politicians'.[71] Other English-educated élite leaders were even more cautious, although during the temperance movement of 1912 some of them attempted to mobilize popular support against the government's excise policy by appealing to popular images of an idyllic past. After significant constitutional reforms were introduced in the 1920s the scene was set for demands that this or that aspect of ancient civilization be recognized or revived. Some of these demands inevitably offended those who were not Sinhala or Buddhist, or who had adopted Western liberal or socialist ideologies. With the emergence of mass politics in the 1950s the balance between forward- and backward-looking ideas of progress became increasingly difficult to maintain.

But mass politics was far from the minds of the new élites at the turn of the century. For them the history that emphasized the achievements of the ancient past appeared to offer a way for Sinhala people or Sri Lankans to achieve progress in the British sense and at the same time create and maintain their cultural pride. If Sri Lankans assessed themselves solely with reference to British criteria of progress, then it was unlikely they could ever catch up, but if aspects of Sri Lankan culture were valuable and unique, then there was nothing to stop Sri Lanka from being great again. This viewpoint also enabled the élite to set themselves above other sections of society. The mass of poor people were obviously degenerate and ignorant; they needed the élite to help them rediscover indigenous culture and meet the challenges of the modern world. The more traditional élites, many of whom were Christian, were portrayed as being too conservative and subservient to the British to provide the leadership the island needed. Historical images thus enabled the middle class to set itself apart from the British, the poor, and the traditional élites, and to assign itself the role of leading Sri Lanka into the new age of progress.

Notes and references

1 I would like to thank Charles Hallisey, Steven Kemper, Elizabeth Nissan, and Jonathan Spencer for their useful comments on earlier drafts of this article.

2 B.S. Cohn, 'The command of language and the language of command', in R. Guha (ed.) *Subaltern Studies*, vol. 4, Delhi, 1985, pp. 276–329; D. Kopf, *British Orientalism and the Bengal Renaissance*, Berkeley and Los Angeles, 1969, pp. 22–42, 167–77.

3 R. Percival, *An Account of the Island of Ceylon*, London, 1803, pp. 4–5.
4 G. Turnour, *The Mahawanso in Roman Characters with the Translation Subjoined*, Cotto, 1837, p. i.
5 J. Davy, *An Account of the Interior of Ceylon*, London, 1821, p. vi.
6 Ibid., p. 293.
7 *The Mahavansi, the Raja-Ratnacari, and the Raja-Vali, forming the Sacred and Historical Books of Ceylon*, 2 vols, London, 1833.
8 Ibid., vol. 1, p. ix.
9 Turnour, *Mahawanso*, p. i.
10 Ibid.
11 The Sri Lankans who provided Upham's version may not have shared the British quest for an 'authentic' version that was as close as possible to the 'original'; see E. Nissan *The Sacred City of Anuradhapura: Aspects of Sinhalese Buddhism and Nationhood*, Ph.D. thesis, University of London, 1985, pp. 324–25.
12 See, e.g. S. Casie Chitty, *The Ceylon Gazetteer*, Kotte, 1834.
13 Turnour, *Mahawanso*, p. ix.
14 K. Malalgoda, *Buddhism in Sinhalese Society, 1750–1900*, Berkeley and Los Angeles, 1976, pp. 50, 132.
15 Turnour's English translation of the Mahavamsa was superseded by revised and extended translations in 1889 and 1912. A Sinhala edition was published in two volumes in 1879 and 1883. For a useful discussion of the consequences of publication of these and other Sinhala and Pali texts see Nissan, *Sacred City*, pp. 324–25.
16 J. Forbes, *Eleven Years in Ceylon*, 2 vols., 2nd edn, London, 1841.
17 W. Knighton, *The History of Ceylon from the Earliest Period to the Present Time*, London, 1845; J. Tennent, *Ceylon: An Account of the Island; Physical, Historical, and Topographical*, 2 vols., London, 1859.
18 For a general discussion of the central role of 'progress' in western thought in the late eighteenth and nineteenth centuries, see R. Nisbet, *History of the Idea of Progress*, New York, 1980, pp. 171–296.
19 Knighton, *History*, p. 283.
20 Ibid., p. 75.
21 Ibid., p. 116.
22 Ibid., p. 44.
23 Ibid., pp. 185–6.
24 For a discussion of why Tennent's book achieved such popularity see Y. Gooneratne, *English Literature in Ceylon, 1815–1878*, Dehiwala, 1968, pp. 80–85.
25 Tennent, *Ceylon*, vol. 1, p. xxxi.
26 Ibid., pp. 6–7.
27 Ibid., p. 385.
28 Ibid.
29 Ibid., p. 401.
30 Ibid., p. 400.
31 Ibid., pp. xxiii–xxvii; Knighton, *History*, p. 5.
32 E. Meyer, 'Bourgeoisie et société rurale à Sri Lanka (1880–1940)', *Purusartha*, vol. 4, 1982, pp. 207–25; P. Peebles, *The Transformation*

of a Colonial Élite: the Mudaliyars of Nineteenth-Century Ceylon, Ph.D. dissertation, University of Chicago, 1973; M. Roberts, 'Élite formations and élites, 1832–1931', in *Collective Identities, Nationalisms, and Protest in Modern Sri Lanka*, ed. M. Roberts, Colombo, 1979, pp. 153–213.

33 Similar processes took place in India, where regional or national histories of religion, caste, and ethnicity were reinterpreted in ways that had direct relevance to the present. As in Sri Lanka, these histories were supported by 'authentic' texts. For examples, see Kopf, *British Orientalism*, pp. 178–213; and R. O'Hanlon, *Caste, Conflict, and Ideology*, Cambridge, 1985, pp. 135–86.

34 D'Alwis's life and career are sketched in Gooneratne, *English Literature*, pp. 123–52.

35 *The Attanagalu-Vansa or the History of the Temple of Attanagalla*, trans. J. d'Alwis, Colombo, 1866, pp. xvi–xxviii.

36 Ibid., pp. xxxiv–viii, xxxix–xliv, liii–lxii.

37 Ibid., p. v.

38 Quoted in Gooneratne, *English Literature*, p. 145.

39 Nisbet, *History*, pp. 286–96.

40 V. Samaraweera, 'Litigation, Sir Henry Maine's writings and the Ceylon Village Communities Ordinance of 1871', in *Senarat Paranavitana Commemoration Volume*, eds L. Prematilleke, K. Indrapala, and J.E. Van Lohuizen-De Leeuw, Leiden, 1978, pp. 191–203.

41 Gunawardana, this volume.

42 *Twentieth Century Impressions of Ceylon*, ed. A. Wright, London, 1907.

43 P. Arunachalam, *Sketches of Ceylon History*, 2nd edn., Colombo, 1906.

44 For a brief account of Dharmapala's life, see G. Obeyesekere, 'Personal identity and cultural crisis: the case of Anagarika Dharmapala of Sri Lanka', in *The Biographical Process*, eds. F.E. Reynolds and D. Capps, The Hague, 1976, pp. 221–52.

45 For a representative sample of Dharmapala's views, see *Return to Righteousness: A Collection of Speeches, Essays, and Letters of the Anagarika Dharmapala*, ed. A. Guruge, Colombo, 1965.

46 Dharmapala, 'History of an Advanced Civilization', in *Return to Righteousness*, p. 479.

47 Fernando, 'History of Ceylon', in *Twentieth Century Impressions*, p. 16.

48 Arunachalam, 'Population', in *Twentieth Century Impressions*, pp. 332–34, 339.

49 Ibid., p. 353.

50 *Buddhist*, Colombo, 13/viii/1893, 20/viii/1893.

51 Dharmapala, 'Buddhism Past and Present', in *Twentieth Century Impressions*, p. 286.

52 Arunachalam, 'Population', p. 325.

53 See An Oblate of Mary Immaculate of the Diocese of Jaffna, *History of Ceylon for the Use of Schools*, Jaffna, 1887.

54 M.G. Francis, *History of Ceylon: An Abridged Translation of Professor Peter Courtenay's Work*, Mangalore, 1913, pp. 7, 14.

55 V. Samaraweera, 'The Muslim Revivalist Movement, 1880–1915', in *Collective Identities*, pp. 261–63.
56 Some Ceylon Tamils saw the outcome differently. Over a decade later a newspaper editorial pointed out that the Moor and Kandyan Sinhalese seats had been created at the same time, and argued that Moors bore the same relationship to Tamils as Kandyans did to Sinhalese. *Hindu Organ*, Jaffna, 13/vi/1900.
57 Perera, 'Ceylon under British Rule', in *Twentieth Century Impressions*, p. 83.
58 Dharmapala, 'A Message to the Young Men of Ceylon', in *Return to Righteousness*, p. 506.
59 Ibid., p. 508.
60 Perera, 'Ceylon under British rule', p. 64.
61 *Buddhist*, 16/viii/1889.
62 E. Nissan, 'Polity and Pilgrimage Centres in Sri Lanka', *Man*, vol. 23, 1988, pp. 256–64.
63 For the Anuradhapura riot see J.D. Rogers, *Crime, Justice, and Society in Colonial Sri Lanka*, London, 1987, pp. 184–87.
64 J.D. Rogers, 'The expansion of sacred space and the imperial response: the Kalutara Bo-tree Agitation of 1891–97', *South Asia Research*, vol 6, 1986, pp. 27–37.
65 J. West Ridgeway to Joseph Chamberlain, 31 January 1902, Colonial Office records, PRO, 54/675 (42).
66 Dharmapala, 'Buddhist Processions', in *Return to Righteousness*, pp. 523–24.
67 J.D. Rogers, 'Cultural Nationalism and Social Reform: The 1904 Temperance Movement in Sri Lanka', *Indian Economic and Social History Review*, vol. 26, 1989; P.T.M. Fernando, 'Arrack, Toddy and Ceylonese Nationalism: Some Observations on the Temperance Movement, 1912–1921', *Modern Ceylon Studies*, vol. 2, 1971, pp. 123–50.
68 *Ceylon Independent*, Colombo, 14/xi/1904.
69 *Idem*, 28/vii/1904.
70 J.D. Rogers, 'Social mobility, popular ideology, and collective violence in modern Sri Lanka', *JAS*, 1987, vol. 46, pp. 583–602.
71 Dharmapala, 'Education in Ceylon', in *Return to Righteousness*, pp. 530–31.

Chapter five

The politics of the Tamil past

Dagmar Hellmann-Rajanayagam

When my son first started school, he told me one day that his friends always called him 'Hitler'. For the children 'Hitler' was the funny German bogeyman from the movies, a good nickname to call someone from Germany, with few of the sinister associations a middle-aged German or Briton might connect with it. For children in Britain one of the darkest periods of German history has passed into the realm of mythology and child's play. It is no longer associated with real Germans, except for the bogeyman figure of Hitler, and it does not stir up national or other passions. Whether it is to be welcomed that the Fascist period has passed into myth so fast is debatable, and it goes without saying that for Germans the problem looks quite different. But what is important here is that facts of history can pass into myth, thereby softening and modifying their impact and removing them from everyday reality: they become literally child's play. But the same does not happen everywhere.

Sinhala Lions and Tamil Tigers are by no means just children's bogeymen; they are perceived as real, dangerous and deserving to be destroyed. These stereotypes are much older than the Third Reich or even the caricature of the Hun. They were dormant for centuries when the Sinhala or Tamil enemy was just a figure of myth with no great significance for everyday life. But the figure has come alive, and we have to ask, how, why and when?

Early reports

From what we can gauge from the writings of early Europeans in Sri Lanka, there lived in the north and east of the island people who spoke Tamil, called themselves Tamils, and were so called because the strangers recognized the similarity to the Tamil people of south India. They were ruled by independent or semi-independent kings who had a traditional rivalry with rulers in other parts of the island and who commonly spoke another language, Sinhala, though the use of both languages was common. That is about all we can say for much of the sixteenth and seventeenth centuries, from these accounts.

What, then, was the Tamil perception of the Sinhala? It is obvious that today they are perceived firstly as cruel, bent on killing or at least driving out the Tamils, and as having been so for centuries; and secondly, as encroaching on Tamil land and thus threatening the concept of the 'traditional homeland'. But this perception seems to be a fairly recent one. In the early eighteenth century, a Dutch governor, Klaas Isaacsz, asked a native from Jaffna, Mayilvakana Pulavar, to write down and have translated a history or chronicle of Jaffna. This man compiled a chronicle, the *Yalppana Vaipava Malai* ('The Garland of Jaffna Events'), out of oral traditions, palm leaf manuscripts of uncertain date, and 'lost works' only preserved in memory.[1] This jumble of myth and tradition, ending with the conquest of Jaffna by the Portuguese and the death of the last king, Cankili, became the standard work of Tamil history in the nineteenth century. While in the Sinhala chronicles the Tamils were the enemy, conversely in these Tamil chronicles, the Sinhala were the adversaries who had to be overcome in order to enable the civilized Tamils to settle, who had to be prevented from polluting Tamil holy places, and had therefore to be driven out, and who instigated rebellions and usurpations against the lawful rulers. The contradiction in this account is that it says that the Tamils got their country as a fief from the 'king of Kandy' in the first place. As this is certainly historically impossible, one has to assume that the author meant by the 'king of Kandy' the only Sinhala king he knew. But the important thing is that there seems to be no visible connection between the 'king of Kandy' and the Sinhala settlers in Jaffna who rebelled against Tamil rulers. Only in the later parts of the *YVM* are the Sinhala further south in the Vanni seen as a sort of fifth column for the southern kings. Although this is only implicit it was spelt out more clearly by later writers. Another interesting feature of the *YVM* is the way in which the Vijaya legend is retold: it is said he was a Saivite Indian prince, married to a Tamil wife, who emigrated to Sri Lanka and built some of the oldest Saivite temples there. But by the nineteenth century these accounts had passed into legend and the Sinhala enemy had become mythical and abstract.

The *YVM* came into its own in the late nineteenth century. When interest in the history and development of Sri Lanka filtered through from the west to Jaffna, it was pounced upon as something analogous to the Sinhala chronicles then coming into fashion as historical sources.[2] To most Tamils, this came as a surprise. Until then, they had seen themselves as part of a greater cultural area which comprised both Sri Lanka and south India. The latter was probably more important than contact with the Sinhala to the south of the island, who were separated by almost impenetrable jungle.

But when the ideology of western colonialism demanded a great past for Sri Lanka, both Tamils and Sinhala were able to present a golden age of culture and fame. In 1834 when hardly anybody in Jaffna had heard of the *YVM*, Simon Casie Chitty wrote his *Ceylon Gazetteer*, which included a discussion of the 'Castes and Customs of the Tamils and the Moors'. He included a short paragraph on Jaffna, narrating the legend of its foundation, but without any detailed list of events or kings.[3] However, Chitty made the interesting remark that it had been the tragedy of the Sinhala never to have been ruled by kings of their own 'race', but always by strangers from south India, referring to the Sinhala kings' custom of taking their wives from south India, and also to the Indian origins of the Nayakkar dynasty in Kandy.[4] He published two articles in the *JRASCB* of 1847: one about the vanquishing of the Buddhists by a Saivite saint from south India, a well-known story from the Tiruvacakam; and one 'On the history of Jaffna from the earliest period to the Dutch conquest', in which he repeats the known tradition.[5] Again, the *YVM* is not mentioned, though the traditional history contained in it was obviously known. About 25 years after the *Gazetteer*, Chitty wrote a sketch of great Tamil scholars and poets, and here he included Indian as well as Sri Lanka Tamils, thus assuming one integrated cultural region.[6]

The interest in history among the Tamil élites, once roused, went on apace throughout the nineteenth century. The *Morning Star*, a bilingual Jaffna paper founded in 1841 by the American missionary Daniel Poor, printed in the years between 1845 and 1855 a long series of articles on the history of Sri Lanka, and mentioned in one of them[7] that the history of Jaffna had been comparatively neglected because (as Rogers shows) the history of Sri Lanka in the nineteenth century was predominantly a history of the Sinhala kings. This started to change in 1879 when Brito translated the *YVM* and put it firmly on the map for future research. By now, western ideas of national differentiation had taken hold; whereas the history of Sri Lanka had, for Tamils at least, been one whole with different facets and contributors, in Brito's work we find the first claims of greater antiquity for the Tamil language – a notion borrowed from European philology. In an appendix to his translation on the development of language in Sri Lanka, he purportedly proved that Tamil was older than even the oldest form of Sinhala, called Helu or Elu, that the latter had developed from the first, and that, therefore, Sinhala was derived from a Dravidian language, not an Aryan one.[8] This academic controversy (which scarcely concerned the bulk of the population) had more to it than met the eye since greater linguistic antiquity might suggest greater cultural antiquity and superiority.

But the time for that had not yet come. As police reports from the time show, both Tamil and Sinhala were generally more concerned with themselves and consequently preferred to assault people of their own 'race'; this showed 'that there is very little race animosity in Ceylon'.[9] Among the Tamils, at least, caste conflicts and riots were much more important than quarrels with the elusive Sinhala, of whom there were in any case hardly any around in Jaffna. By the 1920s, however, the need for a more concrete enemy was felt among large sections of the population. How had this happened?

For Chitty, Sri Lanka was peopled by different 'races' or 'nations' without this fact presupposing political claims of any kind. He enumerated three groups of people in Sri Lanka, the Sinhala, the Tamils and the Moors. *The Tamil Plutarch*, his biographical compilation of Tamil poets published in 1857, is mostly concerned with Tamils proper, whether in India or Sri Lanka, and with the greatness of Tamil literature in general and Christian Tamil literature in particular.[10] Until the 1870s, we thus find an awareness of being Tamil, even an awareness of a historical tradition that differs slightly from that of the Sinhala, yet attached to one political unit, Sri Lanka, and a wider cultural region, India.

Histories of Jaffna

Towards the end of the 1870s and in the 1880s, the picture changes gradually. Though the *YVM* deals extensively with Sinhala history and with the grant of Jaffna to a Tamil by a Sinhala king, it is seen as a chronicle of and for the Tamils. Yet the questions brought up by Brito's translation seem to have engendered comparatively little discussion. Following the *YVM*, however, a spate of 'Histories of Jaffna' began to appear, from about 1878 onwards, all claiming to narrate the definitive history of Jaffna and all drawing largely on the *YVM* and to a lesser extent on other works. Samuel John, a Christian, was the first, followed by Catacivappillai.[11] All these works have some things in common apart from their source material: they hardly ever mention the Sinhala at all, except to enumerate those kings who had a bearing on the fate of Jaffna and, more significantly, to mention the expulsion of Sinhala from Jaffna by Cankili after a rebellion by Buddhists.[12] Generally, expulsions of the Sinhala from Jaffna are attributed to one of two reasons: either because (like the Moors) they pollute temple grounds; or because they instigate Buddhist rebellions. The few Sinhala left after Cankili's last feat become the Goviars, a slave caste in traditional folklore, made up of former Sinhala farmers. In the 1909 reprint of Samuel John's book, his son gives that incident new significance, when he says in the English preface that Cankili's expulsion 'made Jaffna safe for the Tamils'.[13] And a 1927 history complains that the generous attitude of the Tamil kings towards the Sinhala led them to disobedience and rebellion.[14]

It would, however, be quite erroneous to assume that all these histories told the same story because they relied on the same limited sources. On the contrary, fierce controversies ensued over particular points in the history of Jaffna which were described quite differently in the sources. These accounts indicate a range of slightly differing traditions current in the Tamil areas at that time. Examples include the account of the identity of Kulakkottan, the prince who allegedly installed the temple in Trincomalee, the question whether there were one or two Cankilis, the location of Jaffna's capital Cinkainakar, and the origin of the Aryachakravarti kings (were they connected with the Colas or with the Pandyans?). The basic veracity of these often imaginary chronicles was, however, never questioned.

The real turning point came in 1926, when Rasanayagam's *Ancient Jaffna*[15] saw the light of day. Rasanayagam had been working on this book for years and had read an extract of it to the Royal Asiatic Society in 1922 which had caused an outcry among the Sinhala members. Rasanayagam attempted to prove that not only was Sri Lanka's Tamil history the history of Jaffna (he deliberately tried to sever the 'Indian connection' held high by people like Arunachalam and Coomaraswamy by locating the 'Tamil' kingdoms which had influenced the fate of Sri Lanka in Jaffna or Nagadipa), but that practically the whole history of the island was Tamil-Hindu or Dravidian history, or at least widely influenced by Tamil history. This was seen by the Sinhala as an attempt to rob them of their own Sinhala-Buddhist history and tradition.[16] While the Sinhala protested fiercely, the book fuelled the grandiose dreams of some Tamils, though there were other authors, among them S. Gnanaprakasar, who challenged Rasanayagam's arguments after the publication of his book.[17]

The important question to ask here is why the controversy flared up in the 1920s and not a decade or more earlier, when there were enough similar causes for controversy. Between 1921 and 1924 Governor Manning introduced what became known as the Manning reforms, a series of constitutional reforms which emphasized 'communal representation' for those groups recognized as 'legitimate interest groups' by the British.[18] Those eager to secure communal representation therefore had to justify this both to themselves and to the government. Moreover, under an extended franchise, the Tamils saw themselves being reduced from a major community to a minority. Under the circumstances, Rasanayagam's book was perceived as establishing and staking out claims for further use by both Sinhala and Tamils. Whether this was actually his intention is difficult to determine, but given the fact that politicians and academics were often the same people, it would be naïve to assume that developments in one sphere did not bear on those in the other. But, since Rasanayagam's strategy was inclusive – he wanted to subsume all Sri Lankans under the Dravidian umbrella – this seems an unsuitable way to stake out claims to representation based on difference.

The jaundiced view of history as being written for political ends has bedevilled Sri Lanka historiography ever since. History and historiography became a means to substantiate political claims and this was seen as a legitimate objective. The timing of Rasanayagam's book might suggest that this was already the case in 1926, but as it came two years after the reforms, it may easily have been the other way round: political events had shaped a certain perception of history that found its way into print, either to be confirmed or rejected.

A changed perception of history

The change in the perception of history had, however, been brought about somewhat earlier and by slightly different agents: namely imperial education policy and the treatment of the 'natives' who in the wake of western 'oriental' discoveries felt obliged to come up with their own glorious past. The British perceived and defined the existing differences between groups of people as first and foremost differences of 'race' or 'nation'. In the attempt to substantiate this perception scientifically, other characteristics like language and religion were made to align with the criteria of 'race' and 'nation'.[19]

The missionary onslaught on Tamil culture, and the appropriation of Tamil history, made it imperative not only to recover Tamil religion, but also the Tamil-Saiva past. Yet the need for a glorious past necessitated heroism and the conquest of enemies and territory, and here the search for and use of history became pernicious. While the *YVM* was the history of Jaffna proper and its relations, good or bad, but always 'familiar', with the Sinhala, further delving into the past (e.g. by Rasanayagam) and the simultaneous deciphering of south Indian and Sri Lankan inscriptions after about 1875 by official epigraphers brought to light the relations between Sri Lanka and the south Indian kingdoms, notably the Colas who invaded Ceylon in the eleventh century. From vague 'footnotes' in the *Mahavamsa* this became full-fledged history, mentioned (and refused) by Rasanayagam, but avidly appropriated by others. The fact that these discoveries coincided (or were made to coincide) with a period of political ferment and change, gave them added import: the Tamils suddenly had a choice of pasts to select from, and they avidly did so, watched with suspicion by the Sinhala. These histories often clashed, as in the evaluation of the Cola invasion: was this a deliverance or a conquest for the Tamils? The fact that the east holds on to a tradition of Trincomalee being a Cola fief while Jaffna derives its kings from a Pandyan line, makes for interesting speculation.

But whichever past the Tamils chose, for the Sinhala the Tamils became agents of a foreign power. In their eyes, helped on by British perceptions, this was no choice of pasts, but part of a grand design to deprive them of what was theirs: the Cola invaders who allegedly heralded the decline of the Sinhala kingdom, were identified with the Tamils who had lived there before the Colas ever came. One went even further back into mythology and identified (on both sides) a famous Cola king, Manuniticolan, with an equally legendary Tamil usurper of the Sinhala throne in the 1st century BC: Elara, who had been defeated by the Sinhala hero Dutugämunu. And there the wheel had come full circle, and the Sinhala thought they had proof of the Tamils' alienness and cunning. For the Tamils it was more complicated, given their differing traditions, but they, too, managed after a while to portray the Sinhala as the ancient enemies who wanted to drive them out of their country and deny them their historical greatness, whether it be Cola or Jaffna glory.

This choice of 'pasts' has been at once a problem and an opportunity for Tamils ever since: they were free to view and define their identity in quite different ways, *without losing their identity as Tamils*, whereas for the Sinhala there has only been one history available. Even more importantly for Tamil identity, history was not confined to the island of Sri Lanka, but could always be found in India in Tamil Nadu. One could perhaps even say that history held little importance for the Tamils because their identity did not depend on it exclusively. It still does not, but history's significance has without doubt increased since Independence. This fact of having a choice of pasts also partly explains why the Christians were in the forefront not only of historical writing, but also of Tamil nationalism: they had a choice of pasts, too, and being Tamil, or even being Tamil nationalist, was not tied to being Saivite; other identifications existed. This argument seems to confirm Sinhala fears that Tamils look more towards India and Tamil Nadu for succour than towards Sri Lanka and that they therefore cannot be trusted. In a twisted way, it does confirm the orientation of Tamils to India: they look to India for their cultural and religious roots. But at the same time it was this option that prevented them from becoming parochial, and enabled them to be both Sri Lankan nationalists and Tamils. However, once the connection to India, and the choice of pasts, was cut, the Tamils were thrown back upon themselves and upon the tiny (in every sense) area of Jaffna. They became Tamil nationalists and even chauvinists, and finally secessionists, who now again looked towards India, but with a political, instead of a cultural objective.

Immigration myths and the feeling of unity with India on one side and the pride of being uniquely Jaffna Tamil on the other pulled in different directions. But they achieved one result: making Sinhala and

Tamils aware more of their differences than of their similarities. European scholarship and ethnic sensitivities combined to enhance divisions. By the late 1930s the scholarly 'histories of Jaffna' intended for schools had fizzled out;[20] instead we see a spate of laudatory souvenirs with essays and articles on great leaders of 'Eelam' or great Tamils of Jaffna in general, and their achievements for the glory of its history, its culture, its ancient greatness, and most of all, its Tamilness.[21]

The term 'Eelam' (Ilam) seems to have suffered a contraction in the 1930s: it is a very ancient name for Sri Lanka, used interchangeably with 'Ilankai' in the oldest Tamil literature, though the *YVM* seems to prefer 'Ilankai', meaning Sri Lanka without Jaffna, which is always denoted as 'Yalppanam'. Chitty mentions Eelam as the ancient name for Sri Lanka.[22] In the 1920s and 1930s, the term 'Tamil Eelam' comes into vogue increasingly, indicating the areas inhabited by Tamils and considered as belonging to them. It seems that P. Arunachalam, Registrar-General of Ceylon and later a founder-member of the Ceylon National Congress, coined the term 'Tamil Eelam' in 1923, but I have not been able to trace this back to its original source. There is, however, no doubt that the term was widely used in the late 1930s, and it is in this meaning of 'belonging to the Tamils' that the term is currently used in Tamil nationalism. The religious reformer, Arumuka Navalar, whose allegiance culturally was as much to India as to Jaffna, now becomes a national leader of Eelam, and so do P. Arunachalam and his elder brother P. Ramanathan, a lawyer and member of the Executive and Legislative Councils as well as a prolific writer.[23] In parallel to the political development, the historical view continually narrows, from the subcontinent to south India, then to Sri Lanka with Jaffna, and then to Sri Lanka versus Jaffna. By 1951, A.K. Coomaraswamy, Ramanathan and Arunachalam's nephew, a celebrated art historian of India and Sri Lanka and remarkably cosmopolitan and 'un-Tamil', is being represented as a champion of the Tamils of Jaffna.[24]

Ways of using history

The Tamil use of history to justify and defend their position shows decisive differences from that of the Sinhala. While the latter pursue an exclusive strategy, denying the standing of Tamils in the country *per se*, and labelling them alien and foreign intruders, the Tamils followed an inclusive strategy until the 1930s. They tried to prove that the Sinhala were in reality not Aryans, but Dravidians in disguise, and thus had nothing to be snooty about. This did not go down well with those Sinhala who prided themselves on their alleged 'Aryan' ancestry. But by the 1930s and 1940s, an argument had gained weight that it was immaterial whether the Sinhala were Dravidians or not – if they were, they were an inferior sort of Dravidian. The important claim was that the Tamils had been the first people in Sri Lanka, theirs was the highest culture and civilization from which others only copied, and everything great and good in both Sri Lankan and Sinhala culture was by definition originally Tamil. This related not only to language, literature, and architecture, but even to religion: attempts were made to prove that the Sinhala, far from being Buddhists, were in reality Hindus, or that Buddhism was just an inferior kind of Hinduism. The Tamils had created progress and development in the country under the British, and the Sinhala therefore, if not acceding them the right to rule, would at least have to grant them equal political representation. In this, the claim to chronological anteriority, though existent, was muted. This is in sharp contrast to the very chronological myth of Vijaya and of Sinhala settlement.

Again, the choice of histories was both a problem and an opportunity for the Tamils. If they chose, their history, unlike Sinhala history, was not bound to Sri Lanka or even to Jaffna; they could, and often did, look towards Tamil Nadu or south India. But this was an option rejected by many in the 1950s in favour of a Sri Lankan past in the tradition of Rasanayagam. When this option was repeatedly rejected by the Sinhala between the 1930s and 1950s, a period of Tamil introspection began to take shape. This led to the extolling of Tamil virtues over and against Sinhala perfidy, to claims for autonomy, and finally independence. In his famous nine-hour speech defending the demand for 'balanced' (50–50) representation in the 1930s, the Tamil leader G.G. Ponnambalam had mentioned the historical tradition of Tamil independence and the Jaffna kingdom, citing this and the assumed differences of race, language and culture as a reason to grant the minorities (especially the Tamils) weighted representation in parliament and government and thus rejecting the one-man-one-vote system.[25] The argument went like this: the Tamils fell under foreign rule as an independent kingdom; they became a privileged group under the British solely due to their own virtues of diligence and hard labour. This position which is theirs by right must be kept up after Independence. The Sinhala saw this as blatant communalism and a demand for positive discrimination in favour of an already privileged minority, although for the Tamils it spelt nothing more than fair and equal treatment for all.[26] Though by 1947 the '50–50' demand had been sufficiently scaled down to allow Tamil acceptance of the guarantees of the Soulbury constitution and the promise that both Sinhala and Tamil would be made official languages, they never left any doubt that they would always be on the look-out for transgressions of their rights.

It took less than ten years after Independence for trouble to blow up over S.W.R.D. Bandaranaike's 'Sinhala Only' bill in 1956. That prompted C. Suntheralingam, a mathematics professor, former adviser for the pan-Sinhala Board of Ministers in 1936, and MP for Vavuniya, to write a series of articles and letters between 1955 and 1964 advocating autonomy or, failing that, independence for 'Eylom'. Legal, political and historical arguments were used in these articles to substantiate the claim for Tamil autonomy and for the age-old animosity between Sinhala and Tamils. These articles and letters are full of invective against the Federal Party and what he saw as its failure to demand full independence for 'Eylom'.[27] Lord Soulbury, to whom the articles were sent, compared the Tamils with the Scots and suggested a solution on the lines of the United Kingdom or Ulster![28]

The more relations between the two groups deteriorated, the more history became a weapon in the battle to justify Tamil demands for autonomy and, in principle, independence. This began in the 1950s with Suntheralingam and was followed by the Communist Shanmugathasan in the early 1960s. The Federal Party in the 1960s spoke of the three 'umbrellas' under which Sri Lanka had lived until the arrival of the colonial powers, and rejected the 'one umbrella' theory.[29] In 1949 the Federal Party had already based its claim to nationhood on the 'kingdom of Jaffna'. Once recalled, the kingdom of Jaffna was never far below the surface of Tamil consciousness.

But there were other voices as well. Serious scholars researching the kingdom of Jaffna and the origins of Tamil settlement came up with well-researched and well-argued theses which nevertheless drew the enmity of Sinhala reviewers because they established beyond any doubt the existence of the kingdom, even if its chronology was unclear. This happened to Pathmanathan, who published his research on the Jaffna kingdom in the late 1960s.[30] Any author who did not toe the orthodox line that Sri Lanka was the land of the Sinhala, came in for criticism, invective and worse. This created a Tamil backlash, that manifested itself in exaggerated historical claims and the postulate of a 'Tamil homeland'. Scholarly historical research became so imbued with group and communal feeling that it was very difficult indeed not to become assigned to one or the other camp. Whereas in the 1950s the issue could still be side-stepped by avoiding any mention of the Sinhala in works on the Jaffna Tamils,[31] this option became increasingly difficult in a heated political climate. An author like Kadirgamar who wrote a history of Sri Lanka in 1967 and tried to give a balanced view, nevertheless included long passages about the greatness of the Tamil reformer Arumuka Navalar and took pains to point out the faults of the Soulbury constitution.[32]

A new phase began in the late 1970s. History was now finally taken out of the hands of scholars and academics and went into those of the militants on both sides. In earlier times, the lines of communication between historians and politicians were short. History and its significance had been predominantly a matter for élite debate in political or cultural circles, sometimes used to bolster political arguments, though it could be and was used to whip up mass feeling in certain instances. This gradually became not a sporadic, but a regular feature. History became an instrument to fight ideological and military battles, and its character changed. Minor details of fact could no longer be taken into account, and academic research became unimportant. One option after the other closed. Not only had history to justify the claim for independence, it also had to call the young men to battle and to prove ongoing Sinhala perfidy and untrustworthiness.

The claim for independence was supported by delving into the sixteenth century when the kingdom of Jaffna was independent, and into the early nineteenth century when the colony was still administered as three separate units.[33] For the call to battle one went even further back into history: into the epic age of the south Indian Tamils when warring chieftains did their best to exterminate themselves and everybody else and when women urged their husbands, fathers, sons, and brothers to go to the battlefield and die a hero's death. Sinhala perfidy was demonstrated with memories of the time immediately before and after Independence when, it was alleged, D. S. Senanayake had already laid his plans to deprive the Tamils of all their political, cultural and linguistic rights by disenfranchising the Indian Tamils and, more importantly, by 'colonizing' the Dry Zone – the Sinhala *rajarata* (king's country) but also the 'Tamil homeland' – with Sinhala peasants and thus making the Tamils a minority in their own land.[34]

This theme, muted before Independence, gained ground in the late 1950s; the concept of the 'homeland' itself became imbued with mythical and mystical qualities by the movement of the 1970s. This concept of 'homeland' is a comparatively recent one and has to be explored in detail elsewhere. At this time interest in the east as against Jaffna really took off as both groups of Tamils for the first time felt one overriding common interest against the Sinhala.[35] To a great extent this is connected with the increase in the percentage of Sinhala in Trincomalee and elsewhere in the east after Dry Zone colonization.[36] But it contrasts with reports from the beginning of the century, when the Tamils were singularly uninterested in colonizing the Dry Zone despite the best efforts of the British to persuade them.[37] The use of history is now no longer incidental, with interesting snippets being taken to bolster an argument, but it is fashioned and streamlined to serve a purpose, and contradictory details are blacked out.

Dominant themes

Different as the uses of the same historical material might be over the last hundred years, there are certain recurring themes:

1 The tradition of immigration into Jaffna (Nagadipa) which was previously peopled by Dravidian tribes; the independence of the resulting kingdom and its close links with India (when Jaffna went without a king, a new one was called not from among the Sinhala in the south, but from south India; the uniqueness of Jaffna and its autonomy until 1833 are always stressed.

2 The assumed linguistic, cultural, religious and 'racial' difference between Sinhala and Tamils is always made the basis of the argument, whether for an autonomous Jaffna or for a united, multi-ethnic Sri Lanka; the conclusions drawn from these differences can be very different, but the argument remains the same.

3 The Sinhala threat – a theme latent in earlier publications – becomes very prominent in the militant literature, especially in connection with the homeland discussion; most of the earlier literature rarely mentions the Sinhala in any capacity at all,[38] but once the options of historical choice narrow, they turn into the enemy to an ever increasing extent.

Tamil historical consciousness, and the resulting Tamil nationalism, is not simply 'reactive', a product of Tamil responses to Sinhala chauvinism and the Sinhala emphasis on their own history. Tamil nationalism in Jaffna cannot be seen as separate from Tamil nationalism in south India by which it has been influenced and on which it has, to some extent, fed. But what Sinhala nationalism and historical awareness brought about was a heightened sense of being Jaffna Tamil instead of just Tamil, thus leading to a withdrawal from the wider context of subcontinental Tamil culture and history. The choice of pasts is still there, but the options are used less and less. The 'reactive' nationalism consists in singling out one chauvinistic variant of Tamil nationalism which is put across as Jaffna Tamil nationalism.

Conclusion

It is interesting to see the progression: while in the state of innocence, history merely gave the Tamils a heightened self-awareness; it very quickly turned into an instrument first to prove the age-old uniqueness of the Tamils, then to bolster their political claims for separate representation and weighted electorates; from here to the demands for autonomy was a small step, and from autonomy to independence another. The content of the arguments has not changed that much, but the interpretation has. The past has been reinterpreted in a way that makes its acceptance as truth or otherwise vital for the survival of the community. That is why history will not let go and why it seems to have led to a spiral of death and destruction.

It would, however, be quite wrong to say that the distinction between Sinhala and Tamil was a fiction inspired by the British; what happened was that pre-existing differences were reinterpreted in a new fashion that emphasized antagonism and hostility instead of tolerance and exchange. The 'motif' of the Tamil invasion created antagonism on both sides. When it became politically opportune, this antagonism could be drawn on and exploited. We can see the obverse with the Kandyan Sinhala who were not drawn into the vortex of racial differences, because the actual differences between them and the Low-Country Sinhala were not vital enough (or not perceived to be vital enough) whilst overriding common economic and political interests pointed in another direction.[39]

The picture is not as alien as it may seem, since the history of nationalism in the small nations of Europe in the nineteenth century followed similar lines: language, ethnicity, and above all factual or mythical common history, time and again were made the basis for nationalism and national aspirations. We can still see the effects of this kind of nationalism in Spain, Northern Ireland, France, Belgium and elsewhere in Europe. To narrow the comparison further: the Germans, too, have a choice of pasts and histories which have been both a problem (the Third Reich) and an opportunity (the Federal Republic). The problem became acute when *one* historical option was made supreme and normative, excluding all others. The opportunity came when the range of options was acknowledged and the fractured nature of German history and German nationalism taken into account in fashioning German politics after the war.

It has been said that in Europe on the whole other allegiances have proved stronger and thus prevented the worst excesses of a misguided nationalism. The truth of this may be doubted. But one thing seems to be clear. History and historical myth in Europe (with notable exceptions) no longer possess that potential to rouse emotions and instigate action which they still have in Sri Lanka. The European experience of war and a common cultural tradition has now left Europeans with a picture of history as immensely fractured, ambiguous, multi-faceted and ill-fitted to answer to national passions any more. In Sri Lanka, on the other hand, a common cultural background has not prevented national passions being justified and legitimized by history. In Sri Lanka, history is fractured and fragmented and experienced as such, but not as criss-crossing lines of differentiation, but alongside and parallel to the given fracture lines – ethnic, linguistic, and religious – and these are mutually reinforcing. Divisive historical traditions are emphasized to the near total exclusion of those which might unify.

A myth evolved, based on selected facts, which made these facts into eternal and unchangeable 'truth'. What gives history this destructive power in Sri Lanka? And what gives it this power especially with the masses who in the past may not even have known the term 'history' and for whom a 'Tamil' or a 'Sinhala' was never real? The myths are no longer numerous and varied, but boil down to just one; the choice of pasts has narrowed down to that 'reactive' nationalism mentioned above. What can be proved to be 'historical' is right, justifiable, and moral. Whoever possesses history possesses the moral high ground, and possession of history means possession of power and political initiative. Used in this way, history becomes a very powerful weapon indeed to motivate and lead people into action, even into destructive action. The enemy is prefabricated and available on order. That is what has happened among both Tamils and Sinhala: once history was streamlined, old and mythical enemies (the Cinkalar) get easily identified with new enemies (the emerging Sinhala professional and political competition). And since the new enemies are the mythical old ones, they have to be fought with the mythical old weapons: violence, bloodshed, death, and destruction. The past is not past, but alive and kicking and permanently intruding into the lives of present people in a fruitless and destructive way: it is being resurrected, but its lessons have not been learnt.

Notes and references

1 Mayilvakana Pulavar, *Yalppana Vaipava Malai*, with an appendix by Kula Capanatan, Colombo, 1953; hereafter *YVM*.
2 See Rogers, this volume.
3 S.C. Chitty, *The Ceylon Gazetteer*, Kotte, 1834, pp. 104ff.
4 Ibid., pp. 52, 229–30.
5 *JRASCB*, 1847 vol. 2, p. 69; 1847–8, no. B, pp. 69ff.
6 *Idem, The Tamil Plutarch*, Jaffna, 1859.
7 *Utaya Tarakai* (Morning Star), 25/ix/1845, p. 156.
8 C. Brito, *The Yalppana Vaibhava Malai, or the history of the Kingdom of Jaffna*, trans. from the Tamil by C. Brito, Colombo, 1879, App., pp. xxlv–liii.
9 *Administration Report*, 1883, pt. III (judicial), p. 26C (PRO CO 57/90).
10 Chitty, *Plutarch*, pp. 51, 239, 252.
11 e.g., V. Catacivappillai, *Yalppana Vaipavam* (Events in Jaffna), Madras, 1884; Muttutampippillai, *Yalppana Carittiram* (History of Jaffna), Jaffna, 1912; K. Velluppillai, *Yalppana Vaipava Kaumuti*, Jaffna, Vasavilan 1918; S. John, *Yalppana Carittiram*, 3rd edn, Tellipalai, (1909) first publ. in 1879, to name only a few. It should be noted that Christians were prominent in this work.
12 Similarly the Sinhala hardly exist for nineteenth-century religious and social writers.
13 D. John in Preface to John, *Yalppana Carittiram*, p. xxviii.

14 Matiya Paranam, *Yalppana Puvika Vaipavam* (Ancient History of Jaffna), Jaffna, 1927 p. 16.
15 S. Rasanayagam, *Ancient Jaffna*, Colombo, 1926.
16 S. Rasanayagam, 'The kingdom of Jaffna and the Greek writers', *JRASCB* 1922, vol. 29, pp. 17–54; cf. A. Mendis Gunasekera's response, pp. 54–6; Rasanayagam's reply, pp. 58–60.
17 S. Gnanaprakasar, OMI, *Tamilin Purvacarittiramum Camayamum* (The Ancient History and Religion of the Tamils), Jaffna. 1912; first published as a series of articles in the Jaffna Catholic Guardian; *idem, Yalppana Vaipava Vimarcanam* (A Critical History of Jaffna), Accuveli, 1928.
18 K.M. de Silva, *A History of Sri Lanka*, London, 1981 pp. 390–95. For discussion of the reforms see *Sessional Papers* 4 and 28 (1923); PRO CO 57/208.
19 See Rogers, this volume.
20 But cf. C. Rasanayagam, *British Period of the History of Jaffna*, Jaffna, 1934.
21 *Navalar Ninaivu Malar* (Navalar Memorial Souvenir), ed. K.P. Irattinam, Chunnakam, 1938), esp. pp. 34 and 87; C. Ratnarvami Ryyar, *Menmakkal Carittiram* (Mayn Makkal Charittiram: Biographies of Great Tamil Men in Ceylon), Colombo, 1930, esp. paragraphs on Arunachalam, Arumuka Navalar, A. Mahadeva, G.G. Ponnambalam, P. Ramanathan, C. Rasanayagam, C. Suntheralingam.
22 Chitty, *Ceylon Gazeteer*, p. 29.
23 M. Vythilingam, *Ramanathan of Ceylon: The Life of Sir Ponnambalam Ramanatham*, Chunnakam, 1976, vol. 2, p. 541; cited in A.J. Wilson, *The Break-up of Sri Lanka*, London, 1988, p. 8.
24 Ilaventan (E. K. C. Canmukan), *En Nokkil Ananta Kumaraccuvami* (My view of Ananda Coomaraswamy), Colombo, 1971.
25 *Debates of the State Council*, 1939 *(Hansard)*, Ponnambalam on 15th March 1939, pp. 888ff, esp. 908, 991; G.G. Ponnambalam, 'Memorandum on the reform of the Constitution from the All Ceylon Tamil Congress and the Jaffna Association to the Right Honourable MacDonald, P.C., His Majesty's Secretary of State to the Colonies through His Excellency Sir Andrew Caldecott, Governor of Ceylon', 13.7.1938, PRO CO54/954/2, Doc. 469.
26 It has to be said that this '50–50' model generated heated opposition among sections of the Tamils as well, particularly among the left wing and the Communists.
27 C. Suntheralingam, *Eylom: Beginnings of Freedom Struggle. Eleven Documents*, Colombo, n.d. (1967?), pp. 10, 18–9, 39, 49, 70–1. On p. 77 he suddenly talks of 'Eelam'.
28 Ibid., pp. 75, 79.
29 A. Amirthalingam, *'Ilatciyap Patai'* (The Path of Principle), in *Ilankait Tamil Aracuk Katci Velli Vila Malar* (Ceylon Tamil Government Party Silver Jubilee Souvenir), Jaffna, 1974, part II *'Tiyaka Varalaru'* (History of Sacrifice), p. 13.

30 S. Pathamanthan, *The Kingdom of Jaffna*, Colombo, 1978; K. Indrapala, *Dravidian Settlements in Ceylon and the Beginnings of the History of Jaffna*, unpublished Ph.D. thesis, London, 1965; cf. Nissan and Stirrat, this volume.

31 *Nankam Ilankai Tamil Vila Malar* (Souvenir of the Fourth Festival of Ceylon Tamils) Jaffna, 1951.

32 C. S. Kadirgamanathan, *Ilankai Varalaru (Pirittanniyar Kalam 1796–1948)*, (History of Ceylon) Jaffna, 1967, pp. 154–7, 224.

33 e.g. in a PLOTE (People's Liberation Organization of Tamil Eelam) publication: *Makkalin Vitutalaiyai Venretuppom* (We will obtain people's liberation) PLOTE News Coordination Bureau, n.p., 1985, p. 18.

34 A.S. Balasingham, 'Liberation Tigers and Tamil Eelam Freedom Struggle', in *Towards Liberation. Selected Political Documents of the Liberation Tigers of Tamil Eelam*, n.p., 1984, p. 34.

35 See Whitaker, this volume, for the view from the east coast.

36 C. Manogaran, *Ethnic Conflict and Reconciliation in Sri Lanka*, Honolulu, 1987, pp. 4, 84.

37 Durbar of Native Chiefs (Tamil) August 1909, *Sessional Paper* 27 (1909) pp. 3–4, PRO CO57/177; Durbar of Native Chiefs (Tamil) *Sessional Paper* 36 (1910) pp. 7–8, PRO CO57/177.

38 See n. 12 above.

39 See Nissan and Stirrat, this volume, n. 48.

Part II

History at a moment of crisis

Chapter six

Nationalist rhetoric and local practice: the fate of the village community in Kukulewa

James Brow

Representations of the village community

For sixty years policies of rural development in Sri Lanka have been shaped by images of the village community generated within the complex discourse of Sinhala nationalism. Today the village community occupies a place of particular honour in nationalist rhetoric. Visions of the harmonious rural society that is believed to have existed in the past, and which it is the goal of current development policies to recreate, saturate the mass media and animate the 'rituals of development'[1] that continued to be staged almost every day, on a greater or lesser scale, even as the country collapsed into civil war in the mid-1980s. Similar images, depicting village life in the time of the ancient kings as prosperous, virtuous, co-operative, and free from exploitation and discrimination, inform the work both of official development agencies such as the Village Awakening (*Gam Udava*) programme and of non-governmental organizations such as the Sarvodaya Shramadana Movement.[2]

These representations of the village community, however, bear little resemblance to the actual conditions of rural society, either now or in the past. As Gombrich and Obeyesekere assert, referring specifically to the Sarvodaya movement, its 'vision of village society and the past of Sri Lankan civilization is a projection of the bourgeoisie, a fantasy that has no social reality.'[3] 'Projection' in this context is not simply a psychological process. As I have argued elsewhere, the images of agrarian life that are projected in contemporary nationalism form part of a hegemonic discourse, in terms of which the dominant classes justify their privilege to themselves and strive to gain the consent of those whom they command by incorporating them within the 'imagined community' of the Sinhala nation.[4]

Despite their anti-colonial thrust and distinctly Sinhala appearance, the images of the village community propagated in contemporary nationalist discourse derive more from colonial observation and speculation than from the experience of Sinhala peasants. While also drawing on nostalgic constructions of the rural past generated by the indigenous Buddhist revival, the nationalist imagination has appropriated some of its most potent material from nineteenth-century debates among western scholars and administrators. These foreign observers, however, were never able to agree on the fundamental characteristics of the village community, and the legacy of conflicting and often tendentiously imprecise definitions that they bequeathed has afforded ample scope for subsequent ideological manipulation. Among the more influential European writers who addressed the topic in the nineteenth century, Metcalfe's famous assertion that 'the village communities are little republics'[5] stressed political autonomy, while Maine gave priority to the collective landholdings of the 'assemblage of co-proprietors.'[6] Other characteristics attributed to the village community at various times have included autarky, equality, democracy, cultural homogeneity, social harmony, and even material prosperity, and the implication has not been absent that, when the village community really existed, all these features were present at once. Moreover, descriptions of the village community have often uncritically assumed the additional presence of that solidary disposition that Weber emphasized when he defined a social relationship as communal (*Vergemeinschaftung*) 'if and so far as the orientation of social action...is based on a subjective feeling of the parties...that they belong together.'[7] Thus variably constituted, the notion of the village community has served as a rich and volatile ideological concoction, and its evaluation and deployment in political practice have been extraordinarily complex and contentious.[8] In the nineteenth century it was admired by conservatives for the social cohesion it displayed, condemned by utilitarians for the barriers it imposed on individual enterprise, and held up by radicals in exemplary contrast to the social devastation wrought by an unfettered market.

In all of this the ideological potential of the village community was only enhanced by the fact that, although there was little or no consensus about its definition, almost everyone came to agree that it no longer existed. It is true that, as late as the 1870s, some remote villages in Sri Lanka's Dry Zone were still described as 'small agricultural republics',[9] and these were indeed, at that time, still largely self-sufficient, relatively unstratified and culturally homogeneous, if not also harmonious or prosperous, but for the most part the existence of the village community was fixed somewhere in the past.[10]

Samaraweera's careful studies indicate that the decisive incorporation of the village community into the developing discourse of Sinhala nationalism took place between 1925 and 1935.[11] Earlier nationalist intellectuals had already composed a romantic picture of the rural past, inspired by the writings of Maine and others, and had even begun a muted protest against peasant landlessness, but it was not until the 1920s that the political leaders of the nationalist élite, who by then occupied positions of considerable authority and influence, vigorously embraced the cause of the peasantry. They directly attributed the disintegration of the village community to the growth of plantation agriculture and argued that peasants should have priority over capitalists in the distribution of Crown lands. This was an extraordinary move, not least because many of those who made it, most notably D.S. Senanayake, who was soon to become Minister of Agriculture and Lands and later the first Prime Minister of independent Sri Lanka, had themselves greatly prospered from their involvement in the plantation sector.

It was also a move with enormous consequences. Samaraweera links it to the need of the westernized and predominantly Low Country Sinhala élite, against the scepticism of the colonial authorities, to strengthen its claim to represent the people of Sri Lanka as a whole.[12] Expanding on this suggestion, it appears that the decision to champion the interests of the peasantry, even at some economic disadvantage to itself, was crucial to the process whereby the élite sought not only to achieve a rapprochement with the leaders of the Kandyan Sinhala, who had experienced most directly the growth of the plantations, but also to bring together most of the Sinhala subaltern classes, including the peasantry, in an effective alliance of 'national-popular' unity.[13] Ominously, however, this alliance was only accomplished by the exclusion both of the Indian Tamil plantation workers and of the Sri Lankan Tamils in the north.

This hegemonic manoeuvre set the course for much that followed. Samaraweera may be correct in doubting that the élite consciously adopted the cause of the peasantry in order to create a political clientele in the future,[14] but after the introduction of the Donoughmore constitution in 1931 (against the opposition of many of the élite) that is precisely what the peasantry became, and a rural bias was established in national politics that is still evident today. Subsequent agrarian policy has consistently followed the general lines laid down by the Land Commission of 1928, which was dominated by members of the élite and which was convinced, above all, of the importance of preserving the peasantry.[15]

In recent times the commitment to promote the small peasant farm has increasingly been combined with the resurgent Buddhist ambition to create *dharmistha samajaya* (a just society), and in present-day development programmes like that of Village Awakening the stated goals of material welfare and moral uplift are now thoroughly conflated. These goals are legitimated by their placement within the mythological framework of Sinhala nationalism, which sanctifies them with the assertion that the Buddha himself selected the island of Sri Lanka as a place where his teachings would flourish. Structured as a narrative of virtue, degeneration and redemption, contemporary nationalism seeks to restore society to the condition of probity and prosperity it is believed to have enjoyed when righteous kings ruled over harmonious and largely self-sufficient villages.[16] This idyllic social order eventually succumbed to foreign invasion and the corruptions of colonial rule, but the attainment of independence in 1948 brought with it the prospect of national renewal, which is to be accomplished by the re-institution of righteous government and a re-dedication to Buddhist teachings. Revitalization of the village community is thus placed at the core of a nationalist project that shapes its vision of the future to match the dictates of its imagined past.

The aspects of nationalist discourse that have just been summarily described have been well received and widely adopted in Sinhala villages, for a number of mostly rather obvious reasons.[17] In the first place, peasants are doubtless pleased by authoritative representations of the social order in which their own role is accorded such prominence. Second, while harmony and co-operation are by no means the universal, or even the normal, experience of village life, they are held up as ideals of village culture no less than of nationalist imagination. Third, policies of rural development that purport to promote small family farming are congruent with many villagers' own aspirations for the future. Fourth, these policies are commonly accompanied and justified by acknowledgement of the the state's responsibility to provide for the welfare of the common people, which is a central component of villagers' own understanding of moral economy. And fifth, since the nation is itself represented as a nation of villages, there is no contradiction between adopting a stronger identification of oneself as a member of the Sinhala-Buddhist nation and retaining an identity defined in the more circumscribed terms of kinship and the village community.

Nevertheless, despite the fact that nationalist discourse has become pervasive in social life, even in the rural areas, to the point where its adoption has become indispensable to success in almost all encounters with officials and is hardly avoidable even in the mundane round of everyday life, it remains difficult to determine the depth to which a sense of national identity has sunk in the social consciousness of Sinhala villagers. Doubtless there is a considerable range of variation in this regard. It is, moreover, important not to mistake compliance for commitment.[18] The few ethnographic studies that have inquired into these matters indicate that villagers may employ the symbols of nationalism for instrumental reasons of their own that have little or nothing to do with the promotion of nationalist goals[19].

Even in the absence of overt resistance,[20] however, it is evident that the propagation of Sinhala nationalism in the rural areas contributes to a deeply contradictory social process. Social life in the villages has been profoundly disrupted in recent years by massive changes that seriously threaten the persistence of whatever elements of the idealized village community they once possessed. Indeed, implementation of the very programmes that are designed to revitalize the village community, and that are introduced with lavish celebration of its past and future virtues, is itself often disruptive and divisive. But this is hardly surprising in a context where the same government whose policy of economic liberalization is designed to encourage individual enterprise also advocates the use of communal work parties (*sramadana*, the selfless gift of labour) as a basic component of its rural development strategy; and where the virtues of the village community are most stridently promoted by the two major political parties, between whose local branches the conflict has become so intense that it continuously undermines whatever solidarity the villages are able to generate.

In the remainder of this chapter I explore some of these issues more concretely, by examining the impact of Sinhala nationalism on a remote and marginal village that was selected for development under the Village Awakening programme in 1978. I begin with a brief sketch of the village and then describe some central features of the ceremony that marked the official opening of the local Village Awakening project in 1980. The following sections focus on two performances of a very different ceremony held three years later, when the villagers were still struggling with conflicts precipitated by the Village Awakening project. These ceremonies provided dramatic opportunities for them to address critical issues of identity and community, which are discussed in the conclusion with reference to the representations of the past that were constructed and invoked.

Village Awakening in Kukulewa

The village of Kukulewa is located in Anuradhapura District, in the heart of Sri Lanka's Dry Zone. Isolated from major markets and remote from the centres of power, the villages of the Dry Zone were less profoundly affected by the transformations of the colonial period than were the villages of the Kandyan Highlands and the coastal Wet Zone, and as late as the 1950s many of them were still producing most of their own subsistence.[21] Economic stratification within the villages was not pronounced, nor was social differentiation, since all the inhabitants of a particular village were normally members of the same *variga* (sub-caste) and social relations among them were structured by rules of kinship.

The people of Kukulewa identified themselves as members of the Vedda *variga* and claimed to be descended from the union between

Prince Vijaya, the legendary founder of the Sinhala nation, and Kuveni, the aboriginal demon princess with whom Vijaya briefly cohabited after his arrival in Sri Lanka. Descent from Kuveni served to place the people of Kukulewa at the very margins of the Sinhala-Buddhist community, or even beyond them,[22] but their separation was mitigated by the fact that they spoke Sinhala, cultivated paddy as well as chena, engaged in the reciprocal services of the caste system, and occasionally participated in Buddhist rites. In the course of everyday life they were distinguished from their Sinhala neighbours mainly by their greater poverty. Nevertheless their assertion of Vedda descent did promote a distinct sense of identity that was continuously reproduced by a vast repertoire of customary rules and practices, ranging from collective propitiation of the village's protective deity to the norms of reciprocity and mutual aid that governed agricultural activities.

In the last forty years the simple reproduction of the village economy has been steadily eroded by a succession of mostly exogenous changes, the cumulative effect of which has been to threaten the sense of distinct identity that the village's relative autonomy and self-sufficiency formerly served to sustain. Rapid population growth has intensified the pressure on local resources, as a result of which the people of Kukulewa have increasingly been forced to go outside the village to make their living as casual labourers. By the late 1960s, if not earlier, wage labour had become the principal source of income for most Kukulewa villagers. Within the village both wet-rice agriculture and unirrigated cultivation have been largely re-oriented from direct subsistence to cash-crop production, and the employment of fellow villagers for wages, which formerly was considered incompatible with the reciprocities of kinship, has become common.

The expansion of market relations has been accompanied by other changes that have further reduced the isolation and relative independence of the village. State officials have come to intervene ever more decisively in village affairs, particularly in connection with projects intended to raise agricultural productivity. Politically, the struggle to acquire resources controlled by the state led in the mid-1970s to the organization of local branches of the two major parties, and the competition between them now subsumes most of the factional conflicts within the village. On the cultural front, a primary school was built in Kukulewa in the 1950s, and since the late 1960s a small but growing number of village children have continued on to high school. In addition, recent improvements in transportation and communications have brought the villagers within closer range of the mass media. As a result of these developments social life in the village has become more comprehensively encompassed by structures external to it.

The most dramatic of all the events that have contributed to this process of incorporation were those that followed the selection of Kukulewa for development under the programme of Village Awakening in 1978. The Village Awakening programme was the favourite project of the Prime Minister (now President), Ranasinghe Premadasa and, as indicated earlier, it was inspired by the prevailing sense of Sinhala-Buddhist history and the dominant vision of national regeneration. More specifically, it was strongly influenced by the Sarvodaya movement, which seeks to achieve simultaneously both the moral improvement of the individual and the material development of the village, mainly through the inculcation of a spirit of self-reliance and the practice of shared labour.

The Village Awakening programme in Kukulewa took the material form of sixty small concrete houses, two public buildings, and several tubewells that the government built at the northern end of the village. The project, on which Kukulewa villagers were employed as wage workers rather than through the voluntary organization of communal labour, as had originally been intended, was completed at the beginning of 1980, and on January 26th of that year the Prime Minister travelled down from Colombo to attend the opening ceremony. The occasion was celebrated with great pageantry, sponsored by the state, and included a procession, speeches by visiting dignitaries, a musical performance, the unveiling of a commemorative plaque and the planting of a bo-tree, as well as the formal transfer of the keys to the new houses.

Celebration of the national past, and recital of the exemplary lessons it contained, were prominent features of the ceremony. The official speeches recalled that the splendid civilization of the Anuradhapura kingdom was sustained by devotion to Buddhism, and emphasized that prosperity could again be achieved if the people, assisted by government projects like the Village Awakening programme, were to acquire the habits of self-reliance, mutual co-operation and virtuous living that their ancestors had displayed. In this connection much was made of the discovery within the village of a rock inscription, dating from the first century AD, that recorded the dedication of a local tank to the upkeep of Buddhist monks. As the local Member of Parliament pointed out, this endowment by the wife of a royal minister demonstrated not only that Kukulewa had once been a sacred place of worship but also that in ancient times kings, chiefs, and even women had taken a leading role in the work of development. The same speaker also seized the opportunity to assign the people of Kukulewa to their proper place within the Sinhala nation. After acknowledging their Vedda ancestry, he emphasized that they had now adopted Sinhala customs and that aboriginal traditions could no longer be found among them. The Sinhalization of the village was also announced by the name of Samadigama that was officially bestowed on the new settlement. '*Gama*' means village, while '*samadhi*' denotes an advanced state of mental concentration achievable through Buddhist meditation. But perhaps the most decisive act that authoritatively proclaimed the incorporation of Kukulewa within the Sinhala nation was the planting by the Prime Minister of a sapling taken from the sacred bo-tree in Anuradhapura, which is itself believed to have been grown from a sapling taken from the tree under which the Buddha attained enlightenment, and which symbolizes the Sinhala people's mission to maintain the Buddha's teachings in Sri Lanka.

At the end of the day, however, when the distinguished visitors departed, what they left behind was far from the harmonious community of their imagining. It was, rather, a village in which factional conflict had been suddenly and sharply exacerbated by the fact that the sixty new houses were all allocated to the local leaders of the UNP and their immediate associates.[23] For some time afterwards the hostility was very intense, as those who did not receive houses were outraged by what they considered their kinsmen's gross violation of communal norms. In early 1983, when I returned to Kukulewa for the first time since before the Village Awakening programme had been initiated, some of the bitterness and resentment had been pushed beneath the surface of everyday interaction, but it erupted again later in the year, in the weeks leading up to the annual performance of a ceremony called *gambädi rajakariya*. Since 1980 this collective ritual had been celebrated separately by those who had moved into the new houses in Samadigama and those who remained behind in the old village of Kukulewa.

Gambädi rajakariya in Samadigama

Performance of *gambädi rajakariya* was intended to gain the blessings and protection of the gods.[24] At the same time it was a feast to be enjoyed by the people of the village.

A. Dingiribanda, the *kapurala* (priest) who had conducted the ceremony in Kukulewa for many years, explained how this was authorized by the great god Kataragama:

> Valliamma was adopted by Veddas and was brought up by them. But god Kataragama took her away from them by force. He fought with her brothers and defeated them. Valliamma felt very sorry for her brothers, the Veddas, and pointed out to god Kataragama that they had no opportunity to hold a feast on the day she married him. So at her request god Kataragama gave the Veddas permission to enjoy five wedding ceremonies. *Gambädi rajakariya* is one of those five ceremonies, a *maha dana* (major alms-giving) at which many people are fed.

All members of the village community were expected to participate in the celebrations, so when the people who obtained the new houses in Samadigama organized a separate performance of the ceremony, their decision indicated how serious was the rift that divided them from their kinsmen in the old village. Dingiribanda explained:

> Up to 1980 there was only one annual performance of *gambädi rajakariya* in this village. But after the people went to Samadigama they wanted to hold a separate ceremony. Those who got houses there are UNP supporters and there were political differences between us. At that time the Samadigama people and the Kukulewa people were real enemies. They didn't even go to each others' funerals and weddings.

Anticipation and excitement had been rising in Samadigama as the day of the ceremony approached, for there had lately been signs of unusual supernatural activity. The fact that several people had been attacked by demons in the previous few months was not in itself uncommon, but there was one case that commanded particular attention. One day when P.B. Seelawathie was out in the jungle collecting firewood, she was frightened by a sudden apparition. After she returned home she fell ill and was treated for demonic possession. In the course of her treatment she went into trance, and the demon who possessed her spoke through her voice to say that he had been sent to ruin Samadigama by certain people in Kukulewa. The accusation was challenged, but it brought the issue of social relations between the two villages back into sharp focus. Subsequently Seelawathie continued to go into trance, and seemed to show some skill in curing ailments and finding lost objects, so that some people became convinced that she was possessed, not by a demon compelled by sorcery, but by a benevolently disposed god. Then her brother, P.B. Wijeratne, who was secretary of the local branch of the UNP and was believed by many people to be as responsible as anyone for the way the houses had been allocated, also began to go into trance, and intimated that he would do so at the ceremony itself.

On the evening before the ceremony about thirty villagers gathered at the small shrine that had been constructed for the event. Two drummers began to play their instruments and invoke the gods, drawing their attention to the offerings that would be made to them the next day. After a while Wijeratne, who had been sitting inside the shrine with several other men, got up and stepped outside. A few moments later he began to tremble, then suddenly threw his arms up in the air and cried out as he entered the initial stage of trance when the god (*deva*) or demon (*yaka*) mounts his intended vehicle. For several minutes he thrashed wildly about, while those close to him struggled to hold him upright. Eventually he quietened down, still quivering with the presence of whatever god or demon was possessing him but steadier on his feet as he moved into full trance. Then he began to dance to the rhythm of the drums. After a while he approached A. Ukkubanda, the priest who was in charge of the Samadigama ceremony, and asked permission to enter the shrine to make an offering to the major gods. Permission was granted, and someone handed him a few betel leaves. He carried these into the shrine and made his offering. When he came out again he continued to dance for several minutes. Then he stopped and began to speak in the language of the gods, which is not readily understood by all. The priest and the drummers listened closely, and everyone else also clustered around, intent on what was being said:

> I am a very powerful god. I have been in thirty-two villages, including Kukulewa, and everywhere I have watched over the interests of Kuveni's children. Now I have come to this village to give you my message. When the kings built this village and planted the bo-tree here, the village became sacred. The tree is a branch of the Sri Maha Bodhi in Anuradhapura, where the Black God lives. Because of the bo-tree the village is divinely blessed. But you must keep that sacred place very clean. Before you make offerings to the gods you should make offerings at the bo-tree. That will attract the attention of the gods, who will then give their blessings to the village. I will come again tomorrow to give you instructions before you make the offerings.

After he had delivered his message the god left Wijeratne, who was led away to recover himself. The drumming and chanting were concluded a few minutes later. Afterwards the performers, organizers, and invited guests ate together and discussed the arrangements for the following day.

The next morning, as people busied themselves preparing for the ceremony, there was a flurry of excitement when Seelawathie, veiled and dressed entirely in white, emerged from her house and walked down towards the shrine, followed by a procession of about twenty villagers. As she approached the shrine the drummers began to play, and she quickly went into trance. She brushed aside her veil, let down her hair so that it covered her face, and began to dance. She was soon followed into trance by her brother, Wijeratne, who again began to speak in the language of the gods, which his sister helped interpret to the audience:

> The god who speaks through the brother of my vehicle-woman wants to see the two villages united again. He says the people should forget their jealousies and quarrels, and should bring together Samadigama

and Kukulewa into a single community. He wants to see just one performance of the ceremony next year, in which members of both villages participate together.

Excitement spread through the village. Many people believed that Samadigama was about to be blessed. Seelawathie's and Wijeratne's possession seemed to herald the arrival of a powerful god who would take up residence in the village. Some speculated that it might be the return of the same god who had watched over the interests of Kukulewa at an earlier time. That god had used a man named Kandappu as his vehicle, and before that Kandappu's father, who had brought the god's sacred ornaments to the village, had been the medium through whom the god conveyed his messages and afforded his protection. But many people believed that the god had left the village when Kandappu died in 1978, either because of sorcery or because there was no one left who was sufficiently virtuous to be his vehicle. Now people began to recall images of a distant past when, through the mediumship of Kandappu's father, the benevolent gaze of the god had rested on the village and made it prosperous and contented. Word of the god's visit and his promise to return for the ceremony spread rapidly, and more and more people began to converge on the shrine. They came in large numbers not only from Samadigama but also from Kukulewa, and a few even arrived from more distant villages. By the time Ukkubanda began the alms-giving in mid-afternoon, several hundred people were gathered at the shrine.

Accompanied by the playing and chanting of the drummers, Ukkubanda approached the gods, beginning inside the shrine with Pulleyar, Kataragama and the other major gods, and then stepping outside to make offerings to the lesser gods and demons. An offering at the bo-tree was not neglected. Wijeratne and Seelawathie, who again arrived in procession, quickly went into trance. Two men who had come from Kukulewa, sons of Kandappu the former medium, also showed signs of becoming possessed. They began to tremble, as if they felt a god alight on them, but they did not move on into full trance and were led to the side to recover themselves. Then Wijeratne's god began to speak:

I am a watcher for the god who used to live in Kukulewa. The god who spoke through the old vehicle-man is still in the village. He sent me to give you the message that he wants to come again. He has a tender regard for Kuveni's children. But you, the children of Kuveni, are now jealous of one another. Your minds are not clean and you hate one another. You even hate your own kinsmen. You, Kuveni's children, are all one kin group, but you have fallen out among yourselves. All who are kin should be united. The god wants you to come back together.

While Wijeratne's god was speaking Seelawathie remained in trance, swaying slightly from side to side and with her long hair concealing her face. The crowd remained quiet, but pressed in on all sides. Small children were lifted on to their fathers' shoulders to get a better view, and almost everyone gave rapt attention to the words and actions of the gods. After their message had been delivered the two gods danced for a few minutes longer, and then departed. Wijeratne and Seelawathie were laid down to rest and to recover their own senses.

At last it was time for the communal meal. But as preparations were being made to serve the food, most of the visitors from Kukulewa began to drift away. When some were spotted heading down the road they were called back and invited to eat. They seemed to hesitate, and the invitation was repeated. But eventually they moved on again, back towards Kukulewa. One of them called out, and the cry was then repeated: 'We came to see the god, not to eat'.

In subsequent discussions Wijeratne's god's plea for unity between Samadigama and Kukulewa was much applauded. But at the same time many people recognized obstacles to its attainment. Some people, like B. Kandathe, one of those who had obtained housing in Samadigama, thought that the god's expressed wish was itself enough to compel obedience:

> The god wants the people of Kukulewa and Samadigama to perform *gambädi ṛajakariya* together. If that's what the god wants we have no alternative. But it will be very difficult to bring all the people together.

The appeal for unity was also welcomed in Kukulewa, but some people demanded that the Samadigama villagers first take other conciliatory steps. K. Wannihamy, the village shopkeeper and a staunch supporter of the SLFP, was one of them:

> It's good that the god says he wants unity between the two villages. After all, we are all kinsmen. The people of Samadigama are our relatives. There's no point in having two performances of *gambädi rajakariya*. But we won't go to Samadigama to hold the ceremony there. Those people will have to come here. Samadigama isn't even a village. It has no tank, no paddy fields, no land.

Some of the ritual specialists raised other problems. One of them was U. Kalubanda, an *udakki kapuva* (ritual drummer) who now lived in Samadigama but who remained on good terms with his kinsmen and neighbours back in Kukulewa:

> The two villages will never be united. You can call me a dog if that ever happens. When a god comes to live in a village he lays down its

> boundaries (*sima*). The god who used to live in Kukulewa did that, and he chased the demons out of the village. Samadigama does not lie within the boundaries he established. It was thick jungle in those days, and now it's a separate village as far as the god is concerned. So it's not correct for Wijeratne's god to try to bring the two villages together. A very powerful god might be able to unite the two villages, but I don't think such a god would come here. The people are very bad. They are not virtuous. So the gods won't look favourably upon us. The Samadigama people started to hold *gambädi rajakariya* separately three years ago. If they don't continue to do so now the gods may get angry.

According to Ukkubanda, the Samadigama *kapurala*:

> It isn't possible to hold a single ceremony for both villages any longer. Offerings have been made to Kadavara in Samadigama for the last three years, and Kadavara is not like other gods. If offerings are made one year he expects them to be made every year.... Kukulewa and Samadigama are two different villages. Samadigama doesn't fall under the divine protection of the god who used to live in Kukulewa. That god is still there. But because there is no one virtuous enough to be his vehicle he doesn't possess anyone. Samadigama used to be jungle, and it was into that jungle that the Kukulewa god drove the demons that were troubling the village. So Samadigama doesn't have the god's protection. If we want to avoid trouble here we'll have to hold our own separate ceremony.

The real identity of the god possessing Wijeratne was also questioned. Wijeratne's claim that he was a watcher sent by the god who had formerly possessed Kandappu, and that the god himself wanted to return, was not accepted by everyone. In particular, it was challenged by those who feared they would lose the protective power of the god's sacred ornaments if they were removed from Kukulewa to Samadigama.

Gambädi rajakariya in Kukulewa

A few days later the people of Kukulewa held their own performance of *gambädi rajakariya*. On the evening before the ceremony, after a shrine had been built near the centre of the village, close to the tank bund, a few men gathered at the site, where they discussed the arrangements that had been made. Dingiribanda, who had conducted the ceremony for many years, criticized the failure of the *gamaralas* (hereditary village chiefs) to organize the ceremony correctly, claiming that they were supposed to provide a meal for those who had helped in the preparations. He also argued that only those villagers who held shares (*pangukarayo*) in the main field were obliged to contribute to the alms-giving, and that they should contribute in proportion to the size of their holdings. But in fact everyone had been asked to donate the same amount, and again the conduct of the *gamaralas* was deplored.

It took several hours to prepare and cook the food the next day, and it was mid-afternoon before everything was ready. Then a group of men went off to collect the god's ornaments and brought them back to the site of *gambädi rajakariya*, where they were carefully laid out on a table in front of the shrine. After that the *kapurala* began to make the offerings to the gods. At one point he began to tremble and it seemed that a god was about to alight on him, but he recovered himself and continued with the offerings. Instead it was a young man in the audience who began to shake and shortly afterwards went into trance. This was K. Dharmadasa, a resident of Samadigama with close kin in Kukulewa, who had been possessed on several previous occasions. Dharmadasa jerked convulsively about for several minutes, then settled down, and a god began to speak through him:

> I am Kaludakada god. I have come here to explain something to you. There are two people in Samadigama who say they are possessed by me. They are threatening that, because you didn't invite them here, they are going to make trouble for you. Do not believe them. I am here for your protection. As long as I am here nobody can harm you.

At this point U. Sumanapala, one of the organizers of the ceremony, interrupted:

> No, no, we're not afraid. We know that no one can harm us as long as god Kaludakada's ornaments are here.

Dharmadasa then went inside the shrine to worship god Kataragama, after which he stepped back out and began to speak again:

> The gods who speak through the brother and sister in Samadigama claim that the ornaments in Kukulewa belong to them. That is what they said at the ceremony in Samadigama. But I sent my watchers there to prove them wrong.... And my watchers made the sons of my old vehicle-man go into trance.[25] I did this as a protest.

When he had finished speaking Dharmadasa's god began to dance. For a while he danced around the large pots of food that the villagers had prepared, speaking briefly to several of the women who were standing beside them. Then the god left, and Dharmadasa lay down to recover. All the gods had now received their offerings, and the people turned to enjoy their own feast.

When they talked about the ceremony later, there were few people who were convinced that god Kaludakada himself had possessed

Dharmadasa. Most were more inclined to think that it was some emissary of the god. Kalubanda, one of the drummers said:

> You can tell it wasn't Kaludakada himself who appeared at the ceremony. You saw that he didn't even touch the ornaments. If they had been his ornaments he would have worn them. Only the god to whom the ornaments belong can wear them. If someone is not possessed by that god he cannot touch them. They would burn him if he tried to touch them.

Sumanapala explained:

> It wasn't Kaludakada himself who came to the ceremony. It was the watcher who is in charge of the ornaments. Kaludakada sent him to give his message. We're not afraid of the threats made by Seelawathie's god.

But there were also other interpretations of what had happened. U. Menikrala, who had remained in Samadigama, where he was taking on the role of Seelawathie's *kapurala*, believed that Seelawathie's god was responsible:

> The man who went into trance at the Kukulewa ceremony was made to do so by Seelawathie's god. She was possessed by her god on that day. The god was angry that his vehicle-woman had not been invited. Just before the alms-giving at Kukulewa Seelawathie's god spoke through her and said, 'I am going to the alms-giving. I will catch someone there and make him dance'. After that Seelawathie came out of trance. She was conscious all the time that man was in trance in Kukulewa. It was obviously Seelawathie's god who went there.

Such disagreements persisted. Many questions remained unanswered, and people wondered whether things would become clearer in the future and whether Kukulewa and Samadigama would ever be reunited.

Discussion

Images of the past were constantly generated and evoked in the events I have just described. These images ranged from the recent memory of the housing allocations to the recitation of the origin myth of *gambädi rajakariya*, in which god Kataragama recognizes the Veddas' association with his consort by allowing them to hold the feast. In between were various stories about the exploits of Kandappu's father and nostalgic recollections of a time when, through his effective mediumship, the benevolent gaze of the god had rested on the village and made it prosperous. All these constructions of the past were heavy with implications for present-day behaviour. Many of them also spoke directly to issues of community, invoking the authority of the past to define the limits and possibilities of solidarity.

One significant question in this regard was whether or not it was possible to comply with the wishes of Wijeratne's god and to reunite Kukulewa and Samadigama by holding a combined performance of the ceremony in the future. On this issue both the *kapurala*s argued that the possibilities were limited by the previous actions of the god. When a god takes up residence in a village he lays down its boundaries and affords his protection only to those who live within them. The village community, then, is composed of those who enjoy the protection of the same god and who live within the boundaries he has established. Memories of where exactly the boundary runs might at times be in dispute (although there was no indication of that in the present case), but the general point was uncontested: the limits of community are determined by the boundaries marked out by the god, and communal action in the present is thus constrained by divinely authoritative action undertaken in the past.

A second question of comparable import, but one that appealed to secular rather than to sacred tradition, concerned the proper organization of *gambädi rajakariya*. When Dingiribanda asserted the obligation of the *gamarala*s, whose hereditary authority was linked to their holdings of particular plots in the main field, to take the lead in organizing the ceremony, he was recalling a feature of Kandyan Sinhala social organization in Anuradhapura District that had long lost any practical relevance it might once have had.[26] More than that, when he argued that *pangukarayo* (shareholders in the village field) should contribute to the alms-giving in proportion to the size of their landholdings, he was evoking a form of moral economy that not only contrasted with the increasingly impersonal and market-oriented practice of contemporary agriculture but was also one that it would be impossible to institutionalize in Samadigama. The point was not made explicitly, but everyone was well aware that Samadigama had no paddy fields of its own, and therefore no one who could claim the title of *gamarala*. It would not be difficult then to draw the further inferences that no one in Samadigama was authorized to sponsor a collective ceremony such as *gambädi rajakariya* and that Samadigama could not therefore constitute a village community.

These local recollections of the past find their parallels at the higher level of discourse about the national community of Sinhala-Buddhists. Thus the confinement of the village community within the boundaries laid down by the deity corresponds to the mission of the Sinhala people to maintain Buddhist doctrine within the area that the Buddha marked out on the three visits which, according to legend, he made to Sri Lanka.[27] And the image of the village as a moral community in which the *gamarala*s and more prosperous *pangukarayo* are obliged to extend assistance to their poorer kinsmen corresponds to representations of the nation in which contemporary rulers have assumed the responsibility of their royal precedessors to govern virtuously and provide for the welfare of the people. In such ways local constructions of the village community nestle comfortably within the embrace of Sinhala nationalist discourse.

What is remarkable, then, is the meagre extent to which the history lessons authoritatively delivered at the official opening of Samadigama seemed to have penetrated the discursive consciousness of the villagers. In 1983 the attainment of harmony within the village was still discussed in terms of winning the favour of the gods rather than of following Buddhist precepts. No mention was made of the ancient rock-inscription, and only one villager linked the sacred bo-tree to Buddhist practices. For others the tree was the abode of the Black God rather than a core symbol of Sinhala-Buddhist community. No less revealing was the fact that, despite the instruction they had received in history and morality, when the villagers sought to recreate a sense of common identity with their fellows they still addressed them as 'children of Kuveni' rather than as Sinhala-Buddhists.

Thus, despite the congruence between the village community as imagined in Kukulewa and the village community as represented in Sinhala nationalism, specific articulations between local and national discourse were only loosely elaborated. Kukulewa had been placed within the Sinhala nation, and its local pantheon contained within that of Sinhala-Buddhism, but discursive movement between local and national levels was infrequent. This reflected the continued cultural isolation of Kukulewa as compared with most other villages, and the continued attachment of its inhabitants to their Vedda identity. There was no Buddhist temple in the village and, although it did contain a government school, in the 1980s much of the adult population was still functionally illiterate. Moreover, its schoolteachers have generally preferred to reside in neighbouring villages that are better appointed than is Kukulewa. Consequently there was a notable absence from the village of the kind of cultural brokers whose role in linking local circumstances to nationalist discourse has been examined by Spencer.[28] Such local agents of nationalism, typically teachers, minor officials or monks, whose narratives connect local events to the larger story of the nation, were not (yet) active in Kukulewa in 1983.

Under these circumstances the spectacular pageantry that accompanied the opening of Samadigama served to proclaim the incorporation of the village within the Sinhala-Buddhist nation, but it did not effectively colonize the whole terrain on which villagers forged their identities and gave meaning to their lives. Many people in Kukulewa and Samadigama could, indeed, employ the discourse of nationalism when its adoption promised advantages, as in attempts to acquire benefits controlled by politicians and officials, but when engaged in their own internal affairs they reverted to a local idiom which was their own and which, despite the similarities and connections, was only marginally infused with specifically nationalist themes. In this small but significant space the history they produced, and the images of community it served to sustain, were neither wholly subordinate nor clearly oppositional to the dominant nationalism. They constituted, rather, a still viable and at least partially autonomous, if also threatened, alternative.

Acknowledgements

An earlier version of this chapter was presented at the panel on 'Nationalist Discourse and the Uses of the Past in Sri Lanka', held at the annual meeting of the American Anthropological Association in Phoenix, Arizona, on 20 November 1988. I am grateful to Val Daniel, Jonathan Spencer and Mike Woost for their comments, but none of them is responsible for the errors that remain. Field research was conducted from 1968 to 1970 under a grant from the Smithsonian Institution, and in 1983 under grants from the Joint Committee on South Asia of the American Council of Learned Societies and the Social Science Research Council, the Wenner-Gren Foundation for Anthropological Research, and the University of Texas at Austin. P.G. Somaratne provided invaluable research assistance in 1983.

Notes and references

1 N. S. Tennekoon, 'Rituals of development: the accelerated Mahaväli development program of Sri Lanka', *American Ethnologist*, 1988, vol. 15, pp. 294–310.

2 D. Kantowsky, *Sarvodaya: The Other Development*, Delhi, 1980; R. Gombrich and G. Obeyesekere, *Buddhism Transformed. Religious Change in Sri Lanka*, Princeton, 1988, pp. 243–55.

3 Ibid., p. 250.

4 J. Brow, 'In pursuit of hegemony: representations of authority and justice in a Sri Lankan village', *American Ethnologist*, 1988, vol 15, p. 312; B. Anderson, *Imagined Communities*, London, 1983.

5 Quoted in L. Dumont, *Religion/Politics and History in India*, Paris, 1970, p. 112.

6 H. S. Maine, *Ancient Law*, London, 1906 (first published 1861), p. 272.

7 M. Weber, *Economy and Society*, Berkeley, 1978, p. 40.

8 C. Dewey, 'Images of the village community: a study in Anglo-Indian ideology', *MAS*, 1972, vol. 6, pp. 291–328.

9 J. F. Dickson, 'Report on the North-Central Province', in Government of Ceylon, *Administration Report*, 1873, p. 9.

10 J. Spencer, 'Representations of the rural: a view from Sabaragamuva', ms.

11 V. Samaraweera, 'Land policy and peasant colonization, 1914–1948', in K. M. de Silva (ed.) *History of Ceylon, Volume III: Ceylon from the Beginning of the Nineteenth Century to 1948*, Peradeniya, 1973; *idem*, 'Land as "patrimony": nationalist response to immigrant labour demands for land in early twentieth century Sri Lanka', *Indian Economic and Social History Review*, 1977, vol. 14, pp. 341–362; *idem*, 'Land, labor, capital and sectional interests in the national politics of Sri Lanka', *MAS*, 1981, vol. 15, pp. 127–162.

12 Samaraweera, 'Land, labour, capital'.

13 Cf. A. Gramsci, *Selections from the Prison Notebooks*, (eds) Q. Hoare and G. Nowell-Smith, London, 1971; S. Hall, 'Gramsci's relevance for the study of race and ethnicity', *Journal of Comunications Inquiry*, 1986, vol. 10, pp. 5–27; P. Chatterjee, *Nationalist Thought and the Colonial World*, London, 1986.

14 Samaraweera, 'Land, labor, capital', p. 136.

15 M. P. Moore, *The State and Peasant Politics in Sri Lanka*, Cambridge, 1985.

16 Sinhala nationalism is a much more complex, uneven, and even contradictory discourse than this summary presentation may suggest. For present purposes, however, it is sufficient to indicate some of the most prominent themes that characterize its authoritative dissemination in Sinhala villages.

17 Brow, 'In pursuit'.

18 Cf. J. C. Scott, *Weapons of the Weak: Everyday Forms of Peasant Resistance*, New Haven, 1985.

19 Spencer, 'Representations'; *idem, A Sinhala Village in a Time of Trouble*, Delhi, 1990; M. Woost, 'Nationalizing the local past in Sri Lanka: tendentious histories of development in a Sinhalese village', ms.; *idem*, this volume.

20 I am referring, of course, only to the Sinhala-speaking parts of the country. Tamil resistance to Sinhala nationalism is another story.

21 For a masterly account of a village in Anuradhapura District in the 1950s see E. R. Leach, *Pul Eliya: A Village in Ceylon*, Cambridge, 1961; for accounts of the changes that took place in Kukulewa prior to 1970 see J. Brow, *Vedda Villages of Anuradhapura: The Historical Anthropology of a Community in Sri Lanka*, Seattle, 1978; *idem*, 'The changing structure of appropriations in Vedda agriculture', *American Ethnologist*, 1978, vol. 5, pp. 448–467; *idem*, 'The ideology and practice of share-cropping tenancy in Kukulewa and Pul Eliya', *Ethnology*, 1981, vol. 19, pp. 46–67.

22 Cf. G. Obeyesekere, 'The Buddhist pantheon in Ceylon and its extensions', in M. Nash (ed.) *Anthropological Studies in Theravada Buddhism*, New Haven, 1966.

23 At the time there were about 130 households in Kukulewa.

24 The ceremony in Samadigama was held on 3 August 1983; i.e. about a week after the outbreak of ethnic rioting during the last week of July.

25 Dharmadasa is referring to Kandappu's two sons who almost went into trance at the ceremony in Samadigama.
26 Cf. Leach, *Pul Eliya*.
27 Obeyesekere, 'The Buddhist pantheon'; *idem*, 'The vicissitudes of the Sinhala-Buddhist identity through time and change', in M. Roberts (ed.) *Collective Identities, Nationalisms and Protest in Modern Sri Lanka*, Colombo, 1979.
28 J. Spencer, 'Telling histories: nationalism and nationalists in a Sinhala village', ms.

Chapter seven

A compound of many histories: the many pasts of an east coast Tamil community

Mark P. Whitaker

> Although the major identity components of the Sinhalese are their Sinhalese language and their Buddhist religion, and of the Tamils their Tamil language and their Hindu religion, both these populations share many parallel features of traditional caste, kinship, popular religious cults, customs, and so on. But they have come to be divided by their mythic charters and tendentious historical understandings of their pasts.
>
> S.J. Tambiah[1]

> For them too history was a tale like any other too often heard...
>
> James Joyce, *Ulysses*

I remember that in 1984, a supposedly ahistorical American, I sat on a wicker chair in the east coast Tamil village of Mandur watching television. It was the summer of the US Olympic games, and my host Mr Kuruvaltampi had turned on the television to catch the closing ceremonies. Shifting Kuruvaltampi's kids, Kumar and Chandram, from knee to knee, I watched in fascination as a line of prairie-schooner wagons, complete with wooden water casks and buckboards, drove into the centre of the Los Angeles Coliseum. In an explosion of holographic light, America's pioneer past, the pop present, and the sci-fi future were united by the descent of an 'alien' spaceship and the appearance of a tall, silvery extraterrestrial, with (if I remember correctly) the head of an opaque gumball machine. More mytho-hysterically than mytho-poetically, perhaps, the extraterrestrial assured everyone 'out there' (which I took to include even us, in Mandur) that all would be well in the future if only we took with us the spirit of the Olympic games.

Kumar, clearly bored, climbed down from my knee and turned off the television.

It was August in Mandur. The rains were still a month away, it was very hot, and the suffocating wind that blows east off the central highlands was clogging even the nights with its dust. It had been a slow year, a slim harvest, and the political troubles that had exploded the year before, bringing refugees and the army, were making everyone tense. As it was also the festival season, the time when the village's most notable institution, the Sri Kantucuvami temple, would normally draw tens of thousands of pilgrims to the village, the temple officials, of whom Kumar's father's father was one, were worried about whether the festival would again have to be cancelled. The festival, besides being the village's *raison d'être*, also provided a welcome and necessary infusion of cash into its economy. It had been crippled the year before; a far off, and complex, victim of the island-wide rioting that had broken out in July 1983. In August 1984, with civil war already a reality in Jaffna, and with the first scattered attacks beginning to take place in Batticaloa, the Eastern Province's provincial capital, people were again worried that the festival might be shut down.

That night, as Mr Kuruvaltampi and his *maccan* (wife's brother) Bala, turned out the lights and shuttered the windows, I went to my room and tried to write:

> It is odd to think of anything in Mandur changing. For an anthropologist subtly trained in the myth of the eternally rural, Mandur seems to claim all the elements of an unalterable substratum of existence. Its yearly cycle of sowing and reaping, of poverty and gain, simply continues, as the swing of a pendulum does, to clock the passage of an, at worst, corrosive kind of time. Houses are built, white-washed and shingled, only to subside, in little more than a year, into things more pleasantly dusty and well-worn. Bullock carts creak up and down dusty tracks between the compounds, pulled by the same snorting, sweating, fly-infested buffalo. Black crows swoop down upon the cadjan fences, rustle, as always, with tentative abruptness, and raucously jeer at the woman pounding grain. It seems there will always be festivals at the temples, pariah dogs asleep in the wheel ruts, and arguments on the threshing floors.

My writing was interrupted, however, by a sharp, cracking sound, as if someone were snapping apart dry bamboo. Rather concerned, I left my room and found Mr Kuruvaltampi and Bala conversing quietly by the open front door. They seemed to think it might be firing; perhaps the army, south of Mandur. Mandur was hardly a hotbed of separatist sentiment, but the arrest of several of its young men, and the quiet passage of some others into the ranks of 'the boys' (i.e., the separatist guerrillas) made Mr Kuruvaltampi think it was only a matter of time before the army hit Mandur – and seriously, not like the previous July when a patrol had merely relieved a boy of his seat on a bullock cart and thrown him in the lake. So we stood by the door and listened. The firing, or whatever it was, seemed to be getting closer.

There was a rustling over the village. I could hear doors opening and shutting, a baby's cry swiftly muffled, the sound of bare feet pounding on the sand outside the compound. Up and down the road, in the deep village dark (for Mr Kuruvaltampi's house was one of the few that was electrified) I could hear other people at other gates. All along the street, all over the village I imagine, people were doing the same. Listening at their gates; waiting for the army to come. Across the path, and next door, I could hear people whispering, 'Is the army coming?' But soon the whispering stopped, and there were no more runners in the lane. We waited.

Suddenly Mr Kuruvaltampi made a rude, barking noise. A single, explosive, laugh. And with that he was shouting orders. The other *maccan* (see below) were roused from where they slept, or listened, on the front verandah. Two chairs were ordered to be brought out from the living-room – one, as he said, for the compound head (*vitutalivan*) and one for the studying head (*paticcatalivan* – i.e., me). They were placed, as he wanted, on a line with the front door, facing the main compound gate. 'If the army is coming, it will come. But I will not stand and wait; neither will you. We will sit down and greet it.' And so we sat, and talked of the temple, and I tried to remember the stories I'd been told of how the Portuguese had tried to attack the temple four hundred years before only to be turned back by a prayer to its god and a swarm of bees, and of how in 1956 Sinhala rioters riding down the Gal Oya road toward the temple had been stopped at the village boundary by the same god. Yes, we were waiting for the army; and we were waiting for another kind of history.

The army never came that night. The alarm was false, the 'shots' the crackle of fireworks from a temple, miles away, whose festival explosions the wind had carried to us like an advancing patrol. A year later, and again a year after that, the alarms would not be false, and tractors would be burnt, buffalo slaughtered, and people killed in Mandur – killed, as I tend to think of it, by other kinds of history. Yet the question of history – or, more aptly, of histories in collision – that Sri Lanka's post-Independence experience has thrown so powerfully, finally so horribly, into relief, remains. On that night in Mandur, histories, primordial origin stories, myths, 'structures of structuring', charters, or what have you, were thicker than the ghosts that are supposed to hang about village intersections waiting for someone to show them the way home.

In what follows, very briefly, I want to try to pull Mandur's histories apart. For I imagine histories, in Mandur (and in Sri Lanka, generally), like lines of time twisted together into a rope – or, better, all tangled up together into an impromptu, unravellable skein. I will not attempt to qualitatively differentiate, however, between 'history' in our sense – that is, academic accounts of the past produced by those within the discipline of history – and what is often called 'mytho-history', and used to be called 'emic' history. Indeed, for the purposes of this analysis, and in an attempt to escape both historiographic textualism and empiricism, anything that comprises an ethnographically differentiable, and observably effective, use of the past – that is, a 'use' of the past that is shared by some identifiable body of people, whether academics or temple priests, and which constitutes (in the sense of rendering meaningful) a pattern of action in time – shall be regarded as a 'history'. Hence, although I would be the first to join in condemning nationalist histories, whether led by lions, tigers, or prairie-schooners, *for political reasons*, I'm not sure that, as an anthropologist, I can afford to take the high road of empiricism and simply write off such histories as collective fantasies. Nobody ever died of a fantasy, except perhaps by heart attack; whereas, for example, a President who believed that the apocalypse was upon us could very easily make it so. And who would be left to note that no one was saved, that the 'theory' was in error? At the same time, the various histories that have sometimes helped, but most recently tortured, Sri Lanka, are not, I think, best thought of, textually, as 'stories' or 'forms of historical consciousness' or even styles of reasoning about the past. When the Sri Lankan army did finally turn down the road toward Mandur, they were past, I suspect, reasoning about anything. Rather a conjunction of 'histories', of Sinhala nationalism, Sri Lankan electoral politics, development theories, highway construction, local military 'fact' and, if Stirrat and Nissan are correct, perhaps even the face of the demonic (Tamil, not Sinhala) was what drew them.[2] Physical, mental, political, sociological – it was all 'factual' in one sense; it got them there.

In this analysis, however, I shall confine my attention to the Tamil people of Mandur and to the 'histories', in the above sense, that impinged on them. I do this partly because I believe that, as an anthropologist, it is silly for me to play political scientist except when absolutely necessary. Mandur remains what I know about best, and there is certainly enough to know. I do this also because Sri Lanka, whether Sinhala or Tamil, remains a nation of villagers, albeit villagers in villages shot through with strands of the nation and the world. I do this, finally, because I think we can only really see what things mean in the life of people, that is, ethnographically. This is my prejudice, and it is a convenient one since it limits me to what I am least ignorant about.

In 1984, Mandur had, so far as I could make out, seven different histories in operation within it. Some active, some passive, some waiting in the wings, all were, nevertheless, there, affecting people's lives, present in (at least some of) their thoughts, building buildings, determining politics, even directing the water in Mandur's paddy fields, sparking the weird cry of the peacocks in the temple jak tree, and, ultimately, in causal eddies of good and bad action, designing the fate of all. To put a name to them, Mandur's seven histories were: cosmic history, temple history, provincial caste history, nationalist history, colonial history, utopian history, and academic history.

The presence of so many histories in Mandur is not a result of anything particularly odd about the village itself. What people there refer to as the *ur* of Mandur is actually a complex of villages, situated on the western bank of the Batticaloa lagoon. All are wet-rice farming villages, all relatively (some extremely) poor, and all Tamil-speaking, Hindu, matrilineal, and caste conscious. With a total population of about 7,000, Mandur as a whole rings in rather small in comparison to the Hindu Tamil and Muslim villages arrayed, cheek by jowl, on the more populous eastern shore. Its insignificant number of 'white collar' government workers – about 40 in 1984 – indicates not only its poverty, but its only fairly recent (1978) acquisition of a bus connection to Batticaloa and Kalmunai, the Provincial and District capitals respectively. The majority of greater Mandur's people are paddy farmers, and the majority of its paddy farmers are either landless, or own so little paddy land (less than an acre) that they might be best described as rural *lumpen proletariat*, subsisting as they do, and long have, on what they can make as day labourers in other people's fields.

Of course, sitting half-way up the southern side of the peninsula (where most of Mandur's population resides), is one edifice which does render Mandur somewhat unusual. This is the Sri Kantucuvami *kovil*, the temple of Mandur's founder, and the *locus classicus* of at least two of Mandur's histories. The Sri Kantucuvami temple is unusual for being what is called on the east coast a *tecattukovil*, a 'national' or 'regional' temple, and in being owned by four villages and two castes from *outside* of Mandur. And this latter fact, especially, is of signal importance, because the political complexity so many temple-oriented castes and villages can whip up, not only between but within themselves, is considerable. For the temple, in its annual temple festival (*tiruvila*), plays an important role in the distribution of political and social honours, not only in the five villages and three castes directly involved in running the temple, but also in four other villages and at least one other caste as well.[3]

But even the presence of a *tecattukovil* does not render Mandur singular, at least so far as Eastern Province communities go. There are four other acknowledged *tecattukovil* on the east coast, one of which is in Batticaloa itself. And although, as I shall show, Mandur's politically central temple could be said to be responsible for one of the village's histories, it remains that most Hindu (and even Muslim) villages there will have something like it, some local template of a very local kind of history. It is not, in the end, anything unusual about Mandur that gives it seven histories. Rather, it is something about humanity, and humanity's comings and goings in the world, that have 'enriched' it thus.

But let me begin outlining these histories, turning first to three of the four forms of history that have come to Mandur from 'outside' – colonial history also constitutes an 'import', but I shall deal with that presently – and then, in the following section, to the village's more 'traditional' and local forms of history. The 'imports', then, are academic history, of which this chapter is an odd example; nationalist history, which has only recently touched Mandur with its full force; and utopian history, a reaction at once to more traditional historical forms and to nationalist history. These first three forms of history share in being fairly recent additions to the east coast's already complex array of ways of dealing with the past. Now by academic history, of course, I mean simply the attitude and practice that lies behind the documented, generally narrative, descriptive works that characterize the efforts of western or western-trained, empiricist scholars interested in presenting an 'objective' view of the past.[4] My reason for mentioning academic history here, really, stems partly from my own presence as a neophyte practitioner of it, and partly from the ways academic history's products have affected the style, without very much affecting the substance, of more politically powerful forms of historical debate throughout Sri Lanka.

By nationalist history, rather differently, I mean something that is more a political ideology and practice than a disciplinary matrix. Nationalist history, on the east coast, had its initial roots in the polity-building appeals to common Tamilness that have characterized Tamil politics in Sri Lanka since the 1930s (at least), and which have paralleled (often in reaction) a similar effort, of equally long standing, in Sinhala politics. In Mandur, however, as well as in much of the east coast, and despite a formal loyalty to the successive political parties expressive of this sentiment (FP, TULF, etc.), Tamil separatist nationalism, and the accompanying historical dynamic, were often seen with a jaundiced eye – as something perhaps more in the interest of Jaffna Tamils than in their own. This all changed in 1983, when the virulence of the anti-Tamil rioting sent a flood of refugees into the Eastern Province, and, with them, a sense that nationalism was going to be the only recourse, whether dominated by Jaffna or not.

Yet this, in turn, sparked speculation about another possible take on the past, a more radical one, by means of which some hoped to sweep away the social cobwebs embodied both in the more traditional Eastern Province historical forms and the forms of dominance seemingly threatened by both Sinhala and Tamil nationalism, especially insofar as the latter was conservative, *velalar*, Jaffna-oriented – and represented by the TULF. This last impulse, of course, as well as the dynamic of which it is a part, is what I mean by 'utopian history'.

To put flesh on these abstractions, one might turn back to Mr Kuruvaltampi, who sat by the gate waiting for the army to arrive, composing, in a sense, a Batticaloa version of the old nationalism. A long-time TULF supporter, but not above voting for one or another of the major Sinhala parties if advantage could be gained thereby; perennially suspicious of all Sinhala politicians, about whom he frequently complained that the only difference between them was the politeness with which they killed you; as suspicious of Sinhala people in general, whom, he insisted, all carried knives under their sarongs; yet almost as wary of the Jaffna leadership of the TULF, whom he regarded as *velalar* élitists bent on maintaining their own privileges by evoking nationalist necessity; Kuruvaltampi was nevertheless convinced of the inherent and ancient unity of Sri Lankan Tamils, and kept a small file of articles and a well-thumbed copy of the *Ramayana* to which he would make frequent reference as 'proof' of his views. For him, the best evidences of this unity were fully concrete: the ancientness of the Tamil language, the evidence of Tamil residence on the east coast in the 'time before memory', the writings of famous poets like Bharati, and the activities of such organizations as the Rama Krishna mission, in one of whose schools he was educated as a boy. In all this Mr Kuruvaltampi, a relatively well-off landowner, a member of a non-*velalar* yet farming caste, as well as settled and married, could be said to represent standard, conservative opinion on the east coast. Most 'middle-class', Hindu, east coast farmers that I was able to speak with held similar views. What makes opinions of this sort historical is that they stem from the premiss that conflict with the Sinhala is inevitable, and will ultimately lead either to the creation of a separate state (or something like it) or the loss of Tamil identity. What makes 'nationalism' of this kind part of a separate history, in my sense, is that, as many now have suggested, the interaction between Tamil and Sinhala versions of history has formed a pattern of action and reaction, organization and counter-organization, that has dominated Sri Lankan national politics since they began – has created, in other words, a pattern of action that persists through time.

But there is an alternative reaction, and one that has played no small part in the Eastern Province, and indirectly in Mandur, at the time of my research. If Mr Kuruvaltampi, apolitical if left alone, nationalist if bothered, and accommodating if it will do any good, stands within one pattern of action, the *maccan* he depends upon are better fitted, by their present social position and closer proximity to immediate danger, to stand within another – within, that is, utopian history.

The *maccan*[5] are, as a group, unmarried males. The term, literally, refers to 'cross-cousins', male children of one's parents' opposite sex siblings, and therefore, theoretically, on the matrilineal east coast, the unmarried brothers and parallel cousins of an in-marrying male's, or *attan*'s, wife. Men like Kuruvaltampi, both prosperous and strong, often support a number of *maccan*, feeding and providing shelter for them in exchange for labour; all with the aim, supposedly, of allowing these young men time in which to save money to provide dowries for their as yet unmarried sisters. Young men living in the compound of well established *attan* are generally considered boys with a future; often the only recourse for boys from poorer families is day labouring and an eventual marriage to an equally destitute wife. It is, however, frequently a frustrating time of life. For a young man with many sisters, much money to earn, and both his own and his *attan*'s work to attend to, it can be endless drudgery. Kuruvaltampi's wife's 'brother' (i.e. her mother's sister's son), for example, was at once Kuruvaltampi's field manager and general dogsbody, and a Village Council clerk in a nearby village. This meant, in effect, that he spent as much time working for his *attan* as he did for his sister's dowry. He was 32 in 1984, and envisioned completing his sister's dowry house within the next three years 'if things go well with my *attan*.'

Hence it is often among *maccan* that one finds the hope, expressed with varying degrees of articulateness, that things as a whole might change; that, for example, dowry might be done away with, or caste, or even temples. It was also, at least in 1984, the *maccan* who showed the most admiration for 'the boys', the radical separatist guerrilla fighters, whose historical vision is probably best expressed by the much admired *paticca akkal* (or *paticcal*), the local intellectuals.

There is a saying about learned men which neatly summarizes the calling of this small class of general intellectuals: 'If the learned men sit quietly by, who then will ask?' Often town-bred, but also found among village *maccan*, and always circulating freely among the latter, these men differentiate themselves from both the traditional intelligentsia – the astrologers, ayurvedic doctors, classical poets, and local historians that make up the village intellectual élite – as well as from western-trained academics, whom they contemptuously refer to as 'trousered scholars'. Although it is dangerous to generalize – especially since they are, by definition, moored to no doctrine – it could be said that, as a group, they hold to two visions. One is of themselves, as 'activist intellectuals', using their learning to open up village people to alternative social possibilities, and acting as a bridge between village people and the cosmopolitan world of development theorists, nationalist ideologues, and quasi-Marxist revolution. Another is of east coast life, which they see as captured at once by traditional forms of oppression, (such as the caste system, or the very kind of multi-village temple system that Mandur possesses), and TULF-style nationalism, even as it is threatened from the outside by Sinhala nationalism. Their hope, expressed with a degree of sophistication that runs from barely coherent to highly reasoned, is to use the desire for change that has surfaced around the separatist movement to effect a more radical transformation of east coast Tamil, and eventually of Sri Lankan society as a whole.

But it is as critics, and as envisioners of an alternative history, that they are most interesting. In a sense, their critiques seek to incorporate nationalist and academic histories, even as they try to expose traditional east coast beliefs for what they believe they are. Basically, and again this is a generalization, *paticca akkal* see the Eastern Province as a peasant society only just emerging from a past formed, in co-operative parts, of colonial and traditional forms of exploitation. Colonialism, in their eyes, forced the implantation of the apparatuses of centralized government and capitalism; and was abetted in this by a traditional social structure characterized by caste hierarchy and a dearly repressive land tenure system. As outgrowths of this kind of past, the present chauvinist nationalisms, both Sinhala and Tamil, are seen as the successors of these forms of domination. Their violent tenor, which *paticca akkal* recognize as a kind of raw political force suddenly given voice, is thought to have arisen directly from the political incapacity of 'deracinated', 'Cinnamon Garden' élites in the early twentieth century. Lacking a political language to mobilize the masses, these élites are believed to have used their book-learned knowledge of Sinhala and Tamil society to create nationalist 'discourses' which, as one *paticca akkal* put it to me, 'took off on them, like out-of-control magic carpets'. The resulting years of violence and uncertainty, dangerous as they no doubt have been, are nevertheless seen by many of these young men as a time of dramatic historical opportunity.[6]

One of these young men expressed to me his own desire to redirect nationalist discourse toward a more radically transformative end; a goal he felt he could attain by actively participating in the separatist struggle, smuggling into it a combination of neo-Marxist and Tamil nationalist discourse, and eventually creating, thereby, a 'counter-practice', 'deconstructive' of Sri Lankan society as a whole. This 'deconstructive' end he felt was necessary because of the extent to which nationalist discourse, on the one hand, and traditional discourses, on the other, either excluded or appropriated all alternative forms of action and thought. And although this last young man's views are somewhat extreme, they nevertheless characteristically evoke a dream of radical transformation that many young local intellectuals share, and that many more *maccan* harken to.[7]

It is probably best to pause here a moment, and ponder again the night the army did not come. There was Mr Kuruvaltampi, sitting in his chair, waiting to receive the invaders, the threat to his world, in true household-head style; there were his *maccan*, up from their mats on the verandah where they slept, as guards; and there was I, frightened, fumbling for my notebook, wondering whether I could risk a flashlight, still concerned to 'get it right'. There, in a sense, were the three kinds of history; one defensive, one (potentially) creative, and one (supposedly) detached. What a tense, convoluted thing a moment in time can be! Whatever was I writing that night?

But there was more. Mandur, as part of the Hindu world, as the centre of the Sri Kantucuvami temple's political system (a system, moreover, partially composed of a colonial legal tradition it had 'tamed'), and as a multi-caste village dwelling in the midst of a complex provincial caste tradition was obviously, also possessed of, or by, its more 'traditional' histories. Indeed, it is only by turning away from Mandur's 'imported' histories, for the moment, that one can begin to gather a notion of what Mr Kuruvaltampi's nationalism sought to defend, and what the utopian history of the *paticca akkal* would like to transform.

Probably the the best known of Mandur's more traditional histories is its cosmic history, which it shares with most Hindu people. This most common and grand form of history serves people in Mandur as a sort of historical grab bag into which its most inexplicable entities and processes may be placed. It is within cosmic history, for example, that the 'myths', or *purana*, the telling of which pepper normal conversation for moral or didactic effect, are placed. And it is on a cosmic scale that the gods are thought to act, live, and ultimately dissolve. At the same time, it is from some connection to this vaster background of aeons that a number of Mandur's other histories are thought to grow, most especially its temple and provincial caste histories. More than this, however, the knowledge of Mandur's present place in cosmic history, of its imprisonment within the degeneracy of the present age, the *kaliyuga*, serves as a kind of explanation for much that is confusing, painful, and just plain bad about all the other histories in which Mandur is caught. Cosmic history, with its indescribably overarching time-scale, is beyond affecting by humanity or even the gods. As one old, illiterate, *velalar* woman, with whom I was discussing her misfortunes, said to me one day, in the end everything comes down to 'the *kaliyuga* alone (*kaliyukattan*)'.

Mandur, as a part of temple history, however, emerges from this cosmic substratum as a kind of accident. Murukan, second son of the ascetic god Siva, and a product of his momentary outrage, left his famous lance (*vel*) lodged in a jak tree within the jungle that then covered all that is now Mandur. At first found by some passing Veddas, the lance, in glowing through fronds placed over it by the hunters out of some presentiment of its divinity, attracted the attention of a passing group of cultivators of *cirpatar* caste from across the lagoon. Their exclamations, in turn, brought back the Vedda hunters, and an argument ensued over who should have control of the sacred weapon and the temple that would obviously have to be built around it. The argument was settled by Murukan, who, appearing, assigned each his place: to the *cirpatar* as a whole he gave the task of constructing and managing the temple; to the matrilineal 'clan' (*kuti*) that first understood the lance, he granted the role of priest; and the Vedda, who first found the lance, he charged with returning to the temple each year to pay homage and to lead his procession (*tiruvila*). In the following years, under Murukan's inspiration or instruction, the other villages and castes of what was to become a regional complex were likewise brought into the temple order.

Here, of course, we seem to be back in cosmic history, or at least some hazy component of it. And to a certain extent this is the case. The story of Murukan's lance, if pushed far enough, can be hooked by some in Mandur to the classical tale of Murukan's wooing of Valli, his 'Sri Lankan' Vedda mistress. Nevertheless, from the moment Murukan opens his mouth, the tale becomes historical in an entirely different, more trenchantly local sense. The social arrangements put in place by the god are, according to people associated with the temple, precisely those still in place in the present. Power and position within the region surrounding the temple are reckoned to derive solely from the role assumed by each person's ancestors at the creation of the temple social system. Nor is this believed to have been a wholly undocumented event. Local pundits and temple officials, invoking the story to prove a given claim to position within the temple, will frequently mention a text, a *kelvuttu* (literally, 'stone carving'), written shortly after Murukan's intervention, which 'proves' their arguments true.

The key word here, however, is 'arguments'. The story offered above, which seems a straightforward enough 'charter' myth, an origin story offered in legitimation of the present, is actually a set of premisses for the building of legitimation claims. And the number of claims and, hence, of 'stories', is equal to the number of individuals, groups, villages, and organizations at any one time vying for power within local temple society. Hence, different castes within Mandur advance significantly different versions of the tale. At the 'clan' level, the two *kuti* who supply priests to the temple also possess different versions of the 'myth'. So too, at the genealogical level, do two lineages within one clan of the *velalar* caste. And so it goes, right down to the level of individuals, vying for positions that only one person can hold. This pattern, of multiple versions generated by conflicting interests, can also be found between the five villages involved in the temple; and, within each of these villages, again, at caste, clan, lineage, and individual levels.

My point here is that the tale itself is not temple history, but the expressive part of it. The telling of the tale, continuously, variously, and contentiously, is the way local groups and individuals enter into temple history, into the temple's procedures for rendering a changeable present into an 'unchanging' past. Hence, as one might expect, there is a 'history' of this form of history. Ethnohistorical accounts, which reach back into the nineteenth century, reveal a string of conflicts at the regional, village, inter-caste and intra-caste level, all of which, as expressive events, consisted of the advancement of rival claims about what took place at the origin of the temple. Since 1924, when the temple first came to the notice of colonial law, a single complex case, largely a dispute between the four villages and castes that 'own' the temple and the *velalar* of Mandur, has dominated the history of temple history. And these disputes and conflicts, involving villages, castes, clans, lineages and individual men, are not isolated events but form a pattern in time governed by a logic, which I have described extensively elsewhere, that includes economic, political, 'mythic', even devotional elements.[8] The 'story' it tells, as a whole, or at least over the last 100 years, is that of the rise of one caste, the *cirpatar*, at the expense of another, the *velalar*, within temple society. That last 'within', however, is important, because, in this, temple history apparently runs counter to the drift of another kind of history, provincial caste history; and, to accomplish this feat, it utilized, slyly, the power of yet another kind of history, colonial history. Let me run through each of these in turn.

The best description of provincial caste history is probably McGilvray's analysis of what he calls 'Mukkuvar vannimai'. McGilvray says:

> In the Batticaloa area, as no doubt in other South Asian subregions, the 'symbolic language' of the caste system was shaped by the historical circumstances surrounding the establishment of the dominant caste, its ideological resources, and its specialist groups. Here, in fact, a heritage of warrior conquest by a formerly low-ranking Malabar fishing caste, combined with a distinctive non-Brahman Viracaiva (Lingayat) priestly tradition, has produced a regional caste system with a markedly 'political' (or Hocartian) ideology of caste rank and caste honour.[9]

The 'low-ranking Malabar fishing caste' McGilvray speaks of here is, of course, the *mukkuvar*. McGilvray came to his conclusion that caste on the east coast was a phenomenon more to be explained by historical circumstances than by either structural position or ethno-biological substance because of his perception that 'hierarchical' and ethnosociological accounts of caste simply did not reflect east coast beliefs.

So McGilvray turned, instead, to the east coast's own chronicles, particularly to collections of folk tales and temple creation stories. In McGilvray's view it is in the historical competition between two immigrant castes, the *mukkuvar* and the *velalar*, for rights and honours in the regional temples that the dynamics of the east coast's present caste relations can be seen. But while McGilvray's story brilliantly outlines east coast caste politics as a whole, something different happened in Mandur. There, instead of a long-standing competition between *velalar* and *mukkuvar*, the *velalar* were reduced to something of a secondary role, and the *mukkuvar* largely dropped out of 'official' temple history altogether. Indeed, over the last fifty years at least, it has been Mandur's non-*velalar* owners, especially the *cirpatar*, who have acquired the most control over the temple and its political system. Obviously, something happened.

In 1924 the Sri Kantucuvami temple was a more characteristically provincial institution under *velalar* control. This changed markedly, however, when a dispute between the chief temple official and a local native official caused an appeal to the colonial (then British) Government Agent and, hence, to the legal machinery of trust law, which the colonial state had designed for dealing with intractable temple conflicts.

Now a word must be said here about trust law, which I regard as a codification of what I am calling colonial history. The trust law at issue in Mandur's case was Ordinance No. 9 of 1917, subtitled 'An Ordinance to define and amend the Law relating to Trusts'. It was created, according to Jennings and Tambiah, to settle difficulties relating to the various legal concepts of 'equity' emanating from colonial Ceylon's amalgam of English, Dutch, and what they called 'customary' law.[10] With respect to Hindu temples, the purpose of the law was to define, once and for all, their relationship to the colonial government and to avoid the conceptual puzzle, encountered in India, of making jural sense of temples, or 'charitable trusts', that seemed to involve ambiguous legal actors (such as gods) and to be underlain by murky 'charters' or 'schemes'.[11] Since the one difficulty seemed to arise out of an unclear definition of temples as the abodes of 'jural persons' (i.e., their gods), and the other was thought to be due to the absence of any process by which the 'customary' procedures of a temple could be reduced to a settled set of agreed-upon rules, the law was designed to set about correcting these faults by denying the first concept, and by setting up a legal process – 'commissions of inquiry' – by which the second (i.e., the rules) could be supplied. These commissions, which were to be composed of local Hindu notables appointed by the Government Agent, were to afford this miraculous result by gathering evidence relating both to the specific disputes which occasioned the commission being called, and to the temple's history or 'customs'. The latter evidence relating to 'customs' and 'traditions', once properly codified, was then to become its guide in solving the conflict at immediate issue, as well as a 'settled scheme' to be taken into account in the solving of disputes to come. Obviously, it is this use of the the temple's past to generate colonially acceptable legal charters which makes it, in my opinion, a form of history. For, in a sense, the intent of the law, when written, was to effect the incorporation of individual Hindu temple traditions or 'customary' schemes – as troublesome, mystical entities difficult to define and, hence, to regulate – into the legal world postulated by British trust law, and, thereby, into the political and administrative structure of the Crown Colony of Ceylon. Moreover, as the law remains on the books in a relatively unaltered form, that intent, and the ghostly form of history which it constitutes, must also be said to remain.

And this, in substance, is what the law – or rather its application – set about trying to do in Mandur. The initial disagreement subsequently generated two 'commissions of inquiry', one in 1924 and another in 1932, and a court case, begun in 1956 and ending, for the time being, in 1978. The political result of these hearings, for the *velalar*, was grave. Although the official at whom these thrusts were originally directed in the 1920s was a man powerful enough to drive off such attacks, his attempted successors within the Mandur *velalar* community were not. Over the ensuing years, therefore, the *cirpatar*, by skilful use – or, rather, creative misuse – of the 1917 Ordinance, managed to provoke a series of somewhat contradictory legal findings that, none the less, split, and finally overrode, the once unified power of the Mandur *velalar*.

So much for the political consequences. What of the legal? If the law's intent was, as I have described it, to incorporate the temple into colonial (and, later, state) law by remaking it into an institution of a recognizable sort, then the law must be said to have failed. Not that progress was not made in this direction. The presence of local officials at important temple meetings is one sign that relations between the state and the temple were firmed by its application. But in its larger intent – the regularization of temple politics – the law failed because of the nature of those politics. The difficulties were vast, and the nature of temple politics is too complex to describe adequately here.[12] I think, however, an example might provide a clue to their nature.

One problem was the difference between the kind of evidence taken down at both commissions and at the trial, and the kind of evidence required of a member of the temple élite trying to make a case for himself or his group (not always the same thing) in temple terms. In temple practice, legitimacy depends upon the ability to make a historical claim that precisely defines the role of any person's ancestors in the origin of the temple. Such arguments are advanced round about the community before heading into a challenge to see if, and by whom, they will be accepted. This is very important because challenges, or what people on the east coast call *kauravam cantai* ('status battles'), generally go to the individual or group that can mobilize the most support for a position, something which, naturally, will partially depend upon the nature of the tale being told. Now one result of this method of argument is that, often, in so far as a tale may be very well designed as a mobilizer of political support, it may be completely puzzling as 'legal' evidence. So it was in the various cases heard from 1924 to 1978. Varying in content, subtly but tellingly, from testimony to testimony, even as the witnesses did in their political circumstances, the resulting 'evidence' was so inconsistent and contradictory that the creation of a 'scheme', or even the setting of a precedent, became impossible. Indeed, the judge who wrote the 1978 decision declared himself mystified as to the relation between the evidence given and the decisions reached in the two prior commissions, and thought it best to avoid such an embarrassment himself by simply refraining entirely from the whole question of the temple's proper customs. For this reason, among others of a like nature, the effective victors were able to use the power of the court to enforce the results of what remained, to them, a temple *kauravam cantai*; were able to do so in the face of a provincial caste challenge, and against the force of provincial caste history; and were able to accomplish all this while managing to escape any legal alteration by the court of their political system. They, in short, rode the ferry of colonial law without paying the ferryman his legal precedent, an interesting and, if not fortuitous, sly use of one form of history (colonial) by élites within another form of history (temple) to avoid the consequences of a third form of history (provincial caste).

Thus, in outline, are Mandur's seven histories.

Wittgenstein once suggested that people learn their concept of the past by remembering.[13] I like the active sense of that. But it seems to me a dangerous credo if only applied locally. Too often, I suspect, we have been led astray in our consideration of 'history' by our academic experience. History comes in a book, is the product of an interpretation, or of a specific kind of disciplined activity. 'History', so seen, is only a kind of necessary illusion. Necessary because, as Wittgenstein says somewhere else, even if it could be shown that God created the world and all its 'historical' remains last Thursday, we should still have to speak and act as if that were not true or cease speaking sensibly altogether.[14] Our language is simply not set up to do without history. This much, it seems to me, is obvious. But it remains a very twentieth-century remark, a sort of bitter acknowledgement of a weakly 'transcendental' necessity – as if one were to say, 'We need history because, historically speaking, we have always had it. But that does not tell us what it is, or even that it is. Just that we need it. History, then, is whatever we think it is, so long as we have it at all.' One can point to the untruth of this, of course, in any sense that counts. 'History', to use the word in this portentous sense, is as it has been handed to us, as it has been taught to us as a practice and as a body of knowledge. The boundaries of its 'relativism' are the borders of its acceptable variations. And these lines are drawn by industriously territorial scholars and school committees (and, in the US, increasingly by the Supreme Court), and are jealously guarded. Still, this is a sense of 'history' weak enough to cause a certain sense of crisis, a chilling postmodern unease.

One can seek to avoid all this, of course, by settling upon a 'history' that is epistemologically grounded. One can be, for example, an empiricist historian, and declare history to be whatever the 'facts' say it was, while appealing to everyone's common sense in determing what 'facts', in essence, are. But 'sense', especially about what constitutes a 'fact', is much less common than it once was. And even those who decide to take this high road discover a disturbingly various number of routes.[15] Similarly, one cannot simply be a Marxist historian these days; one must declare for or against Althusser; for or against the Marx of 1844 as opposed to the Marx of *Capital*; for or against Wallerstein. In a sense, even the solutions to our uncertainty about the nature of history participate in the plurality of interpretation that precipitated that uncertainty. Honesty demands that plurality be addressed; yet the very plethora of possible kinds of history makes settling for one above the others merely an act of faith. Like Poincaré's scientist, we remain haunted by the ghosts of unchecked hypotheses.

An ethnographer rather than a historian, I would rather escape this difficulty than answer it. I believe it is important to escape because settling a question of essence, which is what the unease about the nature of history amounts to, requires settling upon a descriptive scheme that is liberating only because it is limiting. One can see this, for example, in some of what has been written about Sri Lanka, a hotbed of historical variety if there ever was one. Looked at with one eye upon the essentialist dilemma, Sri Lanka seems a whirling storm of mixed delusion and fact. Some things, like its trade balance, woeful dependence on foreign capital, and political degeneration seem obvious, yet hidden by other things like its chauvinist historical fantasies, with their invocations of ancient texts, nebulous gods, and fore-ordained destiny. The first set of things are 'real' because they are factual; the second set of things, real enough as points of view, are nevertheless about things and entities that do not exist. Seen this way, it seems that if only someone could step outside the fantasy and really see the reality, Sri Lanka's problems might be solved. An editorial in the New York Times even suggested that J.R. Jayewardene, with his then recent settlement with India, had done just that. I wonder, rather, if he did not merely take a chance on another kind of history. Putting the question this way is my tactic for escaping the dilemma of history's essence. For it seems to me that the question of essence, by putting so much emphasis on the relatively trivial question of narrative validity, turns away from observing just what these other 'fantastic' histories are composed of, are used for, and how they interrelate. It was by asking this 'tactical', ethnographic question – and, hence, by focusing on facts of practice rather than presentation – that I was led to Mandur's seven histories.

Let us go back to that moment in Mr Kuruvaltampi's compound. It is a simple event, easily interpretable as a moment in the past history of the Sri Lankan conflict. It is mentionable because I recorded it; and it could prove of momentary interest in a popular history, a footnote or a paragraph to provide background colour. Normally, going into it more deeply would not be required because, after all, nothing happened. The army did not come. Still, if we did, it would seem a clear enough event to an academic historian, to one either in celebration of (an 'absolutist') or in rebellion against (a 'postmodernist') the essentialist historical question. So we are in the compound of a Tamil family. They are frightened because they believe the army may come. The army is Sinhala, and that is truly frightening because the Tamils and the Sinhala, two ethnic groups, have been in conflict for years. The conflict is nationalist in tone. Perhaps it has a disguised class basis; perhaps it has economic undertones. But, essentially, it is a moment in the development of one history, the history of Sri Lanka's ethnic troubles, and we must now, as academic historians, decide where in that vaster drama it fits. We will differ about how to do this, of course. Those of a postmodernist persuasion will see it as a problem of presentation: what is it? Tragedy? Comedy? Farce? Which trope shall we use? More sternly, the absolutist will arrange the facts within his paradigm, cutting some out as too fantastic or unreliable, pasting others together in accordance with his criteria. And all this was also really there in Mandur as well – for it was what I was doing there, and what the *paticca akal* regarded with such contempt.

But the other kinds of histories were also there. Even as Mr Kuruvaltampi, his nationalist dudgeon up, was settling in his chair to meet the army, another danger, from another history, was rearing its head. Ten miles away, in the village of Turainelavanai, a temple political dispute long in the making was reaching its crisis. A group of dissident land holders, displeased with Kuruvaltampi's uncle, a temple official in that village, were out posting leaflets disclaiming his character, and demanding he step down. Within days, in a move familiar by now to temple practice, they would be appealing to the Government Agent in terms of the Trust Ordinance, and slashing away at former historical claims in village compounds. By the end of the year, his reputation damaged, Mr Kuruvaltampi's uncle would be out of office, and Mr Kuruvaltampi's own position in temple society would be so threatened that he would be contemplating a move to Batticaloa. At the same time, caught by still another kind of history, one of Mr Kuruvaltampi's neighbour's *maccan*, who had stepped over to warn us of the shots, was contemplating making a move of his own. Whether to India or into the bush to fight, we never knew, but within days he was gone. He had been upset, I was told, for a long time – chafing at his *attan*, excited by the events of the past year, and not overly interested by his school work or in another day in the fields. So he was off, into another kind of history. Academic, nationalist, temple, colonial, utopian – and who knows, perhaps all these forms of history were crowding into the compound that night as part of the degeneration that will proceed *pralaya*. It would not surprise me in the least.

Notes and references

1 S. J. Tambiah, *Ethnic Fratricide and the Dismantling of Democracy*, London, 1986, p.5.

2 E. Nissan and R.L. Stirrat, 'State, nation and the representation of evil: the case of Sri Lanka', *Sussex Research Papers in Social Anthropology*, 1987, no. 1.

3 See M. Whitaker, *Divinity and Legitimacy in a Temple of the Lord Kantan*, unpublished Ph.D., Princeton, 1986.

4 Examples of the results of this kind of history on the east coast can be found in the work of Raghavan in the 1930s and 1940s, parts of Canagaratnam's work, de Silva's comments on the Eastern Province's agricultural past, McGilvray's attempted reconstructions of east coast caste history, and so forth. See S.O. Canagaratnam, *Monograph of the Batticaloa District of the Eastern Province, Ceylon*, Colombo, 1921; K.M. de Silva, *A History of Sri Lanka*, Delhi, 1981, pp. 63, 304–305, 406; D.B. McGilvray '"Mukkuvar Vannimai": Tamil caste and matriclan ideology in Batticaloa, Sri Lanka", in *Caste Ideology and Interaction*, ed. D.B. McGilvray, Cambridge, 1982, pp. 35–97; M. Raghavan, *Tamil Culture in Ceylon: A General Introduction*, Colombo, 1971.

5 Young unmarried males are, or were, often in more immediate danger because the police and army regarded them with intense suspicion. In Mandur, this was usually unjustified; it is one thing to be sympathetic to a cause, quite another to join it. More often than not, indeed, it was fear of the army and the police, and a desire for protection, that caused people on the east coast to actually join the separatist fighting groups. In any case, my intent here is not to delineate a category of those 'most

likely to join a group', but to describe an attitude toward the past that I found present in varying degrees among many young men in Mandur.

6 One might well wonder at this point, why I call this form of history 'utopian' rather than simply 'neo-Marxist'. While it is true that the story told above is a neo-Marxist one, or even one similar to those found in Liberation Tiger propaganda, it seems to me that the transformative impulse behind it links it to a wider, and in itself not necessarily Marxist, desire to live free of traditional society's structures that is felt by many young men and women on the east coast. See A.S. Balasingham, *Liberation Tigers and Tamil Eelam Freedom Struggle*, Jaffna, 1983; Liberation Tigers of Tamil Eelam, *Towards Liberation*, Jaffna, 1984.

7 The technical language here is not mine. The writings of, for example, Marx, Althusser, Derrida, and Foucault circulate among the English-reading *paticca akkal*, who lecture to the others.

8 See Whitaker, *Divinity and Legitimacy*.

9 McGilvray, 'Mukkuvar Vannimai', p. 35.

10 I. Jennings and H.W. Tambiah, *The Dominion of Ceylon: The Development of its Laws and Customs*, London, 1952, p. 235.

11 A. Appadurai, *Worship and Conflict under Colonial Rule: A South Indian Case*, Cambridge, 1981, p. 174.

12 See Whitaker, *Divinity and Legitimacy*.

13 L. Wittgenstein, *Philosophical Investigations*, New York, 1958, 3rd edn, p. 231.

14 This is, of course, to paraphrase, and greatly simplify Wittgenstein's long argument with Moore in *On Certainty;* see especially L. Wittgenstein, *On Certainty*, New York, 1969, pp. 12–28.

15 This is not to say, of course, that there is not a basic core of facts that most western-trained scholars can agree upon–when, where, and whom will generally turn out the same no matter what western analytic technique is used. Nor do I, a fellow academic, doubt the 'rightness' of this core of facts. My point, rather, is that this core can do little toward providing the sort of answers we turn to history for. Otherwise there would be no debate. And it is the larger questions of cause and consequence that carry with them the onus of asking the question of history's essence.

Chapter eight

Rural awakenings: grassroots development and the cultivation of a national past in rural Sri Lanka

Michael D. Woost

Introduction

In Sri Lanka today, grassroots development has become one of the most prominent staging areas for ideological activities associated with nationalism, a fact underscored by recent analyses of agrarian change.[1] Indeed, on close examination, development in contemporary Sri Lanka appears to be much more than merely the introduction of new technologies and financial supplements to the agrarian and domestic economies. It is a complex array of scarce and unequally distributed material resources, social practices, and cultural activities which provides an ideal context for the dissemination of nationalist ideologies. What has emerged from this tangled discursive web has been aptly described by Serena Tennekoon as a 'celebration of development'.[2] A prevalent cultural feature of this celebration, is the attempt to link various development strategies with versions of a national past in which progressive rural change is framed as a project to restore village society to its former glory as in the times of the ancient Sinhala kings.[3]

While this ideological strategy is an integral feature of state-sponsored development projects, it is equally apparent in grassroots activities sponsored by many of the non-governmental organizations now operating in Sri Lanka. Like their government counterparts, these grassroots organizations generally tend to interpret 'true development' as a process in which the rural society of the past is re-awakened among rural inhabitants. This 're-awakening' generally refers to the effort to help peasants re-discover the traditional values and forms of social organization of their Sinhala-Buddhist ancestors which in turn will allow them to develop their villages without a great deal of outside intervention. According to A.T. Ariyaratne, the leader of the most prominent grassroots organization, the Sarvodaya Shramadana Movement, rural society in the ancient Sinhala-Buddhist past had a socio-economic and political organization dominated by the ethical principles of truth, non-violence, self-denial and sharing.[4] All members of a village community shared equally in the collective labour of cultivation as well as its fruits. Distinctions of caste were merely a part of an equitable division of labour in which even the royalty did their fair share of cultivation work. In this way ancient rural society was economically self-sufficient; it was entirely capable of providing adequately for the needs of all of its members. Based on this view of history, Ariyaratne claims that ancient Sri Lankan society was a progressive one, very much ahead of its time.[5] Although this progressive society is said to have been destroyed through colonial contact and the increasing penetration of capitalism into the countryside, it is claimed that vestiges of it remain in the rural areas. The proper course for development, then, is one which builds on these vestiges of ancient culture and society in an attempt to resurrect the righteous and progressive social order which it entailed.[6]

The widespread use of this construction of the national past in contemporary grassroots discourse is easy to document. However, my concern in this context is not to provide an exhaustive account of development discourse, but rather to examine the practices through which these discourses are disseminated and reproduced out in the countryside where the seeds of these ideologies are sown and supposedly take root. In the light of that concern, I want to turn to a concrete example of the way in which the national past is deployed within the political arena of grassroots development in one village in south-eastern Sri Lanka. While the example clearly shows how state and civil officials use this terrain to disseminate ideologies of the national past, it also demonstrates the extent to which villagers themselves have begun to embrace the national past in order to manipulate the distribution of scarce development resources to their advantage. Thus, even as villagers attempt to limit their ideological domination by turning these ideologies to alternative purposes, they simultaneously aid in the reproduction and dissemination of the dominant interpretations of development, nation, and national history. The example thus reveals contradictions inherent in the reproduction of cultural hegemony.[7]

Suduwatura Ara: theatre of the past

The village of Suduwatura Ara is located in a remote area of Moneragala district in south-eastern Sri Lanka. A small village by most standards, it is home to about 300 people who are divided into 52 households. Homesteads are scattered along a network of rugged paths and cart tracks which generally follow the streams which meander through the valley. Some enterprising villagers have constructed rain-fed paddy fields along these shallow streams, but due to the scarcity of such lands and the absence of reliable water resources, the most economically viable form of cultivation in the area is a mixture of shifting slash-and-burn (*chena*), and permanent plot, dry land cultivation.[8]

Suduwatura Ara is also a relatively new village, having been settled over the last 25 years by migrants from various areas who encroached on what was ostensibly Crown Land. In that, it is like the many other spontaneous colonies that have taken root in Moneragala district over the last 15 to 25 years. Though the district as a whole is still very sparsely populated, its population grew a phenomenal 110 per cent between 1963 and 1981 and is still growing.[9] People have migrated to this area for a number of reasons: many, probably the majority, have come in search of land; others have come to work as wage labour for the multinational sugar corporations now located in the district; and still others have come to seek their fortune in gem mining, a practice which is often combined with either or both of the above.

The inhabitants of Suduwatura Ara are, then, in many respects, like the majority of people who have migrated to the district over the last two decades: they came in search of land. Thus, from 1966 until about 1973, encroachment was sporadic in the area that is now Suduwatura Ara and primarily involved people from a nearby village called Horombuwa, and from a rubber/tea estate known as Gilon. These people moved into the area primarily to work *chena* plots during the main cultivation season, although two families were engaged in the long-term cultivation of sugar cane. They were not for the most part engaged in paddy cultivation. Then in 1974, 13 families, from an Up-Country village called Welimada, moved to the area. These families were quite adept at constructing paddy fields, having come from an area in which paddy cultivation was an important source of income. Thus, upon their arrival, they immediately started clearing whatever land they could lay claim to along the streams which flow through the area in order to construct rain-fed paddy fields. Subsequently, several of these families have become quite successful paddy farmers, which has earned them the animosity of those who had farmed the area before they came. These earlier inhabitants claim that they have lost access to land they had once farmed or that there is now little water for anyone downstream of the Welimada families' holdings since they have dammed up the streams for their paddy fields. As a result, a great deal of personal and political rivalry has developed between the people from Welimada and Horombuwa over a number of issues. These two groups now form the central poles of political conflict in the village with most of the Gilon people usually siding with the Horombuwa faction.

This factional rivalry may at first glance seem to be just another example of typical village-level political wrangling. However, on close inspection, political relations in Suduwatura Ara reveal what is, in all probability, a growing trend within village-level politics throughout the island. For what is striking about the conflicts which have arisen between these factions is that they are increasingly constructed on the terrain and in the language of 'development'. Conflicts over land, for instance, are not simply phrased in terms of tenure and use rights. The key issues are who has worked to 'improve' or 'develop' the land and who is capable of continuing to do so. Furthermore, development itself has become one of the central points over which village-level struggle emerges. Since 'development' has only a limited resource base, what resources do become available are going to be limited. Thus conflicts arise over the designation of beneficiaries of development resources; and these conflicts are structured in the dominant language of development.[10]

This tendency, in which the dominant ideologies of development have increasingly colonized the interpretation of local level conflicts and politics, says something of the environment in which the villagers live. 'Development' has become an integral part of everyday life in the village in many ways. The villagers are inundated with media, both newspapers and radio, coming in from outside, which profess the virtues of a government concerned to develop the nation of villages in spite of the 'terrorist threat'. They purchase development lottery tickets and attend, or at least read about, celebrations of development involving the opening of model villages, schools and agricultural projects in their area and across the island. They were encouraged, and at times even compelled, to participate in the preparations for such events in their own vicinity. Within the village they were the recipients of various development projects: a new irrigation tank had been built; some householders had been given funds to renovate their homes from the Prime Minister's Village Awakening project;[11] development societies were formed in the village under the auspices of government representatives and so on. Such encounters and activities brought the villagers into constant contact with the dominant ways of speaking and thinking about development, progress and the past, ideas which may have drawn on traditional culture but were largely constructed in the urban centres. As I will argue below, given this intense exposure to the discourse of development, it is little wonder that the latter has become such an integral part of everyday social practice and concern. As one man in Suduwatura Ara remarked during an interview, 'we live in the development era'.[12]

One of the most prominent landmarks on the development terrain within Suduwatura Ara was the village's involvement, since late in 1984, with the Small Farmers' Unit of a Colombo-based development organization. The organization was administered by a group of concerned, middle-class, university educators, most of whom had grown up in urban environments very unlike that found in Suduwatura Ara.

Their orientation was largely educational since they had little access to any significant development funds. Thus they arranged numerous 'seminars' in Colombo to teach villagers how to 'become more developed'[13] through their own efforts much as their ancestors were said to have done.

The villagers who were invited to attend these seminars were exposed to a curriculum which linked development with the national past. Villagers were encouraged to work in harmony and to share their labour and in this way they would become developed without outside assistance. They were instructed to engage in collective work efforts to build roads and a community centre; to construct community gardens from which produce could be marketed collectively; to make handicrafts with products from their own area to be sold to other villages not self-sufficient in those goods; to construct smaller vegetable plots called home gardens which would allow them to be as self-sufficient as their ancestors had been. The organization also actively discouraged villagers from cultivating crops for multinationals and from using artificial fertilizers, since doing so would diminish village self-sufficiency. The organization leaders also established a local unit of the organization in the village itself, and asked the villagers to staff it with their own elected officials. These local representatives were to keep the parent organization in Colombo up to date on the progress of development in the village. In addition to that, these local officials were told to set up a number of sub-committees which would organize for specific tasks and goals. For instance, the organization asked the villagers to set up a loan committee in the village with their own funds from which any member could borrow for cultivation inputs like fertilizers and insecticides. Among the other sub-committees was a peace committee which was set up to restore village harmony and work out whatever 'petty differences' existed.

Initially, the villagers were quite interested in these activities. They enjoyed the trips to Colombo and some of those who attended the Colombo seminars returned to the village and organized the construction of a community garden on the village school grounds. Yet this 'honeymoon' was destined to be short-lived. In fact, by the time of my arrival in the village in early 1986, the villagers seemed to have lost all interest in the organization. This had most to do with the ongoing factional disputes in the village. As the local unit was staffed with members from competing factions, the local society soon became the focus of conflict. Members of the respective factions began to compete for control of the society and what little resources it had to offer (in practice, the trips to Colombo). Hence, the local unit soon became ineffectual as a force for organizing any kind of work. Even so, the local officials continued to send reports to Colombo on the progress of development in the village, in spite of the fact that no meetings were ever held.

This waning interest was compounded by a lull in the Colombo seminar schedule: none were held during the first seven months of my stay. Since this was really the only service the organization had to offer, the villagers seemed to feel little need to continue the work advocated by its leaders. As a result, the community garden quickly reverted to a field of weeds, while plans for the community centre were put on hold indefinitely. The loan society also fell by the wayside for lack of adequate funding and the idea of constructing home gardens and compost pits was all but forgotten.

But just when all seemed lost, in July of 1986, the organization sent an emissary to notify the villagers that they could once again expect to be invited to seminars in Colombo. Between August and November four groups were to travel to Colombo to participate in seminars. As a result of these invitations, meetings were held before and after the seminars in Colombo, ostensibly to hear what had gone on during the previous seminar and to select villagers to attend the next one. For the most part this involved people from the Welimada faction and two or three from the Gilon families, but generally speaking the people of Suduwatura Ara did not turn out in droves when meetings were called; attendance was low. Even so, the villagers who had gone to the recent Colombo seminars had been told by the organization's director to have a meeting even if only two people came.

The people who did attend these meetings and seminars often did so reluctantly. Some people grumbled that all of this renewed activity was taking place during the busiest part of the main cultivation season. Others expressed renewed concern about home gardens and compost pits (that had never been constructed) and about the loan society in particular, since the director had asked to see progress reports on all of these things as soon as possible. But most of all there was a great deal of dissatisfaction voiced by the Welimada contingent over the fact that Horombuwa people, who nominally still held seats on the local unit's board, were never in attendance. On that account, there was talk of ousting them and putting in 'more reliable' people, namely Welimada supporters. This is what eventually happened. In September of 1986, the secretary of the local unit called a meeting which was attended primarily by members of the Welimada faction. With this strong show of numbers, they succeeded in posting their own people in all of the offices except treasurer. This was left in the hands of a Horombuwa sympathizer for the time being. Since this person still supposedly held funds belonging to the local unit, it was reasoned that it would be more prudent to wait until he could be present with those funds in hand before they put his position up for grabs, otherwise he might abscond with the goods.

Subsequent to the restructuring of the local board of officers, only supporters of the Welimada faction were chosen to attend the remaining seminars in Colombo, a fact which served to further alienate the Horombuwa people. Yet for their part, the Welimada people were quite pleased with the new situation, at least for the time being. For in a very short time the Welimada people were to learn that in the process of taking control of the local unit, they had also acquired some rather unexpected responsibilities and obligations to the parent organization. These responsibilities and obligations were brought to their attention in late October of 1986: during one of the Colombo seminars attended by their supporters, the director announced his intention to hold a seminar in the village. Suduwatura Ara was to showcase what could be accomplished when rural farmers embraced their social and cultural heritage. Later that same day the director gave a radio interview in which he expounded on the accomplishments of the organization in Suduwatura Ara while at the same time extending an open invitation to interested officials.

One of the director's colleagues also made an intervention in the media at this time supporting the director's contentions. In an extended piece in one of the Sinhala dailies, which was titled 'the nice history of the involvement of the [organization] in Suduwatura', this gentleman made rather extravagant claims for the local society. For example, he noted that the loan society they had started now provided loans for farmers; that the local unit in Suduwatura was the most powerful society in the village (even more powerful than the government sponsored Village Development Committee); that the home gardens 'had produced a bounty of produce for the villagers'. He ended by saying that the only reason the villagers had not reaped their justly deserved monetary benefits from their involvement with the organization was because traders were skimming all of the profits from this bounty for themselves. He wondered aloud whether or not the organization could also solve this problem so that the villagers could truly reap their just rewards from all of this development activity.

In making these announcements the director and his colleagues in Colombo left the Welimada people little room for manoeuvre. They were being compelled to participate in a celebration of development much like those which have come to characterize the emerging theatre state in contemporary Sri Lanka. As it materialized, this local celebration clearly demonstrates the way in which development has become more a stage event than anything to do with shifts in material well-being. But if the celebration of development was to be the stage, the production on display was to be a play of histories involving the restoration and maintenance of the national past.

As one might have guessed, the villagers were in quite a panic upon their return from the seminar. They had been told that up to 150 people would be attending the event. These guests would all need to be housed, fed and entertained for up to four days. Roads had to be cleared, latrines and a community kitchen built, and so on. It seemed a logistical nightmare for the Welimada people, since they would have no support from members of the Horombuwa faction (who were secretly gleeful about the prospect of the Welimada people being seen as frauds). What is more, they somehow had to cover up the absence of development. There was no unity; there were no home gardens or compost pits; the collective garden had returned to jungle and the community building was non-existent. Thus at the village meeting held after the announcement of the approaching event, the Welimada people began to think of ways to cover up the lack of improvements, in order to give an appearance of development accomplished with the help of the organization.

Wimalasena, a young Welimada man who was secretary of the local organization unit began the meeting with the following statement:

> A person from the organization will come later in the month to help us organize. Until then we must clear some of the roads. We can also plant some chillies and distribute them among the other people to plant according to their instructions....And [we can] collect cow dung and put it in polythene bags as evidence of our fertilizer committee....We must cut the grass from a plot, plough it, and quickly plant chillies there. [Chillies] will grow fast and will appear as a nice community garden when the visitors come....We can also mend fences too, that is something worthy....[And everyone must] make compost pits.

Another man interjected with a sense of urgency in his voice:

> Yes, it doesn't matter what you put inside the pit, you can cover with leaves and soil [to give an appearance of a deep compost pit]. We are in a hurry!

Wimalasena continued:

> If we all do that work, at least then we will have something to show the visitors that will please their minds. But now there is nothing worthy to show them.

At that point, Siripala, a member of the Horombuwa faction who was the nominal treasurer of the society, arrived at the meeting. His untimely intrusion created quite a stir and the proceedings came to a halt. Wimalasena immediately laid into him for being late and for having forgotten to bring the account book as had been requested of him prior to the meeting:

> This is the real terrorism in this country. One says 'I'll come' and then never comes on time.

Siripala, attempting to save face, began:

> But I have a lot of personal problems.

Wimalasena simply ignored Siripala and continued his tirade:

> Siripala's defect is this: we can't do anything without the treasurer and he didn't come. I'm telling him in the face. We couldn't know what funds were available or where they were kept. If you would have come we could have collected it all [implies: how can we work in unity with such actions on the part of our officials]. Many are coming to see our work: 75–150. Siripala should work in unity for the good of the organization. You should not be the way you are. We must keep aside our grudges and work as one village.

While Wimalasena had clearly utilized the ideological appeal of village community, his public tirade was meant to ostracize Siripala and those who refused to fall into line on the issue of the conference – fall in line, that is to say, behind the Welimada leadership. This was quite effective. Neither Siripala, nor any of the Horombuwa people for that matter, came to help in the preparations.

As the date of the conference approached, yet another group of people were to go to Colombo for a seminar. Ten people were supposed to attend and I received a letter from a colleague of the director (who I will refer to as Mr D) asking me to 'kindly give these people 50 rupees each' so they could go to Colombo. The organization normally paid these expenses but they were now trying to cut costs for some reason and were requiring the participants to come up with some of their own travel money. I was aware of this fact before I received the letter and had discussed the matter with Mr D, intimating that I could not give the Welimada people any money for these trips, at least not openly, for fear of being seen by the other faction as favouring the Welimada people. I had not told him what the other people were saying about his behaviour towards the Welimada people. I had felt that would only make matters worse. I was more concerned to keep myself clear of such accusations. Frustrated, I finally decided to give the money as requested, but I wrote a letter to Mr D once again explaining why I could not give the Welimada faction money for these things in the future, at least not publicly. I explained that the deep-seated frictions between the two groups made it imperative for me to try and remain neutral in the people's eyes. Mr D had spent a great deal of time in the village himself and was well aware of the frictions there; and what is more, he and I had often sat for hours discussing the various conflicts that were going on. I was sure he would understand. I sent this letter with one of the villagers to hand over to him when they got to Colombo. After that I thought no more of the matter, thinking it settled.

However, the matter was far from settled. When the villagers who had gone to Colombo returned a few days later, I found, much to my surprise, that my position in the village was under heavy assault. I began hearing gossip, relayed through my co-worker, that 'someone had written a letter to the director telling him that there were frictions in the village; that there were divisions among the people like "Welimada People" and "Horombuwa People" (I had not mentioned these categories in the letter at all). Who could have sent such a letter? It was in English, though.' At one point I met one of the more prominent Welimada leaders working with some of the other Welimada people in one of the co-operative plots that was being set up for the conference. She had been in Colombo at the time and spoke to the others about what happened as she worked, telling them about the letter. This was clearly directed at me, since she knew I was listening to the conversations of the workers as I did elsewhere at other times.

Later that day in a meeting of the local unit, the secretary asserted publicly that:

> We have never had village distinctions (*gam bedaya*) in our village, yet a report has gone there [to the organization in Colombo] that there is a 'Welimada Yaya' and 'Horombuwa Yaya', that there are divisions like that. [But] I don't know who wrote that.

They obviously knew that I was the one who had sent the letter, and wanted me to know indirectly that they knew I had done this, but they would not confront me openly with it.

The meeting went on and more preparations were made for the up-coming conference, while the chairman and secretary of the local unit admonished everyone to 'work in unity'. They noted that the director had sent word that they must put aside their divisions and attend to the work at hand. At one point they were discussing how they would pay for the workers to have tea and 'short-eats' while clearing the road for the conference. One person suggested that the chairman ask me for a contribution, but the treasurer quickly spoke up that this was not a proper thing to do. This seemed quite strange, since such requests had hardly been considered improper on previous occasions. I wasn't sure what this change of attitude meant, but I was soon to find out. I realized the villagers had felt deeply threatened by the revelations in my letter. It was as if I had betrayed their trust, which indeed I had done, however inadvertently. Some of the Welimada faction were now very cool towards me. One fellow who had borrowed money from me prior to going to Colombo (to buy parts for his bicycle) even came by immediately upon his return and paid back the money he had borrowed saying he didn't need it after all. Others were telling my co-worker that I had misunderstood the village: 'There are no divisions... in this village. Mahataya has it all wrong. You must explain to him.' Others asked him if I was against 'progress' in the village. I was very distressed about the matter and wondered how my friendships would be affected, to say nothing about my work in the village.

A day or so later I realized that much more was going on here than just this letter business. One of the people who had gone to the Colombo seminar told my co-worker another aspect to the story which caught me totally off guard, but which also helped to explain better some of the villagers' reactions to the incident. Apparently the director had got the letter from Mr D and had called all of the Suduwatura participants to his office and read the letter in front of them. By all accounts he was angry. He scolded Mr D for 'asking money from the *suda* [white person]'. He continued, speaking to all present:

> If I was told about money, somehow or other wouldn't I have found it and given it? It doesn't matter if you ask from a Sinhala person. You [addressing Mr D] could have asked from someone in the Education Department [in Moneragala town] at least. Don't ever go to ask money from them (*okungeng*). Why do you go on being slaves to these aliens (*paradesa karayo*)? Don't ever degrade [cheapen] yourself by doing so. They just pretend to be good. Though they seem kind while they are here, when they go back to their own countries they (*ovun*) expose themselves as they really are. I know how they are (*ovunge häti*) because I have travelled to many countries. Never believe them.

As might be expected, under the circumstances of the impending conference, the director had felt threatened by my letter, a letter he was never supposed to see. The fact remained that he and his colleague, to whom I had addressed the letter, were both aware of the lack of unity in the village, the failure of the programmes to develop the village, and that efforts in the media to claim otherwise were just so much propaganda for their organization. Thus he was threatened by the prospect of this alien creating problems during the conference, possibly even revealing the truth to the media. Clearly I had become a threat to their goals. For that reason, it was in the director's interest to pass off his reservations about me to the villagers and to try to isolate me somehow. The most effective way to do this seemed to be through a nationalistic discourse, which portrayed me as a meddling alien interfering in things which were more properly the province of the Sinhala people.

So with his words of anger and frustration the director had addressed everyone in his captive audience as Sinhala people, admonishing them for not relying on their own people for help. In short, he scolded them all for degrading themselves and, by association, all Sinhala people, by asking me, an alien, for money. What is more, the effects of the director's nationalist interpolations were all the more powerful for the fact that he was able to situate them in the realm of common sense, thereby connecting them with real everyday concerns. In his view it was common knowledge, or should be anyway, that the historical experience of the Sinhala people had shown foreigners to be untrustworthy and exploitative. This was not some abstract rhetoric about the glories of the past, but was instead a serious practical discourse about dealing with foreigners in serious practical situations. As the director viewed the matter, the actions of those gathered before him were indications of a serious lack of common sense; they had disregarded, or were ignorant of, what every Sinhala person should know about dealing with foreigners. And this was a situation for which they should all feel shame, for they were in effect degrading their own people by their actions. That the villagers took his comments seriously, then, should come as no surprise. It helps to explain the cool way the Welimada people behaved towards me upon their return, the refusal at the village meeting to ask me for money, as well as the return of the loan. They had returned to the village armed with a new common knowledge in which my position as representative of the 'other' was a much more threatening one. This conflicted with all the other day-to-day relations within the village community in which I was treated with deference, as a possible benefactor or patron. But in the discourse of the nation I was no longer simply a benefactor to be manipulated; I was an 'other' to be regarded with suspicion, never to be relied upon, always having ulterior motives. And judging from their cool demeanour towards me upon their return from Colombo, the Welimada villagers were convinced, at least for a time, that this was the way I should be construed.

As might be suspected, this added a whole new dimension of tension and stress to the preparations for the conference, a dimension which had to be dealt with if the conference was to be successful. There were even rumours that the conference might be postponed. In an effort to avoid such an embarrassment, an emissary was sent to Suduwatura Ara to implore the villagers to put their differences aside, or at least to hide them during the conference itself. The Horombuwa people were specifically asked to keep their dissensions quiet during the conference so as not to create a scene in front of the media. A similar campaign was waged to convince me that I had been mistaken in observing factional differences and disputes. Villagers emphasized to me and my co-worker that 'there are no distinctions in our village, we are one family'. And the emissary from the organization assured me at the end of his mission in Suduwatura Ara that 'the dissensions have been ironed out and now they are all working in unity'. A better summation would have been that the villagers were now ready to represent themselves to the world as a harmonious village, on the road to progress. This aspect of the celebration had been worked out to almost everyone's satisfaction. The hope was that I would not intervene any further to rupture the contours of that fragile representation.

In the final days prior to the conference, the worries over the letter incident subsided, or at least took a back seat to the more immediate worries and concerns regarding the preparations for the conference. These preparations went on frantically. The kitchen and latrines began to materialize and road crews cleared a path for the visitors. A great deal of effort was also put into covering up the lack of development in the village. Something resembling a collective garden was planted near the meeting site. Welimada householders also constructed fake compost pits and home gardens near their houses as part of the planned cover-up. Amazingly enough, these preparations were completed, but only hours before the first guests were to arrive. Nevertheless, all seemed ready for the drama that was about to begin. And on 6 December 1986 the national past went on display in Suduwatura Ara.

The event was supposed to be organized around various educational classes but the real focus of the event was the long stream of officials and celebrities who had been invited out to observe the events and give a speech. These people were also taken on impromptu tours of the village to witness the improvements that had occurred (compost pits, home gardens, etc.). In addition, representatives of four other villages involved with the organization attended. These representatives were asked to give up-to-date reports of their own development work as part of the event. They told about the development that had been accomplished through association with the organization. All of these narratives noted in one way or another how their involvement had restored village unity and co-operation which in turn had allowed each village to approach self-sufficiency.

After these speeches the director gave a speech of his own, likening these accomplishments to those of the ancient kings:

> I remember talk about the great irrigation works of the ancient kings like Dutugämunu and Parakramabahu. Some say these works could only be done with the help of giants, that common people could not accomplish such great feats....But our works [those recounted in the reports] show that we are the giants of today. Impossible works, you ask? There are no impossible works for the Sinhala people.

One of the director's colleagues joined in on the chorus:

> This is indeed a historical landmark when one thinks of the... 2,500 years since Prince Vijaya came and established our nation. All of those who came with him were small farmers just like yourselves.... Thus this conference marks only the second time since Vijaya's arrival that there has been such a conference of small farmers....Indeed this event turns a new page in our history as a people.

Here the speaker very clearly likens the present meeting and the activities being carried out there to the very establishment of the nation itself. Thus the activities of the farmers present at the conference were deemed to be as patriotic as those of the very first small farmers who came to the island with Prince Vijaya. Both groups of farmers played an important role in history: one established the nation, the other revived it.

However, the climax of the whole affair came when the District Minister arrived to give his speech. After remarking about the progress of development made possible through organizations of this sort, the minister noted that the event provided an important opportunity for people to come here and gain a knowledge of the history of the area:

> It does not matter if some already know this history, for hearing it again, over and over, will only strengthen their pride in the nation. Then the seed of pride in the nation would undoubtedly germinate in their minds.

He then attempted to situate the new village of Suduwatura Ara into national history in a very specific way – through reference to the 1817–18 rebellion against British rule which had started in this very region. Using this piece of history he attempted to explain why Suduwatura Ara was so underdeveloped:

> I believe that even the people of this area do not know why [it] became so sparsely populated, so deforested, or why so many villages went extinct....In the uprising of 1818, in the effort...to protect the freedom of the nation...I must say that Suduwatura Ara is a place that sacrificed many lives proudly. That's why this area is so sparsely populated...and why the tanks here need renovation.... Before the British imperialists came there was a population with self-reliance who were proud of their nation. We must once again... unite like those days when we worked in our paddy fields, sharing our labour. In that way Suduwatura can step up the ladder of improvement.

The Minister was especially adept at this kind of national historical discourse. He well understood the importance of the opportunity before him as did the director and the other officials who attended. It is not surprising then, that after the speech the minister requested a guided tour of the recently 'renovated' village irrigation facilities. As a crowd stood looking down on the tank bund, the Minister noted that what lay before everyone present was a testament to the will of the Sinhala people. The tank thus became a visual aid in the dissemination of a national identity. One would be hard pressed to think of a better way to pull all of the ideological threads together in one image.

The next day the conference closed with an eloquent, if rather stridently nationalist, speech by one of the co-founders of the movement and current deputy director of the organization. He began his speech by lauding the qualities of the Suduwatura Ara people and then turned his attention to an assessment of the conference itself:

> The ethical and hard-working qualities which have been revealed here in this village are indicative of the personalities of people born and brought up in our villages. No other country in the world has the spiritual development that we have, and here we are making it known to the world that it is the Sinhala Buddhists who have...had a spiritual superiority (*sresdanvaya*) for over 2,500 years. For that reason,...[the community that]...can protect the Sinhala nation and Buddhism is the Sinhala nation with its historically important human qualities and superiority. And our fathers, mothers, brothers and sisters here in Suduwatura Ara have demonstrated by their efforts and hard work that they are a part of that community.

Does ideology really work in mysterious ways?

What becomes plainly apparent in this is that ideological practices are not created equal: ideologies operate at different levels and with varying degrees of effectiveness. This is most evident in the contrast between the oratory witnessed at the development celebration in Suduwatura Ara and the ideological buzz which surrounded the letter incident involving the villagers, the organization and myself. In the case of the former, we witness a kind of rhetorical overkill. The speeches delivered to the audiences in Suduwatura Ara were well stocked with seemingly overwrought connections between past and present: the connection between the conference and the coming of Prince Vijaya to establish the nation; the attempt to link the people of Suduwatura Ara with patriots who had given their lives in the Great Rebellion of 1818 against the British. These and other similar couplings of past and present often brought smiles to the faces of people in the audience.

While it is easy to be sceptical of the effectiveness of these inflated comparisons and to wonder whether they are ever taken seriously by those who create them, let alone by those who sit and listen, it is prudent to keep in mind that this inventive hyperbole is taken as evidence of rhetorical skill. Those who speak at development rituals like the one held in Suduwatura Ara are expected to make speeches like these, and speakers are judged according to their ability to do so effectively. The minister is a case in point. Nearly everyone I spoke with after the conference said what a 'great speech' he had given. Other speakers were mentioned, but none compared favourably with the minister. He had captivated his audience with his account of history and its links with Suduwatura Ara. Other speakers were said to be too 'flowery', and often such comments were made by other speakers right after the speeches had been made. What we have in this case is a genre of ideological discourse, fundamental to the celebration of development itself. Indeed, it almost seems that the celebration's only reason for existence is to act as a conveyor of such discourse. One needs only to engage in a cursory examination of the newspaper coverage of other larger and more extensively advertised celebrations to recognize this general trend.

However, the question remains of the effect of this kind of ideological practice on its audience. At first glance one may be inclined to dismiss all of it on the grounds that no one could possibly take such florid talk seriously. Yet it must be remembered that while such articulations may seem far-fetched, they actually fall on ground in which emotionally-charged notions and images of the nation and the national past have previously taken root. In this light, celebratory forms of discourse linking the national past with the present may reinforce sentiments, desires, values and beliefs which are either emergent in rural consciousness or already firmly rooted there. Thus, the overstatement and repetition which one observes at celebrations of development perform very useful functions in reinforcing the dominant ideology. And the impact of such figures of oratory is all the more powerful when heard emanating from voices of authority, speaking with rhetorical skill and finesse. There is admittedly no guarantee that this will work in all cases, or that it will work evenly on all those who hear it: ideological domination offers no such guarantees.[14] It demands repetition, over-statement and continued ideological vigilance to create and maintain its hold, however tenuous or tenacious, on popular consciousness. That, in effect, is what the process of hegemony is all about. It is a moment in the process of social ordering, which, as Gramsci argued, can only be characterized as an 'unstable equilibrium'.[15] To paraphrase Stuart Hall, it is a state of play in the ideological struggle, which on that account requires continual reworking and reconstruction in order to maintain its necessarily incomplete coherence.[16] In short, hegemony is never a given or 'permanent state of affairs, but has to be actively won and secured'.[17]

It is on this broader landscape of hegemony that the letter incident I described becomes significant. In that instance the power of the ideological appeal appeared more immediate and forceful. I attributed that to the way in which the director managed to situate his interpretation of the problem in the structures of common sense. But it also illustrates the manner in which ideological gaps constantly occur in common sense which have to be filled or re-filled. The villagers and the director's colleague had to be forcefully reminded of who they were and where their obligations lay. They were Sinhala people with a history of colonial rule by aliens who still threaten their way of life; indeed, in my case, I was construed as a threat to the very revival of pre-colonial society in Suduwatura Ara. In a certain sense the people who were scolded by the director had not done their homework: they had not been very efficient in applying the ideologies of nation and the national past they had been exposed to elsewhere to relationships in their everyday lives. They had to be shown and/or reminded that such notions have a very practical value. As I have already indicated, this practical, common sense appeal had a powerful impact on those who heard it and subsequently relayed the director's comments back to their friends and allies. But I want to emphasize that this encounter with the director was only one of many like it that occur in the area of development. I have limited myself here to one example, but it is the overall effect of these seemingly isolated examples that is of interest in the analysis of the process of hegemony. Hegemony is not a state of affairs, but the outcome of a multiplicity of practices like these.

Overall, then, the celebration of development which was mounted in Suduwatura Ara in December of 1986 provides ample evidence of how important such rituals are for the public display and dissemination of dominant constructions of national identity and the national past. With effort and initiative on the part of the villagers themselves, Suduwatura Ara was made to embody the images of the rural envisaged in élite constructions of the past. The village then provided an ideal stage upon which the play of national histories could be locally performed and represented in such a way as to invoke the Sinhala-Buddhist past as a model for the future. Suduwatura Ara became, in effect, a symbol of that past in the present, which could be paraded before the public eye as evidence of the potential for progress inherent within the model of ancient Sinhala-Buddhist society.

But what claims can we really make regarding the effectiveness of this ritual activity in the struggle to construct a nationalist social order? This is an important question given that few people in the village really believed that the makeshift compost pits and gardens which had been hurriedly constructed represented true progress for the village. The interpretive key to this aspect of the event lies, I believe, in Wimalasena's plea to his fellow villagers that they must work hard to 'have something to show the visitors that will please their minds'. The implicit motive was to represent themselves as progressive people, concerned with development, and ready to work in unity as their ancestors had done. In this way the presumably powerful outsiders who would attend the event might be impressed enough with their work to donate some money or equipment to their society (or faction). However, if they failed in this effort they would be the shame of the entire island in addition to losing any hope of bringing development resources into the village. This view of the situation is a concrete result of the way the struggle over development takes form for the majority of rural Sri Lankans. In an economic environment in which the resources of development grow increasingly scarce, the only choice left to the Suduwatura Ara people was to participate in the celebration while trying very literally to embody the values of those who controlled access to what resources might be available. In a very real sense, it was a case of playing by the rules of what was perceived to be the only game in town.

This leads to another equally relevant question. If we are to conclude that the villagers take these celebrations seriously, but for their own reasons, what can we say about the relevance of the celebration of development to the ideological quest for social order? Is this aspect of the quest for cultural hegemony simply a pipe-dream of the élite? Whatever the villagers' motivations, conscious or otherwise, their actions and efforts on behalf of the organization effectively made them collaborators in the production and reproduction of the emergent theatre state. And since the celebration of development can be seen as an increasingly important cultural tool in the ideological work of hegemony in Sri Lanka, the villagers thus filled a critical role in the ongoing production and maintenance of nationalist hegemony. For that they were rewarded with a valorous and patriotic position in the national past.

Acknowledgements

An earlier version of this paper was presented at a panel on 'Nationalist discourse and the uses of the past in Sri Lanka', at the American Anthropological Association meetings in Phoenix, November 1988. The research on which this paper is based was supported by the Social Science Research Council and a Fulbright-Hays Doctoral Research Fellowship – 1985–1987. The essay has benefited from earlier readings and comments by James Brow, Jonathan Spencer, Ana Alonso, and Ted Swedenburg.

Notes and references

1 J. Brow, 'In pursuit of hegemony: representations of authority and justice in a Sri Lankan village', *American Ethnologist*, 1988,

vol. 15, pp. 311–327; N.S. Tennekoon, 'Rituals of development: the accelerated Mahaväli development program of Sri Lanka', *American Ethnologist*, 1988, vol. 15, pp. 294–310.

2 Tennekoon, 'Rituals of Development', p. 295.

3 The 'national past' to which I am referring should not be thought of simply as a text which can be read. By the 'national past, I mean to indicate the complex and contradictory set of discourses and practices, all of which attempt to project some image, notion, or rendition of the past as it relates to the nation and its people.

4 A.T. Ariyaratne, *Sarvodaya and Development*, Moratuwa, 1980, p. 5.

5 A.T. Ariyaratne, *Sarvodaya Shramadana: Growth of a People's Movement*, Moratuwa, 1970, p. 16. The object of the present discussion is to trace the effect of this sort of ideological representation of Sri Lanka's rural past, rather than assess its accuracy. For critical discussions see D. Kantowsky *Sarvodaya: the Other Development*, Delhi, 1980; J. Spencer, 'Representations of the rural: a view from Sabaragamuva', paper presented at conference on, 'Symbolic and material aspects of agrarian change in Sri Lanka', Anuradhapura, 1984.

6 V. Fernando and J.H. De Mel, *Development Consortia in Sri Lanka: a Critical Examination of NGOs and NGO Umbrella Organisations*, Colombo, 1985, p. 1; Ariyaratne, *Sarvodaya Shramadana*, p. 16.

7 R. Williams, *Marxism and Literature*, Oxford, 1977; S. Hall, 'Signification, representation, ideology: Althusser and the post-structuralist debates', *Critical Studies in Mass Communication*, vol. 2, 1985, pp. 91–114.

8 P. Vitebsky, *Policy Dilemmas for Unirrigated Agriculture in South-eastern Sri Lanka: a Social Anthropologist's Report on Shifting Cultivation in an Area of Moneragala District*, Cambridge, 1984, mimeo.

9 S. Abeyratne and J. Perera, 'Change and continuity in village irrigation systems: a case study in the Moneragala District, Sri Lanka', *Agrarian Research and Training Institute Research Study*, no. 75, Colombo, 1986, p. 11; Department of Census and Statistics, *Census of Population and Housing 1981: Moneragala District Report*, vol. 1, part XXII, Colombo, 1981, p. xiii.

10 M. Woost, 'Nationalizing the local past in Sri Lanka: histories of nation and development in a Sinhalese village', ms.

11 See Brow, this volume.

12 *api sanvardhana yugaye jivat venava.*

13 *vädi diyunu karanava.*

14 S. Hall, 'The problem of ideology – Marxism without guarantees', in B. Mathews (ed.) *Marx: a Hundred Years On*, London, 1983; *idem*, 'Culture, the media and the "ideological effect"', in J. Curren, M. Gurevitch, and J. Woolacott (eds) *Mass Communication and Society*, Beverley Hills, 1977.

15 A. Gramsci, *Selections from the Prison Notebooks*, (ed. and trans.) Q. Hoare and G. N. Smith, New York, 1971; Williams, *Marxism and Literature*.

16 S. Hall, 'Race, articulation and societies structured in dominance', in UNESCO, *Sociological Theories: Race and Colonialism*, Paris, 1980.
17 Hall, 'Culture, the media', p. 333.

Part III

The politics of the past

Chapter nine

J.R. Jayewardene, righteousness and *realpolitik*

Steven Kemper

Chronicles and power

Sinhala people look back on an extraordinary civilization that began with the establishment of Buddhism in the island some 2,500 years ago. They know quite a lot about that civilization because people they regard as their ancestors have written things down – donations of property, astrological and Ayurvedic treatises, poetry and works on poetics, monastic rules, stories of the Lord Buddha, and historical accounts. Historical writing stands out for several reasons. First, there has been quite a lot of it – some three dozen histories in all – and the writing begins at a precocious moment in the south Asian past. The most important of these histories, the Mahavamsa, constitutes 'the only early historical literature in the realm of South Asian culture'.[1] Second, historical writing plays an epistemological role to which other forms of writing do not aspire. Histories (*vamsas*) stand behind the authenticity of knowledge, relationships, and practices. As a result, historical writing has always had genuine political importance. In what follows I want to concentrate on the political uses of historical writing, and more particularly on the politics of commissioning a new extension of the Mahavamsa. The practice culminates in J. R. Jayewardene's decision to compile the *Mahavamsa, Nutana Yugaya* soon after his election in 1977.[2]

The idea that a historical account can legitimate the authenticity of knowledge, relationships, practices, and sacred places derives from the way higher knowledge was traditionally preserved in south Asia. Knowledge did not survive from age to age through the unembodied transmission of ideas and values. It was passed between one generation and the next along lines of teachers and students. The root *vamsa* of the word Mahavamsa has several primary senses – generation, descent – which lead naturally to another of its senses – history. Knowledge survives because human relationships are organized to guarantee its protection and exclusivity. In the Hindu tradition, the most reliable kind of knowledge is so regarded because it is 'that which is heard', ([Skt.] *sruti*), as opposed to less reliable traditions preserved in the *smrti* literature, 'that which is remembered'. The relationship between persons exists to make hearing a certain kind of knowledge possible, not as independent of that knowledge and not as an open channel to relay any kind of knowledge. The Buddhist *dhamma* (teaching) has been preserved for twenty-five centuries along lines that run from teacher to student. Knowledge gained directly from the Buddha is better than knowledge gained from a monk who has himself gained it from the Buddha. But the Buddha is gone, and relying on a descent line which begins with someone who has heard it directly is the best one can expect in diminished circumstances.

Historical accounts have come to do quite a lot more than warrant knowledge. *Vamsas* also serve to glorify and castigate, to point a moral, and to explain a present-day relationship or practice. Taken at their own words, *vamsas* want to edify. Here the epistemological function of historical writing is linked to its political importance. Historiography in Sri Lanka has always done something besides simply recording the past. To call such traditions Whiggish or ideological puts contemporary conceptions of historical writing on materials that share few of our intentions. The point is not that the ancient histories are unreliable – although the extent of their reliability is always at issue – but that they demonstrate a characteristic way of legitimating present-day arrangements. In some cases the historical accounts that warrant and the ritual or texts that are warranted meld into one another. A fourteenth-century work on the Tooth Relic, the *Dalada-sirita*, begins with the history of the relic – its sojourn in India after the death of the Lord Buddha, its journey to Sri Lanka, and its growing significance in the medieval Sinhala state. The last chapter presents the rites to be observed for the Tooth Relic. 'If the title of the work is an indication of its nature and contents, one may reasonably infer that it is both a history of the Tooth Relic and an account of the rites to be observed in its worship. The word sirita means both "life history", "life story", and "rite".'[3]

The Mahavamsa guarantees the authenticity of a certain kind of Buddhism, Theravada Buddhism, by tracing out the human connections that link the monks of the sixth century AD to the Buddha himself. The descent of the Theravada monks is intertwined with the history of the Sri Lankan state. It records not two histories but one, for the Mahavamsa assumes the mutual necessity of kings and clerics, as well as society's need for both. Kings patronize the religion and observe its ceremonies; clerics educate kings and bend their policies in the direction of wisdom. Until the eighteenth century – which is to say of an ancient tradition, until the recent past – the chronicle has concentrated exclusively on the doings, both pious and impious, of these two groups of actors. Kings rush by, dynasties rise and are eclipsed by others, south Indian armies advance and withdraw. Before it is done, the Mahavamsa recounts over 150 kingly reigns and 25 centuries of Buddhist history. Mahanama, who compiled the first part of the Mahavamsa in the sixth century, made these episodes sound distinctly religious themes, emplotting the narrative in ways that point a moral. Each chapter concludes with a moral reflection that puts the political, economic, and religious contents of the chapter in a doctrinal context – the flux of worldly affairs is unending and without exception.

The chronicling has never stopped because the Mahavamsa has been periodically updated. Last things quickly become the last things before the last, the chronicle falls behind events – often by centuries – and a new generation of monks picks up the task of recording events on palm-leaf manuscripts. The updating has been neither regular nor very frequent; but it requires only a single king and a scholarly monk to undertake an extension. The act of updating the chronicle often comes at moments of reform of the *sangha* (monkhood), although there have been several reformations of the religion without a corresponding extension of the chronicle. Scholarly monks have extended the chronicle five times since its first compilation in the sixth century. When the Kandyan kingdom fell in 1815, the circumstances that supported the chronicling changed forever. The Mahavamsa tradition, strictly understood, ends with the abolition of the Sinhala monarchy.

In another sense nothing at all changed. The British monarch simply replaced the local one. Large portions of the Sinhala aristocracy held on to their privileged positions. The monkhood declined in Kandyan areas, but it survived. In the Low Country, Sinhala castes, previously excluded from ordination, established new monastic groups of their own, and the religious life blossomed.[4] Some monks clearly saw their interests in opposition to British rule, especially because of the identification between colonial rule and aggressive Christian missionary activity. But other monks, and perhaps even those monks who were in principle hostile to the government, looked to the Crown as a plausible source of authority and patronage – perhaps not as reliable and certainly not as righteous as the traditional monarch, but the best one could find. For its part, the colonial government took on some of the traditional responsibilities and prerogatives of the monarch. At its initiative, the Ven. Hikkaduwe Sri Sumangala, the outstanding monk of his day, and a learned pandit, Devarakkhita Batuvantudawe, translated the Mahavamsa from Pali into Sinhala in 1877, and added a supplement which brought matters up to 1815. That supplement added a 101st chapter to the text. Counting this extension as the fourth, the fifth was more eccentric. In 1935 Ven. Yagirala Pannananda advanced the narrative from the fall of Kandy to the period just before Independence. He called his work the Mahavamsa, Part III[5] (the first two parts being the Mahavamsa proper and its extensions which Geiger edited as the Culavamsa), and undertook the task at his own initiative. After the fact, it has become a piece of the tradition.

The updating of the chronicle has occurred under a variety of circumstances, but most often it has happened during a time of reformation or resurgence. Mahanama compiled the first part of the Mahavamsa after Theravada Buddhism and the monks who espoused it had been returned to a position of privilege in Anuradhapura. Buddhist revivals in the twelfth and thirteenth centuries gave rise to the first two extensions of the chronicle. The eighteenth-century extension came during a moment of great religious enthusiasm in the Kandyan kingdom when proper ordination had been brought from Thailand and the *sangha* reformed. Even under British rule, the late nineteenth-century extension of the Mahavamsa coincided with the resurgence of Buddhism. The pattern is clear. In the traditional scheme of things, updating the chronicle is more than putting the record straight. It is itself part of the act of reform. Anyone familiar with the gradual, but inexorable return of Buddhism to political life in independent Sri Lanka has to suspect that Jayewardene's interest in extending the Mahavamsa is in some way a return to the traditional scheme.

In reforming the monkhood, the king finds himself in a curious position. He must believe that the monks have fallen into corruption or heresy, but he is himself a layperson, and no authority on either proper behaviour for monks or orthodox belief. The king needs an upright monk to put things right. In practice, the monk designs and guides the reformation, writes a new code of regulations (*katikavata*) for the reformed life of the monkhood, and the king backs him up. The political issue, of course, is which monk the king chooses to reform the monkhood and why he chooses him. The choice puts a single monk at the top of the ecclesiastical hierarchy, favours the monks who are tied to the reformist monk, and drives off the monks who fall under suspicion. What becomes of the property of monks who are expelled from the order is unclear, but it undoubtedly gave the king material means to make friends. The political potential of reform is not its most salient characteristic, but an inescapable part of the process. The king brings credit on himself by showing respect for the dispensation of the Buddha. But he does so at a price because reform makes enemies as well as friends. The Mahavamsa speaks of some thirteen reformations before the British conquest, usually offering no details about the repercussions of reform.

When a king and monk reform the monkhood, the act of reform and the code of regulations it produces are self-conscious appropriations of

Buddhist tradition. Latter-day kings in Sri Lanka and south-east Asia have looked to the Indian emperor Asoka as a paradigm of a righteous king who unifies and reforms the monkhood.[6] When the king and his cleric reform the monkhood, they enjoy the reflected glow of Asoka. *Katikavata*s themselves have a self-conscious way of following in the tradition, presuming the existence and force of previous *katikavata*s even though the need for reform assumes that those codes are not being followed. So it is with the initiative to update the Mahavamsa. The act puts the leader in a noble tradition. When the eighteenth-century king Kirti Sri Rajasinha resolved to 'fulfil the duties of a king', as the Mahavamsa puts it, he thought of the Mahavamsa and decided to update it.[7]

J.R. Jayewardene updates the Mahavamsa

It is useful to keep this self-conscious tradition in mind in turning to the new Mahavamsa. By the time Jayewardene took office in 1977, the circumstances that gave rise to earlier extensions of the chronicle had changed irremediably. A long colonial period had come and gone. Sri Lanka had become a parliamentary democracy, and Jayewardene had been elected to the office of Prime Minister not raised to the kingship.[8] But the turbulence and decline that marked the previous administration made reform a compelling idea. Critics charged the 1970–77 Bandaranaike administration with autocratic rule, political victimization, favouritism to party faithfuls, and abuse of power.[9] Jayewardene was elected on a promise to establish a *dharmistha* (righteous) government. He talked of clean government, ethical conduct in public life, respect for the rule of law, the independence of the judiciary, and freedom of the press. Where the Bandaranaike government had tightly controlled the economy, the UNP manifesto proposed to open it up, and encourage foreign capital investment in order to create employment. Once elected, Jayewardene said he would develop the nation, bringing Sri Lanka the economic expansion and prosperity that Singapore had enjoyed in the 1960s and 1970s. The process would entail dismantling state-run corporations and getting the government out of commercial enterprises, large and small. But the manifesto also proposed to maintain existing welfare measures – subsidized food, free medical care, and educational services, as well as cheap public transport.

At the same time as it reduced the ideological difference between itself and the Sri Lanka Freedom Party, the UNP developed the theme of righteous leadership. Addressing an election rally at Panadura, Jayewardene declared that he had been an *ahimsawadi* (devotee of peace) for life, although he acknowledged having done a little boxing in school. 'I have told my candidates', he went on, 'that liquor will be anathema in the next Parliament, bribery a thing of the past, and that we shall rule according to the '*sadacharya*' [tradition of virtue] of the country. Any member of his party who failed to adhere to the code for members will have no place even for an hour in the National State Assembly. A code of ethics has been prepared for the Prime Minister as well.'[10]

Righteousness has served as a counterpoint to powerful leadership throughout Sri Lankan history. Indeed Jayewardene's code of ethics recalls the *dasarajadhamma* (the ten kingly virtues of medieval Sri Lanka). But the call to righteous leadership had never appeared before in a election manifesto. The UNP 1977 campaign manifesto promised righteousness in government in the same breath as it announced its support for free education and food subsidies. If the constitutional changes that followed his election can guide us, Jayewardene also intended to increase the power of his office. At election time he emphasized that the public could expect proper behaviour from his government, not that he would soon increase the powers of the office he sought.[11] Jayewardene would lead an exemplary life. He expected the same of his ministers, Members of Parliament, and the Buddhist monkhood. Creating a *dharmistha* society would be the work of disciplined leaders, some in government, some in the monkhood. The monks would set an example for the members of his government, and they would set an example for the people. Drawing on his personal credibility, Jayewardene made himself the paradigm example. Vote for the UNP, he argued, because I am its leader.[12]

The call for a *dharmistha* society naturally evoked the paradigm of Asoka, who himself invented a variety of neologisms constructed from the root *dhamma*. S. J. Tambiah has argued that the Asokan model continues to exert great power on the Theravada societies of south and south-east Asia up to the present time.[13] Recalling Asoka's rule played a part in the expressive politics of newly-independent India, despite the fact that India lacked a substantial Buddhist community. In the Indian case where Hindu, Muslim, Sikh, and Christian held sway, invoking Asoka had virtue by default. It put none of the major communities at a disadvantage, but celebrated the moral intentions of the new state in a diffuse and non-doctrinal way, harking back to a period of righteousness almost two thousand years before the British imposed their own conception of good government on India.[14] In contemporary Sri Lanka, invoking Asoka strikes a very different chord because here what recommended Asoka was not his inoffensiveness, but his capacity to exemplify both morality in government and the rising force of Buddhism in the national life. In the production of a culture of righteousness, it is hard to overlook the presence of Anandatissa de Alwis, the Minister of State in Jayewardene's government. He took over responsibility for government information and broadcasting after a career at the J. Walter Thompson advertising agency where he created the first advertising campaigns aimed at rural Sinhala.

Jayewardene was nothing if not eclectic. He told President Reagan on a state visit to Washington that he was Sri Lanka's 193rd head of state; at a dinner party on that same occasion, he toasted Reagan, saying that his favourite song was Frank Sinatra's 'My Way'.[15] He invoked the Buddhist past at the same moment he invited foreign capital to Sri Lanka, saying 'Let the robber barons come'. When events began to overtake Jayewardene's administration, the invocation of righteousness became more ironic than eclectic. As he was commissioning a new President's flag, centered around a symbol that is both Asokan and Buddhist, the *dhammacakka* (wheel of righteousness), the major ethnic minority was beginning to rebel against the hegemony in Sri Lankan life of the Sinhala majority. He also sponsored several expensive and meritorious ceremonies which entailed lighting 84,000 oil lamps (*asu haradahe pahan pujava*) in honour of the Buddha. When I have talked to people about the ritual, most have spoken of being impressed by Jayewardene's piety. One person said that it was by such acts of piety that Jayewardene had managed to remain in politics so long. The number 84,000 recalls Asoka's legendary charity, which the Mahavamsa says resulted in his building 84,000 *vihara*s (monasteries) to equal the divisions of the *dhamma*.[16] Jayewardene's political opponents were unpersuaded by his resemblance to Asoka – one characterized him as wanting 'not to be a "Dharmasoka" [an Asoka of Righteousness], but an "Agamethisoka" [an Asoka who holds the office of Prime Minister]'.[17]

Asoka's name does not come tripping off the tongue of Sri Lankans much more often than Frank Sinatra's, but calling on his image was part of a process by which the new government created Buddhist culture, giving Jayewardene the advantages of the imperial style into the bargain. Jayewardene moved Parliament to Jayawardhanapura, an area just outside Colombo, which had been the centre of power in the Kotte kingdom of the fifteenth and sixteenth centuries. In so doing, he struck a connection between the one-time capital and himself simply because it was Jayewardene's good fortune to have inherited a surname that matched the medieval capital's name. But Jayewardene's affinity for Asoka is more than a happy coincidence.[18] There is something unmistakable in the way Jayewardene made use of popular feeling for Buddhist moral leadership; as his enemies frequently pointed out, there is also something unmistakable about the monarchist imagery of Jayewardene's administration. One of the complaints people in Sri Lanka made most often about Jayewardene is his presumptuousness. After his election, for example, he asked people to address him as *devavahanse*, a phrase that is translated into English as 'Your

Excellency', but which carries a divine and kingly connotation in Sinhala. Describing himself as the inheritor to the Sinhala monarchy, Jayewardene made speeches that sounded eerily similar to arguments Sinhala kings are known to have made.[19] He took a sapling from the sacred bo-tree in Anuradhapura, and had it replanted in the foothills of Sri Pada (Adam's Peak), the mountain in Sabaragamuva where, according to tradition, the Buddha left his footprint. That sapling itself put forth nine more saplings in short order, which Jayewardene had planted in the administrative capitals of the island's nine provinces.[20]

Shortly after his election, he began a food drive by travelling to Panduwasnuwara, close by 'the mellowed, time-worn bricks and stones of King Parakramabahu's palace', as a newspaper account had it, 'nestled below the hill where the ashes of King Vijaya are believed to be buried'.[21] There, at the *Vap Magul* ceremony that initiates the sowing season, Jayewardene appeared, along with his Ministers, his sarong pulled up in a *vahal pata* (tied above the knees to allow him to work in a muddy paddy field), and his hair restrained by a *jatava* (turban). Other members of Parliament appeared in *amudhaya*s (loin cloths). With this striking act, Jayewardene signalled not only the UNP's traditional interest in increasing food production and helping the peasantry, but also a new sympathy for the way of life and religious beliefs of the majority of Sri Lanka's people.

Besides making personal examples of himself and his supporters, Jayewardene set out to foster a *dharmistha* society by enlarging the activities of the Ministry of Cultural Affairs and creating a Department of Buddhist Affairs. E. B. Hurulle, who was to become the Cultural Affairs Minister, said soon after the election that his ministry would carry the burden of creating a *dharmistha* society.[22] Although the Cultural Affairs Ministry had existed since the first Bandaranaike administration, there had been no attempt, Hurulle said, to revive Sinhala civilization. *Daham pasala*s (*dhamma* schools) had received stepmotherly treatment. Hurulle's Ministry would correct this indifference, appointing cultural officers in each electorate to foster culture at the village level. Asoka had done the same thing.

Shortly after his election, a delegation of leading Buddhist laypeople from the All-Ceylon Buddhist Congress called on Jayewardene. The group presented him with a list of seven proposals which had been approved at the annual meeting of the Congress. As it had since the 1950s, the Congress expressed its concern over the behaviour of Buddhist monks and recommended the establishment of both ecclesiastical courts (*sanghadhikaranaya*) to keep monastic disputes out of civil courts and a *Buddha Sasana Mandalaya* (Buddhist Affairs Committee) to watch over all matters relating to the *sasana* (Buddhism as a historical phenomenon). Jayewardene was agreeable. At the same time the delegation urged the need to make Sri Lanka a Buddhist Republic. 'As the goal of the Prime Minister was to create a *dharmistha samajaya* [a righteous society], the deputation reminded the Prime Minister that the setting up of a Buddhist Republic should be the ultimate aim of a Buddhist renaissance in Sri Lanka'.[23] To this proposal Jayewardene was not agreeable.

When the group returned four days later to continue their deliberations, Jayewardene put his own plan to them:

> The Prime Minister reminded the delegation that all Buddhist matters would be referred to and handled by the new Department of Buddhist Affairs office. Steps would be taken for the propagation of Buddhism through the Sri Lankan embassies abroad...the Prime Minister said some of the matters raised by the deputation were really those that should be discussed with the Minister of Education and the Minister of Cultural Affairs. He would therefore ask the Congress to take up those matters with the two Ministers concerned.[24]

In quick order Jayewardene staked out the high ground as a Buddhist leader without letting Buddhism or Buddhist leaders define social and economic policy. His plan was to pursue two transformations at once. Sri Lanka was to become a fast-developing economy, and it was to become a *dharmistha* society. The trick was keeping the two transformations separate. To accomplish this Jayewardene put the responsibility of supporting the *sasana* on the Ministry of Cultural Affairs and the Department of Buddhist Affairs, while himself attending to the business of business. As an individual Jayewardene would be exemplary, as a national leader he would be Lee Kuan Yew.

Jayewardene argued that a *dharmistha* society depends on individuals acting as individual moral agents, not on government legislation.

> The Buddha never for a moment thought it was possible to reform society through legislation. There were many in society who did not understand that. Such persons were asking why would not the government bar the killing of animals, consumption of liquor, and the like in a Buddhist country like Sri Lanka.
>
> As the leader of the government he had set an example to others of fair play in administration, not taking revenge on political opponents, ensuring freedom and liberty for all people. There was a code for conduct for the Cabinet and the government party....
>
> The government could help Buddhism in two ways – helping in the spread of Dhamma and Buddhist organizations. That was being done by the government.
>
> There were times when he wished to become a Buddhist priest [*sic*] away from the bustle and hustle of politics. But still he had a little

> craving for power that was why he had not made his mind up yet. If he became a priest he would go to a forest hermitage and meditate.[25]

The President said that he would urge people neither to drink alcohol nor to eat meat. But he would initiate no legislation towards those ends. The same free-enterprise spirit he proposed for the economic order he envisioned for the moral order. The state should not determine the morality of its citizens, nor should it allow Buddhist monks to make policy.

Monks should act as moral exemplars. They should not, as has been increasingly the case since the 1930s, involve themselves in politics. On this topic Jayewardene made his position perfectly clear. When Ven. Muruttetuwe Ananda led a strike in 1986 of the nurses' union – the Public Service United Nurses Union – of which he serves as President, Jayewardene denounced the action as contrary to Buddhism. Saying that the Ven. Ananda's activities violated the Buddha's teachings about the proper relationship between monks and women, Jayewardene refused to meet the nurses' delegation as long as it was led by the monk. The deeper problem for Jayewardene has been the very involvement of monks in political activity, whatever their contact with women in such activities.

As with the other UNP leaders who preceded him, Jayewardene has viewed the monkhood conservatively. He has made no secret of his sympathy for forest monks, in part because they are known for their self-discipline, in part because they are apolitical. But village monks too, on his account, should set examples not of activism, but of individual moral responsibility:

> The President was speaking at a meeting which followed the opening of a 3-storeyed building at the Wanawasa Sangha headquarters at Wathurawila. 'I can fashion only one person and that is myself. To others I can only set an example by my words and actions,' he said.
>
> The President said that he had not known the history of the place when he received the invitation....But he said, his interest grew when he read a book entitled, 'The Forest Monks of Sri Lanka' by an American Michael Cerithers [*sic*]... This was a very important book. It revealed the ideas of the forest monks, their meditation, their way of life and the difficulties they have undergone in following the teachings of the Buddha.
>
> He intended to ensure that this book was translated into Sinhala and published and distributed... so that all people could gain some knowledge about the way of life of these monks. That was the real Buddhist way of life – not talking politics and abusing ministers, MPs and officials.[26]

Jayewardene's conception of Buddhism as a religion of individual responsibility justified his disinclination to make Buddhism the state religion. His understanding of 'the real Buddhist way of life' led to his wanting to remove Buddhist monks from political campaigns and secular vocations. It also legitimated his returning Vidyalankara and Vidyodaya universities to *pirivena* (monastic school) status, from which S.W.R.D. Bandaranaike had elevated them. When Vidyalankara *pirivena* was re-opened in 1980, Jayewardene spoke at the opening ceremony recalling his opposition in the 1950s – along with D. S. Senanayake, R. Premadasa, and N. M. Perera – to making the *pirivenas* into universities. 'From that day to the present,' a reporter quotes Jayewardene as saying,

> his views regarding what might be called the 'plunder' of the *pirivenas* did not change...he was entirely in agreement with Ven. Walpola Rahula and Ven. Yakkaduwa Pragnarama about the need to take back the *pirivenas*. Lord Buddha has clearly defined the way of life one should follow. One's aim according to the teachings of the Lord Buddha should not be to become a doctor, lawyer, or a Member of Parliament or the President, but to wean away greed, anger, and ignorance.[27]

Appreciating the full force of Jayewardene's words requires knowing that over the last thirty years Buddhist monks have become regular figures on political platforms, speaking for candidates of both the left and the right. A few monks have themselves run for office. They have had their rights as citizens – despite their being world renouncers – confirmed by the Supreme Court. They vote. They have taken secular jobs – mainly as teachers, although a notorious few have aspired to become doctors, lawyers, and union leaders. One monk in the 1960s took out a license as a barber. And a disproportionate number of monks interested in politics and secular employment have been educated at Vidyodaya and Vidyalankara universities.

Entertaining such views – opposing the political and economic activities of monks, their support for political candidates, their attempts to guide government policy, and their campaigns to make Buddhism the state religion – makes it necessary for a Buddhist leader to find visible ways to support the religion. There are a variety of ways of doing so – from his and his Ministers' regular presence at Buddhist occasions to more substantial acts to patronize the traditional religion of the state. Jayewardene's government has directed considerable resources – governmental, UNESCO, and private Sri Lankan donations – towards restoring Buddhist temples and relic mounds. From 1977 to 1987 the government spent Rs. 1000 million on the Cultural Triangle, the area between Anuradhapura, Polonnaruwa, and Kandy, renovating the

Jetavana *vihara*, Abhayagiri *vihara*, *Dalada Maligava* (the Temple of the Tooth Relic), *Natha devale* (shrine), Gadaladeniya *vihara*, and Lankatilaka *vihara*. It declared, or planned to declare, a huge number of Buddhist places 'sacred areas'. Although Mr Bandaranaike had established the Ministry of Cultural Affairs, its efforts were limited by lack of funds. The Jayewardene administration gave the Ministry more funds, and created the Department of Buddhist Affairs in 1981 to direct state support to favoured Buddhist monks, to publish biographies (*caritaya apadana*) on the occasion of the death of less important monks, and to support *daham pasalas* (*dhamma* schools). With patronage came constraint. The department also took over the registration of Buddhist monks and pursued the implementation of the ecclesiastical court system.

It was in the midst of all of these gestures of concern for Buddhism, that Jayewardene's government announced its intention to bring the Mahavamsa up to date. The idea of extending the chronicle came from a student at the Ceylon Law College who put the plan to a civil servant in the Ministry of Cultural Affairs, Nalin Ratnayake, who became in turn the mover behind the project. Ratnayake called a public meeting – of scholars, laypeople, and the press – to lay out the proposal to take up the writing of the Mahavamsa once again. Dr Nandadeva Wijesekera, an anthropologist, pandit, former Commissioner of the Official Languages Department, and former ambassador to Burma and Laos, was elected chair and editor-in-chief. Mr V. W. Abeygunawardana, a newspaperman and former editor of the UNP party newspaper, became secretary. The Ministry of Cultural Affairs gave Wijesekera a budget of Rs. 485,000 to begin work. When the Secretary to the Ministry of Cultural Affairs held a press conference to publicize the project, he indicated that President Jayewardene 'had taken an interest in the project'.[28]

By January of 1978 an advisory board had been appointed. From this board a sub-committee – Ven. Tallale Dhammananda, Ven. Poruna Vajiranana, Prof. D. E. Hettiarachchi, Prof. Sirimal Ranawella, Prof. Gunapala Senadhira, Prof. Amaradasa Liyanagamage, and Prof. Karunaratna Vijayatunga – was chosen and given the task of constructing an organizational structure for writing the new Mahavamsa. The Ministry had stressed that the board should be faithful to the traditional forms of *vamsa* writing. But the committee wanted substantial changes. Previous instalments of the chronicle had been organized chronologically, and such was the original plan for the contemporary extension. One chapter was set for each of the eleven national leaders, from the British governors who exercized power after 1935 to the Prime Ministers since Independence. Instead the committee decided to organize the new Mahavamsa topically. The model was the

University of Ceylon History of Ceylon, itself patterned on the *Cambridge History of India*. The change suggests the force of professorial authority in the committee's deliberations. It also created the need for expertise and the participation of a large number of authors, editors, poets, and advisors. Where previous instalments of the Mahavamsa had been written by one hand, the new Mahavamsa required the contributions of fifty-seven people.

The committee made a second important change. It added a Sinhala text to the Pali stanzas that served as the language of the previous parts of the Mahavamsa. Opening this part of the Mahavamsa, the reader finds Pali *gathas* (stanzas) treating the high points of the chapter, followed by a fuller account in Sinhala prose. The Pali preserves only the highlights of what the Sinhala says more fully, but its use preserves the traditional idiom. The committee decided that Pali, lacking a technical vocabulary, could not cope with some developments of the modern world. The chapters were composed in Sinhala, not Pali, with the exception of a few chapters written in English. In other words, the new Mahavamsa is essentially a Sinhala work, intended for Sinhala readers. The language is simple Sinhala (*sarala Sinhala*), not the literary language which ordinary readers have difficulty following.

The change in language level was not made casually. Some members fought the change, and others argued for another course, using the purified form of Sinhala, Hela, associated with the work of Munidasa Cumaratunga and the rise of Sinhala nationalism.[29] The faction favouring ordinary Sinhala prevailed. Instead of sacred learning accessible only to highly-educated monks or Hela known to even fewer, the new Mahavamsa was written in ordinary, demotic Sinhala. The Committee's hope was that a person who can read a Sinhala newspaper – which in a literate society means most Sinhala – can also read the new Mahavamsa. The editor stressed his intention that the chronicle 'follow in the tradition' (Pali *pubbalikhita*). But the tradition to which the new Mahavamsa attaches itself is a tradition which has itself changed many times. The practice of including a Sinhala paraphrase, for instance, began with Ven. Yagirala Pannananda. The *Mahavamsa, Nutana Yugaya* adds new emphasis and a committee of authors, and it aims at a large audience. But even if most copies of the *Mahavamsa, Nutana Yugaya* sit unread in libraries, the Jayewardene government's righteous decision to extend the chronicle reached its intended audience.

Righteousness and *realpolitik*

Commissioning the *Mahavamsa, Nutana Yugaya* draws on the power of the past twice over. Recording the history of the 1935–1977 period, the new Mahavamsa traces out and celebrates the process by which

Buddhism re-emerged in the national life and electoral politics.[30] Independent of the edifying content of the historical writing itself, the act of calling for an updating of the chronicle exploits the past by appropriating a historical paradigm – the righteous Buddhist leader who renews Buddhism, reforms the monkhood, and brings the historical record down to his time. I want to concentrate on this second way of using the power of the past. It exemplifies the way a consummate politician brings together righteousness and *realpolitik*.

The formula is simple enough. The leader shows his personal concern for Buddhism, directs patronage to the monks, and makes institutional arrangements for the protection of both the religion and its virtuosi. But he also comes down hard on the monks as a political force, constraining their power as a group. And in particular he acts against a certain kind of monk. Nowadays these politically-active monks are usually young, and often university-educated. They have bedevilled politicians for the last forty years. While maintaining their public responsibilities to Buddhism, Buddhist kings have had to contend with politically-engaged monks through most of the island's history. Righteous leadership is not weak leadership. Consider the great twelfth-century reformer Parakramabahu. He recovered control of the capital at Polonnaruwa by treachery and force of arms, and then unified the monkhood, expelling corrupt monks and issuing a *katikavata* which imposed unity and orthodoxy on a monkhood rent by divisions. His name means 'strong arm', and that strength served him in dealing both with his political enemies and the monkhood. Jayewardene's achievement derives from finding ways to make this formula work in a democracy.

Jayewardene's government created a new constitution in 1978. It promised 'Buddhism the foremost place', making it 'the duty of the state to protect and foster the Buddha *sasana*, while assuring to all religions the rights granted in Articles 10 and 14 – freedom of thought, conscience, and religion, and freedom of speech and assembly. The 1978 Constitution did not make Buddhism the state religion, but it preserved the priority that the Constitution of 1972 returned to Buddhism. Buddhism enjoyed a growing measure of expressive hegemony in the Jayewardene years. Government officials frequently appeared as guests at Buddhist occasions, where they spoke of their government's commitment to the religion in a way never before heard from Hindu, Christian, or Muslim members of government. The Ministry of Cultural Affairs concerned itself with Sinhala and Buddhist culture, to the exclusion of minorities and minority religions. The Department of Buddhist Affairs was well-staffed and centrally-located; equivalent departments for Hindus and Muslims were not; Christians had no department. The Jayewardene government was expressively Buddhist. It addressed its pronouncements to a public it assumed was Sinhala and

Buddhist. After the 1983 Sinhala attacks on Tamils, government communiqués urged the Sinhala not to fear for their lives or property.[31] A prominent Minister spoke to the nation of the hardship faced by the Sinhala, now forced to queue up for food. He said nothing of, or to, the 70,000 Tamils in refugee camps.

The government directed patronage to monks through both the Ministry of Cultural Affairs and the Department of Buddhist Affairs. The total amount was not great. District Ministers had some Rs 2,000 each year to spend on rebuilding and maintaining monasteries. The Department of Buddhist Affairs urged those funds be given to a single monastery in each district. When a high-ranking monk died, the Department allocated funds to celebrate his funeral in a suitable way. The Department's original plan was to use its resources to finance funerals for monks who die in poverty; it came to use these resources to stage grand funerals for high-ranking monks. Asking monks to serve as poets, editors, and advisors to the new Mahavamsa was another kind of patronage. The honoraria were not large, but altogether the Mahavamsa Compilation Board chose over fifty monks to contribute to the chronicle's creation. In so doing, the government signalled its support for a certain kind of Buddhist monk – senior, high-ranking officials of the various fraternities and scholarly monks – and a certain kind of Buddhism – the kind that is lived out in monasteries, not on political platforms or behind police barricades.

Jayewardene created the Department of Buddhist Affairs by putting together disparate functions that had been left to the Public Trustee and the Ministry of Cultural Affairs. The Department thus took over the regulation of all monks, a task fundamental to long-term government plans to issue identity cards to legitimate monks and to impose ecclesiastical courts on them. Both goals will serve to discipline the monkhood – the identity cards will allow civil authorities to discriminate genuine monks from men who take on the robes temporarily. The ecclesiastical courts have been in the offing for almost fifty years because the project is very hard to put into practice. Legislation for that system of justice still sits in the Legal Draftsman's office and, before it can be implemented, requires the establishing of *katikavata*s for each *nikaya* (monastic community).

Since the late 1930s middle-class Buddhist laypeople have urged the *nikayas* to draw up codes of regulation for their governance and for settling disputes between their own members. What prompts this interest in self-governance is the litigiousness of Buddhist monks, and the unseemliness of world renouncers fighting over incumbencies. Proposals to make the monks govern themselves are reformative, not simply a redistribution of authority. In the words of a prominent Buddhist activist and lawyer:

> It is clear from the cases argued at the civil courts, and from past case records connected to incumbency disputes, that a great decline has begun in the order of the *sangha*. The case records reveal how monks have made nasty allegations against one another....The decline of the *sangha* society, and the disgust of laymen towards the *bhikkhus*, have become obstacles for the development of Buddhism.[32]

The solution is the *katikavatas*, but they are also the problem. The proliferation of monastic communities since the fall of the Kandyan king leads to each group's wanting to govern itself by its own *katikavata*, and democratic political realities require the recognition of these divisions. Where reform traditionally used a *katikavata* to unify the monkhood, making it, as the Culavamsa puts it, 'as uniform as milk and water',[33] reform under democratic circumstances perpetuates divisions. Reform nowadays also requires waiting until each monastic community produces its own *katikavata*.

Most of Jayewardene's concern for the monkhood has been directed at high-ranking monks, not the monkhood at large. Negotiations for the devolution of power to District Councils began in the early 1980s, but Sinhala public feeling would have nothing of it. The government attempted to win Sinhala-Buddhist support by creating, and then conferring with, a small group of senior monks, the Supreme Council (*Uttaritara sabha*). The Supreme Council remained opposed to any kind of power-sharing with Tamils in the north and east, and the government's deliberations with them were largely ceremonial. The government was represented by Jayewardene and his Minister of Cultural Affairs, not the Ministers of State, National Security, or anyone directly involved with reaching a settlement besides Jayewardene. But the very act of consulting the monkhood was unprecedented, making senior monks privy to and part of any prospective settlement.

To politically-aggressive monks, Jayewardene's government has shown the back of the hand. The unhappy decline of a group of Buddhist monks and Catholic clergy, 'Voice of the Clergy', (*Pävidi Handa*), is a good example. The group came together in opposition to Jayewardene's plan in 1982 to defer Parliamentary elections in favour of a referendum. In December 1982 Ven. Daramitipola Ratanasara organized a Pävidi Handa meeting in Gampola. For several reasons the meeting never occurred. The proprietor of the meeting hall where the group planned to meet was approached by young men who demanded that he not rent the space to the clergymen. On the day of the meeting clergy arrived at Ven. Ratanasara's monastery, unaware that the meeting had been called off, and were set upon by a mob. Local police arrived to inform the crowd that no meeting would be permitted in the monastery.[34] Gampola police went on to seize 20,000 of the group's petitions, preventing the clergymen from publicizing their views. In February 1983 the Supreme Court ordered the Superintendent of Police in Gampola to pay Ven. Ratanasara Rs. 10,000 for violating his constitutional rights.[35] In March Jayewardene's Cabinet decided that the state should pay the fine and that the Superintendent should be promoted.[36]

Jayewardene's government recognized a reality that earlier UNP leaders only dimly perceived – Buddhism and its practitioners had become intrinsic parts of the political life of the nation. Under these circumstances, the Jayewardene government acted to give the advantage both within the monkhood – as in the case of the ecclesiastical courts – and in its dealings with the monks – as in the compilation of the *Mahavamsa, Nutana Yugaya* – to a certain kind of monk. In 1967 the Senanayake government made available to high-ranking monks an old colonial house to serve as a lodging place when official duties took them to Colombo. In 1977 the Jayewardene government commissioned the writing of the *Mahavamsa, Nutana Yugaya*, and chose the same house, *Charikaramaya*, as the headquarters for updating the Sinhala chronicle. The twenty-odd monks who became the core of the Mahavamsa Compilation Board were many of the same monks whose high offices entitled them to board at *Charikaramaya*. In this building the representation of the past is melded into the politics of the present.

Notes and references

1 H. Bechert, 'The beginnings of Buddhist historiography: *Mahavamsa* and political thinking', in B. L. Smith (ed.) *Buddhism and the Legitimation of Power in Sri Lanka*, Chambersburg, 1978, p. 3.
2 *Mahavamsa, Nutana Yugaya*, Colombo, 1986.
3 A. Kulasuriya, 'The minor chronicles and other traditional writings in Sinhalese and their historical value', *Ceylon Historical Journal*, 1978, vol. 25, p. 12.
4 See K. Malalgoda, *Buddhism in Sinhalese Society, 1750–1900*, Berkeley, 1976; L. A. Wickremaratne, 'Religion, nationalism, and social change in Ceylon, 1865–1885', *Journal of the Royal Asiatic Society* 1969, vol. 56, pp. 123–50.
5 Gonagala, 1935.
6 S. J. Tambiah, *World Conqueror World Renouncer*, Cambridge, 1976, pp. 54–72, 159–78.
7 *Cv*. II. 99: 76–80.
8 Jayewardene was made President under the new constitution of 1978.
9 Jayewardene summed up these charges in a campaign speech: 'Bad examples, treating one's kith and kin, political incarceration without trial, taking over or controlling the mass media are things that must be shunned by a just government', *Daily News* 2/v/77.
10 *Daily News*, 14/vi/77.

11 *Daily News*, 2/v/77.
12 *Daily News*, 16/vi/77.
13 Tambiah, *World Conqueror*, pp. 515–30.
14 See M. Marriott, 'The cultural policy of the new states'. in C. Geertz (ed.) *Old Societies and New States*, Glencoe, Ill., 1963, p. 39.
15 'Visit of Sri Lankan President Jayewardene', *Department of State Bulletin*, vol. 84, no. 2090, September 1984, pp. 65–8.
16 *Mv*. 5: 78.
17 J. R. P. Suriyapperuma, the SLFP candidate for Minuwangoda, in a campaign speech in Gampaha; *Daily News*, 1/vii/77.
18 Jayewardene included an early article on Asoka in a collection of speeches and writings, *Buddhist Essays*, Colombo, 1982; first published 1942, pp. 86–94.
19 See, for example, the government publication *Golden Threads*, Colombo, 1982, which contains numerous kingly remarks and images. Such references often appear in English and seem to be intended for foreign consumption.
20 L. A. Wickremaratne, 'Shifting metaphors of sacrality: the mythic dimensions of Anuradhapura', in B. L. Smith and H. B. Reynolds (eds) *The City as a Sacred Centre*, Leiden, 1987, p. 57.
21 *Daily News*, 11/x/77.
22 *Daily News*, 1/x/77.
23 *Daily News*, 5/ix/77.
24 *Daily News*, 10/ix/77.
25 *Daily News*, 10/i/80.
26 *Daily News*, 4/ii/86; cf. M. B. Carrithers, *The Forest Monks of Sri Lanka*, Delhi, 1983, p. 190.
27 *Daily News*, 4/i/80.
28 *Sun*, Colombo, 19/ix/78.
29 See Nissan and Stirrat, this volume.
30 The irony of course is that the UNP which opposed the political emergence of Buddhism in the 1950s is the party which celebrated that transformation in the new Mahavamsa thirty years later; see S. Kemper, *The Presence of the Past: Chronicles, Politics, and Culture in Sinhala Life*, Ithaca, forthcoming.
31 E. Nissan, 'Some thoughts on Sinhala justifications for the violence', in J. Manor (ed.) *Sri Lanka in Change and Crisis*, London, 1984; G. Obeyesekere, 'The origins and instutionalization of political violence', in ibid.
32 P. Goonesekera, *Vihara Niti Vittiya* (A Compendium of Monastic Law), Colombo, 1961, p. 47.
33 *Cv*. 73: 22.
34 Petition of Ven. Daramitipola Ratanasara, Supreme Court of Sri Lanka, 9 December 1982.
35 *Divayina*, 9/ii/83.
36 *Island*, Colombo, 3/iii/83.

Chapter ten

Newspaper nationalism: Sinhala identity as historical discourse

Serena Tennekoon

Introduction

National identity is most vigorously affirmed when it becomes most problematic. In Sri Lanka, the dramatic escalation of ethnic conflict between the Sinhala majority and the Tamil minority, especially during the last few years, has generated a national identity crisis. This chapter explores the impact of political events on the cultural co-ordinates of Sinhala nationalist identity, which in turn influence the perceptions and practices of politics.

As in many nation states where national identity is defined emphatically in the features of a majority ethnic identity, in Sri Lanka since Independence national identity has continued to be conflated with Sinhala-Buddhist identity. This ambiguity is preserved most strikingly in language: *jatiya* (denoting group or kind) refers to ethnic group as well as nation.[1] Throughout this chapter, unless otherwise indicated, I will translate *jatiya* as nation, thus maintaining the original ambiguity.

The official installation and popular reaffirmation of a predominantly Sinhala-Buddhist national identity and the concomitant peripheralization of minority ethnicities in both symbolic and material practice, contributed to the development of a Tamil nationalist movement. The militant and separatist turn of Tamil nationalism in the last two decades has, in turn, threatened the hegemony of the Sinhala and provoked among them a crisis of identity. It is this identity crisis that erupted in the rhetoric of the three newspaper debates analysed in this paper.

The newspaper debates which appeared in 1984–5 must be situated also in the context of the anti-Tamil riots of July 1983. The July riots[2] marked a critical juncture in the ethnic relations between Sinhala and Tamil. Soon afterwards, the guerrilla war between Tamil militants and the largely Sinhala government forces escalated into a 'National Security' issue and each community's perception of the other as enemy hardened with each ambush, bomb explosion and massacre.

The July riots and their turbulent aftermath highlighted fissures among the Sinhala community as well. This was particularly evident in the diverse ways in which Sinhala identity was reassessed from political platforms, seminar rooms and the mass media. For many, initial shock gave way to rationalizations and the reassertion of Sinhala nationalism. The July riots were interpreted as righteous violence and Tamils (both militant and civilian) were cast as *agents provocateurs*. The victims became the victimizers. Moreover, the severity of the violence (which became apparent initially through exposure in the foreign media) was minimized and adverse publicity was attributed to Tamil propagandists. According to this line of rationalization, the recovery of Sinhala moral esteem was more important than understanding what happened.

This position was challenged by a minority of activists, bilingual intellectuals, and academics, whose political sympathies ranged from the liberal to the left. These women and men represented several groups and organizations (which were multi-ethnic) and were concerned with studying the ethnic conflict dispassionately and contributing towards its speedy and just resolution.[3] In general, these individuals recognized the economic and political grievances of the Tamil minority and were also critical of Sinhala nationalist excesses. The newspaper debates discussed below illuminate a particular confrontation between this group and the opposing faction of Sinhala nationalists.

A highly literate population and a long-established tradition of newspapers notwithstanding, there is a paucity of research on the press in Sri Lanka.[4] A remark made by some westernized Sri Lankan university students and recorded by Marshall Singer in the late 1950s may still explain the invisibility of the Sinhala press in the English language social science literature: 'If you want news, you read the English press; if you want gossip, you read the Sinhala papers'.[5] If, as Benedict Anderson argues persuasively, 'the nation [and nationalism] was conceived in language, not blood', and if 'print-literacy' is a significant factor in the origin and circulation of nationalism, then any analysis of contemporary nationalist trends in Sri Lanka can hardly ignore the most widely read Sinhala press.[6]

During the latter half of 1984 and early 1985, the '*Kalina Samvada*' (Contemporary Controversies) pages of the Sunday *Divayina* became the forum for three newspaper debates on Sinhala history, culture and identity. The Sinhala daily, *Divayina* (hereafter *Dv.*), and the Sunday *Divayina – Divayina Irida Sangrahaya* – as well as their English counterparts are published by the Upali Newspaper Group which was established in 1981 by a Sinhala millionaire entrepreneur, Upali Wijewardena. Although both daily and weekly *Divayina* are newcomers on the competitive Sinhala newspaper market, recent (1985) readership figures indicate that they are the most popular Sinhala newspapers.[7] In the absence of survey data on readership preferences, the success of *Divayina* may be attributed partly to its selective criticism of government policies which is coloured with a strong sense of Sinhala nationalism. While such editorial policies may be formulated in response to the perceived needs of a nationalist readership, invariably they also inform and influence mass opinion. In this regard, the *Divayina* newspaper debates represent not only a cross-section of the views of the Sinhala intelligentsia, but also an example of the media's participation in the generation and maintenance of a particular kind of nationalist discourse.

All three debates concerned aspects of historical relations between Sinhala and Tamil. It is my contention that appearing as they did at that particular time, these newspaper debates constituted a culturally familiar mode of discourse within which Sinhala identity and nationalism were examined and reaffirmed.

Since much of the controversy highlighted nationalist versions of history and culture, throughout this chapter I shall use the terms 'history', 'myth', and 'past' loosely to refer to the various interpretations of the past which were debated. My intention is not to sift facts from fictions or myths from history, regardless of the extent to which such exercises are even possible. I treat history as a mode of discourse which reveals 'as much *about* the nature of interpretation itself as it is *about* the subject matter which is the manifest occasion of its own elaboration'.[8] I analyse history as a cultural-political construct which is caught in the process of (re)composing national identity and examine how the Sinhala have selectively appropriated their past in order to understand the present and shape the future.

The Kingdom of Jaffna: 'something they never had'

The first controversy was sparked by a comment made by a prominent Sinhala lawyer, Gamini Iriyagolla, in the course of an extensive interview which was published soon after a bomb explosion – which was attributed to Tamil militants – at the Madras Airport in August 1984. Iriyagolla, who has written and spoken on subjects ranging from state irrigation policies to Tamil nationalism, on this occasion attempted to refute Tamil claims to a traditional homeland in the north and east. He was especially critical of the notion that an independent Tamil kingdom had been established at Jaffna around the thirteenth century, from which time on Sinhala and Tamil rulers had administered their separate kingdoms until western colonialism transformed domestic politics. Dismissing the Tamil nationalist use of history,[9] Iriyagolla charged,

> They [the Tamils] are fighting to restore the independent Tamil kingdom they say they once had. Yet there was no such thing. And we cannot give them something they never had.[10]

Iriyagolla's denial was premissed on a widely-shared understanding of Sinhala identity through time (history) and space (geography), derived mainly from sources such as the mytho-historical chronicle, the Mahavamsa.[11] In post-colonial Sri Lanka, the search for Sinhala national identity remains oriented to a past when they apparently retained undisputed hegemony over the entire island. And within the parameters of such an imagination, it would indeed be difficult to admit the possibility of a separate Tamil kingdom in thirteenth-century Jaffna as well as (by extension) a politically autonomous Tamil region in the north and the east today.

Iriyagolla's reconstruction of history was challenged by Carlo Fonseka, a member of the Medical Faculty at the University of Colombo, who is perhaps better known as a leftist activist and social critic. Armed with the works of two Sinhala historians (K.M. de Silva and Vijaya Samaraweera), Fonseka declared that, contrary to Iriyagolla, Sri Lanka had been politically unified only by four Sinhala kings, and that in the thirteenth century an independent Tamil kingdom had indeed held sway in the north.[12]

Although the initial dispute was between Iriyagolla and Fonseka, it provoked a number of *Divayina* readers to offer their own historical readings and counter-readings. At a fundamental level, Fonseka's critics implicitly agreed that in the thirteenth century, Jaffna appeared to be outside the political control of southern Sinhala administrations. Beyond this, different interpretations abounded: that the kingdom of Jaffna was short-lived; that it was not an *independent* kingdom but a client state of a neighbouring south Indian kingdom; and that it was not a *Tamil* kingdom, because although the population may have been Tamil, their rulers were of Aryan (that is non-Dravidian) stock.[13] Whatever the historical evidence, these claims resonated with the Sinhala political consciousness of 1984. For example, the emphasis on thirteenth-century Jaffna as a puppet regime of a south Indian kingdom was strikingly congruent with the widely-shared notion that Tamil Nadu 'harboured terrorists' today and, if unchallenged, would control the separate Tamil state of Eelam tomorrow. At stake then was not a mere historical detail – the medieval kingdom of Jaffna – but Sinhala hegemony in modern Sri Lanka now endangered by Tamil separatism.

The issue of whether or not in medieval times the north was under Sinhala political control spilled over into a related consideration, the question of original inhabitants. Some contributors to the *Divayina* controversy became preoccupied with establishing the pre-Tamil existence of Sinhala settlements in the north. In this regard, a couple of contributors utilized evidence of ancient Sinhala-Buddhist ruins in the north and east to prove that the Tamils were mere latecomers.[14] And despite some attempts to demonstrate the fluidity of ethnic identities through history,[15] anti-Tamil sentiments surfaced in the rhetoric of P.L. Gomis' 'The original invaders of Lanka were Dravidians'.[16] Gomis insisted that the Dravidians could not have been the original settlers of Lanka because they constitute a small population today. This, he claimed, proved that the Dravidians came to Lanka as invaders and never as permanent settlers:

> It would be accurate to define the Dravidians of the North [of Sri Lanka] as descendants of South Indian invaders who came to plunder weak Sinhala kingdoms. They multiplied at random and were unable to sustain a continuous, independent kingdom of their own ....This is their true inheritance [*janma jatiya*] which continues to guide even today's Tamil extremists as they murder and plunder from South India.

As is evident in this passage, the past was closely and constantly juxtaposed with the present. Mytho-historical details were not important in and for themselves but as antecedents or models for the understanding of present events. History was a mode of discourse which both facilitated and framed the discussion of ethnic relations in general and Sinhala identity in particular.

Some of the participants in this debate were sensitive to these meta-historical issues. For instance, Carlo Fonseka pondered that whether a Tamil kingdom existed in the north was ultimately irrelevant to the present ethnic crisis.[17] Another contributor, M.T. Samaranayaka, heightened the absurdity of 'splitting historical hairs' to solve the ethnic crisis by extending the search for 'original' inhabitants to pre-historical limits.[18] The sole Tamil participant in this debate, K. Kandasami, having identified himself as a casualty of the July riots, also agreed with Fonseka, conceding that 'we only need history to build the future'.[19] And, impatient with the surfeit of history, a (Sinhala) contributor, Susil G. Seneviratna, attempted to change the mode of discourse:

> It is my belief that the debate on whether there was a historical Tamil kingdom is not concerned with clarifying historical issues. If the Tamils are claiming their rights, it is clear that we [Sinhala] are directing this debate to prove that they don't have such rights. As a result we are covering up the gravest problem we face today and avoiding coming to grips with it. I would like to invite our intellectuals to stop obfuscating the issue and discuss it directly.[20]

It is not entirely clear whether the absence of 'direct' discussion on contemporary nationalist politics was due to a lack of enthusiasm on the part of the *Divayina*-reading Sinhala intelligentsia or to the exercise of editorial discretion. If indeed it was the case that *Divayina* readers preferred to contemplate the prevailing conflict tangentially through historical situations rather than directly through the terms of the present, then it would seem that for the Sinhala, the past constituted a significant mode of discourse within which they believed the present (and the future) could be negotiated and redefined.

Sinhala Culture: the 'double-headed serpent'

Even while the Kingdom of Jaffna and the antiquity of Tamils and Sinhala were passionately disputed, a second storm was already brewing in the same newspaper. The Sinhala Culture controversy was sparked by a Sunday *Divayina* editorial titled 'Intellectuals and seminars'. Referring to a recent seminar on Sinhala Culture, the editorialist questioned its relevance and suspected its motives.[21]

The seminar at issue here was held on 19 September 1984 at the Colombo Public Library and was organized by a group of mainly leftist Sinhala intellectuals of the Open Arts Circle and the Workers' and Peasants' Institute. According to some of the participants, the original topic for discussion 'Do the Sinhalese have a Culture?' was later modified to 'Do the Sinhalese have a Great Culture?'. This qualification was important but it was also misleading. For the purpose of the seminar, Great Culture referred to culture in the Great Tradition (*maha sampradaya*). The seminar organizers could hardly have been ignorant of the politics of that concept, of its unmistakable resonance of superiority and high culture, but they refrained from problematizing the very classification of Great and Little Traditions. Thus it was hardly surprising that the seminar was controversial on several levels.

Central to the controversy were two seminar papers presented by Newton Gunasinghe, a Colombo University sociologist, and Charles Abeysekera, a social scientist, literary critic, and human rights activist. Gunasinghe maintained that contrary to popular assumptions the roots of modern Sinhala culture did not stretch in an unbroken line to the Anuradhapura period of Sri Lankan history (circa 250 BC – 1017), but only to the Kandy period (circa eighteenth century). Focusing on the Kandy period, he examined the relationship between the mode of economic production and selected cultural traditions and concluded that Kandy period culture – and, in extension, modern Sinhala culture – belonged to a Little Tradition (*cula sampradaya*).

In making the distinction between Great and Little Tradition cultures, Gunasinghe did not refer to anthropologists like Robert Redfield or

Milton Singer, McKim Marriott, M.N. Srinivas or Gananath Obeyesekere[22], but offered his own definition. According to his first criterion, a Great Tradition produced works of lasting artistic value, whereas the merits of a Little Tradition culture fluctuated with the shifting socio-economic conditions which produced them. Second, the works of a Great Tradition were removed from the activities of daily living, while Little Traditions were intimately connected with and reflected the stuff of humdrum life. Finally, Great Tradition cultural productions were the achievements of full-time specialists supported by the economic surplus generated in their societies. In contrast, Little Tradition artists were amateurs who also had to engage in economic production.[23]

Abeysekera's paper was not especially concerned with the problem of Great and Little Tradition terminology. Even so, his analysis was influenced by some of Obeyesekere's work.[24] Abeysekera contrasted 'village Buddhism' with the Buddhist cultural identity created in the twentieth century. By the early twentieth century, he argued, Sinhala culture had fractured into several regional cultures whose common feature was a syncretistic form of 'village Buddhism' which was considerably different from the original, textually preserved doctrine of the Buddha. Having discussed some of the significant factors (such as the Buddhist reform movement) which shaped modern Buddhist identity, Abeysekera concluded that,

> What we recognize as Sinhala culture today is not something which is naturally linked to the unbroken 2,500-year-old historical evolution of the Sinhala. Rather, this culture has changed during the last 100 years in response to various economic and political needs. In the course of this development this [new] Sinhala culture has displaced village Buddhism to a secondary position.[25]

The *Divayina* editorialist objected to the focus of the Sinhala Culture seminar. He contended that to explore the question, do the Sinhala have a culture, was absurd: 'For not only do the Sinhala (like other peoples) have a culture, but, according to the experts, when compared to other cultures, Sinhala culture enjoys a great and unbroken tradition'.[26] The editorialist then caricatured the seminar participants as 'intellectuals perform[ing] like peacocks on seminar platforms', implied that they were being manipulated by 'external' powers, and accused them of deliberately misleading the public instead of 'providing the general public with the strategies and strength to deal with the shattering assault on [our] nation and culture'.

This editorial proved to be a mere prelude. A week later, the matter of 'ulterior motives' was pursued in stronger prose. Sinhala intellectuals of the sort who were critical of Sinhala culture were accused of being sponsored by wealthy, 'two-faced' organizations which mask their real and sinister intentions (of weakening the Sinhala) with pious concern for their problems. The editorialist also alleged that motivated by greed rather than patriotism, Sinhala intellectuals had prostituted their professional skills to the highest bidders. In short, they were traitors.[27]

These two editorials set the tone and the agenda of the debate which followed. For example, next to the second editorial was published a lengthy article by Sarath Wijesuriya headlined, 'Lurking behind social science, Devadattas hurl rocks at culture'.[28] According to Buddhist legend, Devadatta, the Buddha's evil cousin had made several unsuccessful attempts on the Buddha's life – on one occasion, toppling boulders in his path. By comparing social scientists to Devadatta, Wijesuriya cast them as the (un-Buddhist) villains of this drama and symbolically elevated Sinhala culture to a quasi-sacred status beyond critical debate.

The theme of traitor-intellectuals publicly disparaging their already maligned culture circulated for several weeks in articles which were both passionately nationalistic, aggressively populist and anti-intellectual. For example, consider Gunawardena Suriyaracchi's rather apocalyptic vision:

> Sinhala culture, once a football for hypocrite-experts, has now split into a double-headed serpent of Great and Little Traditions. It is truly astonishing that this split began to emerge only recently. Having masticated all that is edible of Sinhala culture, they are now swollen-headed with pride and denigrate even its unchewable dregs. But does any one of these false experts try to rescue Sinhala culture from the abyss into which it has fallen?[29]

Again, echoing the suspicions of the editorialist, C. Rajapaksa concluded his rambling critique of Gunasinghe's Little Tradition thesis, charging that Little Intellectuals [*cula ugatun*] were selling the country to foreigners for dollars.[30]

A cartoon version of this theme also appeared in the Contemporary Controversies page. It figured two balding men, positioned back to back and sharing the same lower torso. One man, dressed in western clothes, looked smug clutching a wad of dollars in his left hand and a sign announcing, 'Culture is for Sale' in his right hand. The other was dressed in the loose *kurta* which comprises the top half of 'national dress' for men. He was sour-faced and carried a sign which exclaimed, 'There is No Culture'.[31] This then was the traitor-intellectual, a Janus-faced opportunist who, by virtue of his westernized training was not only presumed incapable of understanding his *real* culture but also guilty of deliberately distorting that culture for a fistful of dollars.[32]

It would be misleading to characterize this *Divayina* controversy as entirely polemical and divorced from the presentations made at the Sinhala Culture seminar. For some contributors were concerned with the substantive issues raised in the seminar rather than their allegedly sinister implications. For example, Nalin de Silva – an academic and social critic who was also a participant in the Sinhala Culture seminar – criticized Gunasinghe's choice of the Great and Little Tradition classification. Calling attention to the colonial origins of such western social-scientific concepts, de Silva argued they were inappropriate to the Sinhala context.[33] Another, Mangala Ilangasinghe (who professed to be no sociologist but engaged in the study of history and education) challenged Gunasinghe's findings on the mode of economic production in the Kandy period and also his choice of Little Tradition cultural forms.[34] In a similar fashion, Mendis Rohanadeera – also an academic – objected to Abeysekera's attempt to locate the development of modern Sinhala culture in the political and economic (class) processes of the twentieth century. His critique was based on the assumption that the ancient roots of Sinhala-Buddhist identity were self-evident and the development of this identity through history was therefore unproblematic.[35]

When compared in style and tone to the explosive prose discussed earlier, these critiques were undoubtedly more tempered, and the arguments couched in social science rhetoric. However, I am not suggesting that the latter were ideologically innocent. In fact, the Sinhala Culture seminar itself as well as the responses it elicited were bound by competing ideological claims: in general, both Abeysekera's and Gunasinghe's analyses were located within neo-Marxist paradigms while their critics were guided primarily by nationalist/populist considerations.

The entwinement of nationalism and social analysis hinted at in Rohanadeera's contribution referred to above was more explicitly articulated by Nalin de Silva. In another article, de Silva reflected,

> In the context of the present national problem it would have been better if this question (whether the Sinhalese have a Great Tradition culture) was discussed under a different topic. The theme of the seminar should have been, the Sinhalese have a great cultural heritage that they can be proud of but should not impose on other ethnic groups. Those who claim that the Sinhalese have an inferior [*pahat*] culture will never have any credibility with the people.[36]

Accordingly, critical analyses of one's own culture at a time of national crisis (in this case, the Sinhala–Tamil conflict) were deemed at best counter-productive or at worst destructive. Unlike the ideal Weberian intellectual for whom politics and science (scholarship) were separate vocations,[37] Sinhala intellectuals were expected to act politically as nationalists not traitors, and as defenders of their cultural heritage, not its critics. It was because Gunasinghe and Abeysekera flouted these implicit requirements and chose to deconstruct prevailing notions of Sinhala culture at a time when Tamil nationalism appeared to threaten Sinhala identity, that their explorations proved to be so explosive.

Ethnicity, social scientist and national heroes

Many of the themes which had already emerged in the two foregoing debates were reopened in a third *Divayina* controversy. This dispute began over a volume of essays, *Ethnicity and Social Change in Sri Lanka* (*ESC*), published in English and Sinhala by the Social Scientists' Association (SSA) in 1984. This collection was the product of a seminar held in 1979, before the July riots. Although the editors of *ESC* had hoped that, 'the papers in this volume will at least force some of the exponents of Sinhala and Tamil nationalism to look more closely at the myths, misinterpretations and misunderstandings that have nourished their ideologies',[38] the nationalist backlash which ensued demonstrated otherwise.

This controversy was concerned with reconstituting a Sinhala identity perceived to have been defamed by Marxist academics. As such, it was a continuation of previous arguments in a new guise. Central to the new dispute was the reinterpretation of two important Sinhala nationalist heroes – Anagarika Dharmapala and King Dutugämunu. Anagarika Dharmapala was one of the leading figures in the early twentieth-century Buddhist reform movement which contributed the first wave of modern Sinhala nationalism. King Dutugämunu (Dutthagamani Abhaya) was the epic hero of the Mahavamsa and is best remembered for his victory over Elara, the south Indian ruler of the northern kingdom, in the second century BC.

Dharmapala: 'no savage blood is found'

The reappraisal of Dharmapala's life and work was provoked by Kumari Jayawardena's essay in *ESC*, in which she explored the links between merchant capital, the rise of a Sinhala petit bourgeoisie, the religious and cultural revival of this period, and their communalist implications. With specific reference to the revivalist ideology, she claimed that,

> [R]ather than being swept away by the winds of nationalism and national unity, the older forms of identity were given a new lease of life, resulting in communalism, casteism, a distortion of history, a revival of myths of origin, and hero-myths along with the creation of visions of a past "golden age".[39]

The most fundamental of these myths was the three-pronged notion of Aryan-Sinhala-Buddhist identity which pervaded the speeches and writings of the reformer, Anagarika Dharmapala. Jayawardena pointed out that Dharmapala believed the Sinhala to be descendants of the Indo-Aryan race who were pure and more civilized than other racial groups in the area; that Lanka was Sihadipa, the island of the Sinhala people who claim descent from (the Indo-Aryan) Prince Vijaya; and that Lanka is also Dhammadipa, the island of the *dhamma*, where the dying Buddha predicted his teachings would flourish: 'Racial purity and religious purity were thus combined and the "pure Aryan Sinhalese" became the appointed guardians of the "pure doctrine" of Buddhism'.[40]

Jayawardena was by no means the first social scientist to offer a critical appraisal of Dharmapala and the Buddhist reform movement.[41] Nevertheless, the timing of the *ESC* publication and its availability in Sinhala help explain the outrage it provoked.

Ven. Kahawatte Ananda[42] proved to be Jayawardena's most persistent and bitter critic. He lambasted her for 'dynamiting our national heritage' by maligning Dharmapala and the Buddhist-nationalist movement. Specifically, he objected to her treatment of the notion of Aryan origin. Pointing to Jayawardena's implication that Dharmapala's comment, 'the Sinhalese ... in whose veins no savage blood is found ... stand as the representatives of Aryan civilization' was racist, Ven. Ananda accused her of confusing the Sinhala meaning of *arya* ('those who do not indulge in lowly, animal-like behaviour') with Hitler's 'fundamentally different concept of a superior Aryan race'.[43] However, Ven. Ananda continued to use the Sinhala term *arya* in a racial sense: he ascribed the Buddhist meaning of *arya* (which is related not to race but noble conduct) to the Sinhala *jatiya*. Furthermore, that Ven. Ananda was convinced of the (northern) Indo-Aryan origins of the Sinhala was explicit in his angry reaction to a discussion of the close ties between ancient Sri Lanka and (Dravidian) south India in the *ESC* essay by Susantha Goonatilake:

> Supposedly our ancient Sinhala culture and society was based on south Indian culture and society. Supposedly we inherited our irrigation system from south India ....What better distortion of history to support the cause of Eelamists.[44]

These vigorous reaffirmations of their Aryanness fit into the broader context of Sinhala cultural-political preoccupations of this period according to which the ethnic conflict was perceived as a replay of ancient Aryan-versus-Dravidian conflict.[45]

Having angrily dismissed Jayawardena's analysis of the myth of Aryan origins, Ven. Kahawatte Ananda also challenged her exposition of Sihadipa (the idea that Sri Lanka is the island of the Sinhala). In her essay, Jayawardena had claimed that according to Sinhala-Buddhist ideology taking shape at the turn of the century,

> Sri Lanka was the *land of the Sinhalese* and ... non-Sinhalese who resided there were allowed to do so by grace and favour of the Sinhala master 'race' who had prior rights of possession and were the exclusive 'sons of the soil'.[46]

Referring to this passage, Ven. Ananda accused Jayawardena of deliberately making false allegations.

> What is she trying to show the world by imputing to Anagarika Dharmapala things that neither he nor any other reasonable Sinhala ever intended? No one will reject the notion that this country belongs to the Sinhala. It is the Sinhala who have lived in this country since ancient times. At that time the term Sinhala encompassed all who lived in this country. The Sinhala have never let anyone live here subject to their grace and favour and they have treated other [ethnic] groups like their own brothers.[47]

Ven. Ananda's confused remonstrations point to the central problematic of Sinhala identity: it is at once inclusive and exclusive. Sinhala (ethnic) identity is conflated with Sri Lankan (national) identity. On the one hand this is a linguistic problem, for a single term, *jatiya*, continues to denote both ethnic group and nation. However, as the passage quoted above as well as many of the arguments already discussed in this paper testify, this limitation is not a mere linguistic one but also ramifies through Sinhala culture and politics.

Jayawardena had specifically related the concept of Sihadipa to Dharmapala's chauvinism toward ethnic minorities. In particular, she had cited Dharmapala's comment: 'Look at the Administration Report of the General Manager of Railways ... Tamils, Cochins and Hambankarayas are employed in large numbers to the *prejudice of the people of the island* – sons of the soil, who contribute the largest share'.[48] Both Ven. Kahawatte Ananda and a new entrant to the controversy, Minuwangoda D. Liyanage, believed that Dharmapala's sentiments were justified. Liyanage, in particular, characterized the (early twentieth-century) minority leadership as loyal colonial lackeys who would have come under inevitable attack during Dharmapala's anti-colonial campaign: 'The shot intended for the crocodile often strikes the birds who prey on the crocodile's back. That is the fate of those who eat the filth on the back of crocodiles'.[49] The image of parasitic scavenger birds clearly disparages the minorities – very likely, privileged and opportunistic Tamils. It also refers obliquely to the traitorous, foreign-funded social scientists attacked earlier. The 'other' on this occasion are not only despicable, they are also polluted.

The anti-colonial campaign was closely linked to the Buddhist revival. In her essay, Jayawardena had focused on the economic underpinnings and caste dimensions of the revival movement and its operations. She revealed that many leaders of the Buddhist revival belonged to the *goyigama* (cultivator) or *karava* (fisher) castes and had made their money in the arrack rental business, mining, and in coconut, cinnamon and rubber plantations. One of their chief targets was the colonial policy on liquor which was held responsible for the decline of Buddhist values.[50]

Ven. Kahawatte Ananda saw Jayawardena's analysis as a sinister attempt to disparage the Temperance Movement and the Buddhist revival as an arrack renters' campaign. He also accused her of rousing casteism among the Sinhala by pointing to the caste affiliations of the revivalists. Finally, he declared that she exposed her ignorance of the revival movement by belittling the significance of the nationalist dimensions of Dharmapala's work.[51]

While this defence of Dharmapala and the Buddhist revival represents a cultural response to the political crisis between Sinhala and Tamils, its main arguments are not unfamiliar. The Sinhala press – and the *Divayina* in particular – has frequently bemoaned the rapid commercialization and westernization of Sinhala society (produced by the 'Open Economy' policies introduced by the UNP government in 1977) and the concomitant destruction of 'traditional' culture and moral values. In this respect, the situation facing the Sinhala today becomes analogous to the colonial situation which Dharmapala attacked. Furthermore (as in the case of the Sinhala Culture debate) those social scientists who dared to question and criticize existing paradigms of traditional Sinhala-Buddhist culture by applying 'western' modes of inquiry, became the complicit agents of western culture and perpetrators of their own culture's destruction.[52]

Dutugämunu: facing 'Tigers' with new 'Geigers'

While Dharmapala is an important national hero for the Sinhala today, his fame is eclipsed by the popularity of that other controversial figure in this debate, King Dutugämunu. Artists and poets through the ages have retold the saga of Dutugämunu, changing the details to suit the tenor of their own times. Accordingly, in recent years, politicians, monks, and occasionally academics, have contributed their versions of Dutugämunu which reflect modern nationalist politics.[53] In the modern Sinhala consciousness, Dutugämunu symbolizes the epitome of Sinhala-Buddhist nationalism: he had saved his nation (*jatiya*) and religion (*Buddha sasana*) from an invader alien in 'race' as well as religion. And his war against the south Indian king, Elara, is a paradigmatic reaffirmation of Lanka as Dhammadipa and Sihadipa.

Leading up to the July riots, Dutugämunu's heroism and nationalism bore distinctly anti-Tamil overtones.[54] However, since then, and particularly through the latter half of 1984 when Tamil militancy increased, Sinhala politicians began to reinterpret Dutugämunu's relevance for the present. They were particularly anxious to dissociate him from any racist implications and instead emphasized his successful unification of ancient Sri Lanka. It is within this web of shifting interpretations that the *Divayina* exchange on Dutugämunu must be analysed.

Dutugämunu was brought into the discussion by Ven. Kahawatte Ananda. He objected to the treatment of the king in *ESC*, and alleged that Dutugämunu's nationalism had been distorted as racism. The guilty social scientists were then denounced as 'traitors':

> All their intellectual efforts are aimed at attacking the Sinhala.... Although [these social scientists] engage in intellectual perversions for their own enjoyment and to receive foreign funding, they commit traitorous acts against the people of this country.[55]

According to Ven. Ananda, Susantha Goonatilake had committed just such an intellectual perversion in his essay in *ESC*, when he observed that, 'Dutugämunu himself marched in war with a Buddhist relic in his spear, as complete a symbolic act as could occur illustrating the use of religion to defend the state's power at the expense of even a fundamental reversal of the teaching'.[56] Ven. Kahawatte Ananda did not quarrel with this 'fact': after all, it is stated in the Mahavamsa (35:1). Neither did he appear to object (on this occasion) to Goonatilake's argument that the king had exploited Buddhism to buttress state power. Instead, he picked on a seemingly innocuous detail, namely, that the (original) Pali word, *konthaya* was mistranslated as 'spear' and not, properly, as 'mace'.

What was at issue here was not an alleged mistranslation but a dispute between a section of the Sinhala-educated intelligentsia represented by Ven. Kahawatte Ananda and the bilingual but mainly English-speaking intelligentsia of the Social Scientists' Association. According to the former, the latter were unqualified to interpret Sinhala socio-cultural reality by virtue of their English-language fluency and their choice of expression in that language. Furthermore, this was also a quarrel over reclaiming Sinhala identity from a neo-colonial class of (English-writing) intellectuals who – like the Tamil nationalist propagandists – were apparently bent on denigrating the Sinhala. Ultimately, the issue of (mis)translations manifested shame and status concerns: Anglicized intellectuals were accused of building their fame and fortunes on the shame and ruination of the Sinhala. Thus, the

Divayina debates represented a forum where tables could be turned: Sinhala honour could be vindicated and the traitorous culprits publicly shamed.

Linguistic distortions of history were soon linked to more serious, allegedly deliberate, distortions of Sinhala identity. Ven. Ananda referred to another essay in *ESC*, by W.I. Siriweera, which dealt with the historical permutations of the encounter between Dutugämunu and Elara. He rejected Siriweera's critical assessment[57] of some recent chauvinist representations of the myth, with the accusation: 'these social scientists are attacking the majority community and Buddhism with a vigour unmatched even by the Eelamists'.[58]

Ven. Ananda's comments drew support from like-minded defenders of Dutugämunu. For example, Minuwangoda D. Liyanage flung his accusations not only at today's social scientists but also at an older generation of scholars including the late Sinhala historian, G.C. Mendis. According to Liyanage, Mendis had dismissed the Dutugämunu episode – and the Mahavamsa itself – as myth devoid of any historical value. He mused on the irony that it took a foreign scholar, Wilhelm Geiger (the German translator of the Mahavamsa) to teach the Sinhala to appreciate their own history.[59] Like Ven. Ananda, Liyanage too symbolically lumped the 'traitorous' social scientists undermining Sinhala identity with Tamil militants. He lamented sarcastically, 'unfortunately, we no longer have Geigers from foreign lands to tell us about ourselves. Instead of Geigers, today we have Tigers!'.

Or, as another participant in the debate, Vijita Karunaratne, preferred (drawing his analogy directly from the story of Dutugämunu), academics who belittled the hero-king were modern-day Elaras. Karunaratne also made vivid symbolic connections between Dutugämunu's war against Elara and the Sinhala-Tamil confrontations of the 1980s:

> Dutugämunu united the country and destroyed Elara, an invader who ruled just one part of the country. Is this racism? If it is, then won't the anti-terrorist measures taken today also be considered racist? In this case, since it will be racist also to kill Tamils in the possible event of an invasion from Tamil Nadu, must we curl up and remain silent?[60]

In this passage, a hypothetical invasion from Tamil Nadu wears the face of Elara, the Tamil ruler from the second century BC. And in the image of silently curling up is conjured a well-known anecdote from Dutugämunu's childhood. According to the Mahavamsa, when King Kakavannatissa ordered his two sons to promise that they would never fight the Tamils, the young Prince Gamani refused and curled up in bed. To his anxious mother he complained that he could not stretch out as long as there were Tamils to the north and the ocean to the south.[61]

None of the contributors to *ESC* had claimed that Dutugämunu was a racist. Indeed as R.A.L.H. Gunawardana argued, the meaning of Sinhala identity has changed over several centuries and ideas of 'race' and 'ethnicity' as we understand them today are modern fabrications.[62] Siriweera – and others who discussed Dutugämunu – pointed to how the king used Buddhism to legitimize state power and how later interpreters of the Dutugämunu saga imbued it with nationalist and racist innuendos suited to their own times.

In symbolic transformations such as those recounted above, the ethnic polarization of the present is defined in terms of past rivalries, and in that process, the past itself is rearranged in terms of the policies of the present. History/myth is of the past but not in that past; it is rooted and flourishes in the present.

There were other recitations of the Dutugämunu myth in the *Divayina* which did not address the *ESC* essays directly but were obvious ramifications of this controversy. In general, these writers were concerned with locating the myth within the historical context of the Mahavamsa, and rationalizing Dutugämunu's war against Elara as a war of unification, rather than a Sinhala–Tamil conflict. In their effort to exonerate him from any implications of racism, they invariably raised the issue of Dutugämunu's conscience.

Ven. Dediyawela Tilakasiri's article titled, 'Was the author of the Mahavamsa a racist?', was one such intervention. He referred to the Mahavamsa account of Dutugämunu's conscience, which was troubled by the carnage of Tamils in the war against Elara. According to the Mahavamsa, *arahats* had comforted the king, arguing that he was only responsible for taking one-and-a-half (Buddhist) lives – for only 'one' had observed the Five Precepts and the 'half' had sought the Three Refuges. Critical of this numerical sophistry, Ven. Tilakasiri observed,

> The Mahavamsa author has tried to console the King using a weak argument based on the Five Precepts and Three Refuges. It is obvious that his arithmetic is faulty. However, we should not be so foolish as to suggest that, therefore, the Mahavamsa must be consigned to the flames. We should study it in its proper context.[63]

Lionel Sarath was similarly concerned that it was not Dutugämunu but his interpreters who were racist. He asserted that the prominence accorded to Dutugämunu's campaign in the Mahavamsa was motivated by political considerations of his time.[64]

Others not only attempted to exonerate Dutugämunu from racism but also idealized his nationalism. Both Nalin de Silva and Robert Alagiyawanna used King Dutugämunu as a model against whom today's politicians were evaluated and found wanting.[65]

The emphasis on Dutugämunu's alleged racism, his unification of ancient Lanka and his troubled conscience is neither accidental nor pre-determined solely by the 'objective' imperative of history. Certainly, the reproduction of these highlights of the Dutugämunu myth was made possible by their prior existence in Sinhala historical consciousness. However, as Obeyesekere has argued, there is a close link between cultural and political attitudes and myth-making. He demonstrates that the historical development of the motif of the king without a conscience coincided with the prevalence of anti-Tamil attitudes among the Sinhala.[66]

While Obeyesekere's analysis of the recent reinterpretations of Dutugämunu may be accurate for the period up to July 1983, the redefinition of Dutugämunu in the *Divayina* as well as in political speeches from 1984 onward suggests that attempts are well under way to restore the king's troubled conscience. In rehabilitating Dutugämunu, his apologists have created a symbolic equivalence between this national hero and the Sinhala nation. By highlighting the motif of the virtuous king who reunited a politically fractured Lanka, they have rationalized the war against Tamil separatism. Through this mythic discourse, they have rescued the much-maligned moral integrity of Sinhala identity and strenuously revived nationalism. Therefore, the literary act of expunging racist connotations from Dutugämunu resembles symbolically a collective exorcism of the stigma of racism attributed to the Sinhala particularly since – and because of – the July riots.

The dialectics of nationalist discourse

In this chapter I have explored in detail how three newspaper debates focusing on cultural issues refracted the current political antagonisms and anxieties of the Sinhala. In these debates, culture (as it entwines historical, religious and linguistic strands) and politics are dialectically engaged. It is apparent that political convulsions – such as ethnic conflict – do not merely spark cultural controversies; nor do the former only provide the turbulent background for the latter. Rather, politics is *figured* prominently in culture. In turn, these politically textured reaffirmations of culture and history are evoked to bestow legitimacy on preferred political arrangements. It is in this dialectical engagement of culture and politics that nationalism is (re)generated.

The nationalist discourse explored in this paper is a past-oriented one. Since this orientation is situated in and informed by the present, the selection and interpretation of the past is contingent on the present. As was often demonstrated in each of the debates, it was the crisis of Sinhala identity in the 1980s that found such impassioned expression in

Sinhala cultural history. This is not to deny that, to a certain extent, the past (as both myth and history) is independent of present exigencies and yields common features through interpretations ventured over time. Nevertheless, the past can be imagined only through some present, just as each present is also shaped by past presents. In general then, both past and present are mutually constitutive.

On a more specific level, as the *Divayina* debates reveal, the past is what the present is not but was and should be. The recent resurgence of popular interest in the thirteenth-century kingdom of Jaffna, the origins and definitive features of Sinhala culture, the lives and works of national heroes, historical relations between Sinhala and Tamils, and the real relevance of the Mahavamsa, all provide complex models of the past for the present and future.

The preoccupation with the past-as-paradigm tends to be inversely related to an orientation to the present, and by extension, also to the future. The less satisfactory the present the greater the desire to perfect it in the image of a preferred past. Such a paradigmatic orientation to the past is hardly peculiar to the Sinhala, as scholars of other ancient mytho-historical traditions (for example, Judaism) will attest. But be that as it may, the Sinhala predilection for past-ward forms of discourse is firmly grounded in that culture's own historical consciousness.

Within the mytho-historical tradition of the Sinhala chronicles, an ideal Buddhist socio-political order formed the frame of reference for historical interpretation.[67] Thus, epic heroes such as Dutthagamani Abhaya of the Mahavamsa were intended to serve as model kings for the chronicler's royal patron, as well as to inspire future leaders. The assumptions underlying this narrative technique were probably similar to those which informed the didactic temporal structure of the Jataka tales – present to past to present. In these tales, the Buddha links a specific problem in his present to its karmic antecedent. The present is made intelligible, and therefore rendered changeable, through the proper understanding of its preconditions.

The past-ward mode of discourse through which contemporary issues of ethnicity and nationalism were debated in the *Divayina* controversies represents a modern manifestation of this Sinhala historical consciousness. The extent to which such modes of discourse produce inclusive (rather than exclusive) and progressive (in contrast to regressive) forms of nationalism hinges not on evocations of the past *per se*, but on the motivations and manipulations of monks, politicians, scholars, newspaper editors and readers. For it is they who, through widely available and influential media such as newspapers, reinterpret the past to recharge nationalism with varying symbolic significance.

Notes and references

1 Although some Sinhala have begun to distinguish between ethnic (*jana vargika*) and national (*jatika*), for the most part, this remains an academic classification which has yet to enter popular usage.

2 Sinhala rationalizations of the July riots have been examined in E. Nissan, 'Some thoughts on Sinhalese justifications for the violence', J. Spencer, 'Popular perceptions of the violence: a provincial view', in J. Manor (ed.) *Sri Lanka in Change and Crisis*, London, 1984.

3 For example, the Committee for Rational Development (CRD, a multi-ethnic group of concerned young intellectuals) brought out a volume in Sinhala and English titled, *Sri Lanka's Ethnic Conflict: Myths and Reality*, Delhi, 1983.

4 See W.A. Wiswa Warnapala, 'Press and politics in Sri Lanka (Ceylon)', *Journal of Constitutional and Parliamentary Studies*, 1975, vol. 11, pp. 125–155. The only significant work on the Sinhala press is Kalukondiyave Pannasekera's 9-volume *Sinhala Puvat Pat Sangara Itihasaya* [History of the Sinhala Press], Colombo, 1971.

5 M. Singer, *The Emerging Elite*, Cambridge, Ma. 1964, p. 113.

6 B. Anderson, *Imagined Communities*, London, 1983, p. 133.

7 According to a 1985 market survey, the daily *Divayina* readership is estimated at 1,798,000, while the readership of other Sinhala dailies, *Dinamina* (of the state-owned Associated Newspapers Group) and *Davasa* are respectively, 1,696,000 and 1,338,000. In the Sunday newspaper category, the Sunday *Divayina* with a readership of 3,698,000 has overtaken the ANCL's *Silumina* (3,256,000) and the Independent Newspaper Group's *Riviräsa* (2,314,000), private communication, 1986.

8 H. White *Tropics of Discourse*, Baltimore, 1978, p. 4.

9 Tamil nationalist ideology is clearly articulated in the literature of expatriate nationalists; for example, S. Ponnambalam, *Sri Lanka: The National Question and the Tamil Liberation Struggle*, London, 1983. For a critical analysis of Tamil ideology see Radhika Coomaraswamy, 'Nationalism: Sinhala and Tamil myths', *South Asia Bulletin*, 1986, vol. 6.

10 *Dv*., 12/viii/84.

11 Other recent reinterpretations of the Mahavamsa in the press include a debate in English on the 'Mahavamsa mentality', *Daily News*, 24/v/85, 10/vi/85 and 5/vii/85, and a popular history serial appearing in the *Dv*., titled 'Sinhalavamsaya' (The Chronicle of the Sinhala), which dramatized stories from the Mahavamsa.

12 *Dv*., 19/viii/84.

13 *Dv*., 2/ix/84.

14 Perera in *Dv*., 26/viii/84, Obeysekera in *Dv*., 2/ix/84. A former Minister, Cyril Mathew, attracted considerable publicity to ancient Buddhist ruins in the north and east (as evidence of the prior existence of Sinhala settlements) and launched archaeological projects to protect these ruins from alleged Tamil vandalism. See his *Sinhaluni! Budu Sasuna Beraganiw* [Sinhalese! Save the Buddhist Religion], Colombo, 1981.

15 Ivan in *Dv*., 9/xi/84, Kodituwakku in *Dv*., 16/ix/84.
16 *Dv*., 7/x/84.
17 *Dv*., 2/ix/84.
18 *Dv*.,2/ix/84.
19 *Dv*., 9/ix/84.
20 *Dv*., 14/x/84.
21 *Dv*., 23/ix/84.
22 See Obeyesekere's critical application of this terminology in 'The great tradition and the little in the perspective of Sinhalese Buddhism', *JAS*, 1963, vol. 22, pp. 139–153.
23 *Dv*., 21/x/84. Each of Gunasinghe's three criteria can be contested without specific reference to Sinhala culture. However, it was not his criteria but their implications for Sinhala culture which were at issue.
24 Obeyesekere, 'The great tradition'.
25 *Dv*., 28/x/84.
26 *Dv*., 23/ix/84.
27 *Dv*., 30/ix/84.
28 *Dv*., 30/ix/84.
29 *Dv*., 11/ix/84. This translation appears rather convoluted owing to the fact that I attempted to capture the tortuous but vivid prose of the original.
30 *Dv*., 11/ix/84.
31 *Dv*., 28/x/84.
32 Such rejections of western-derived social-scientific analyses are part of the ongoing nationalist reaction against colonial and neo-colonial traditions of academic inquiry and the politics of knowledge. The most recent contribution to this debate is Goonatilake's controversial critique of the 'ethnic studies industry'. But while western colonial and neo-colonial impositions of authoritative meaning – what Edward Said forcefully described as 'orientalism' – are overthrown, 'authentic' nationalist interpretations are installed in their place. Unself-critical in their turn, the nationalists stereotype 'the west' as 'other' and ignore the origins and historicity of their own nationalist premisses. See S. Goonatilake, 'The ethnic studies industry', *Lanka Guardian* 1987, vol. 10, nos. 12 and 13; E. Said, *Orientalism*, New York, 1978.
33 *Dv*., 4/ix/84.
34 *Dv*., 4/ix/84.
35 *Dv*., 11/ix/84.
36 *Dv*., 30/ix/84.
37 M. Weber, 'Science as a vocation', in H.H. Gerth and C. Wright Mills (eds) *From Max Weber*, New York, 1958, p.145.
38 'Introduction', in *ESC*.
39 K. Jayawardena, 'Some aspects of class and ethnic consciousness in the late 19th and early 20th centuries', in *ESC*, p. 87
40 Ibid., p. 89.
41 Obeyesekere had published two essays in which he discussed Dharmapala. However, both were available only in English, perhaps one of the reasons why the Sinhala-educated intelligentsia had ignored them. G. Obeyesekere, 'Personal identity and cultural crisis: the case of

Anagarika Dharmapala of Sri Lanka', in F.E. Reynolds and D. Capps (eds) *The Biographical Process*, Paris, 1976; *idem* 'The vicissitudes of the Sinhala-Buddhist identity through time and change', in M. Roberts (ed.) *Collective Identities, Nationalisms and Protest in Modern Sri Lanka*, Colombo, 1979.

42 In the opinion of some SSA members, Kahawatte Ananda was a pseudonym used by a controversial (lay) Sinhala sociologist.

43 Jayawardena, 'Some aspects', p.88; *Dv*., 6/i/85/.

44 *Dv*., 4/xi/84.

45 Aryan and Dravidian racial stereotypes continue to be articulated throughout Sinhala society. In late 1983, a Sinhala politician affirmed that all Aryans (in this case, north Indians and the Sinhala) are physically similar by declaring that the late Prime Minister Indira Ghandi and President J.R. Jayawardena shared similar noses (*Daily News*, 8/x/83). Newspaper articles have linked the Sinhala with (Aryan) north Indians, who are defined as allies, in contrast to the (Dravidian) south Indians and Sri Lankan Tamils – the 'other' – who are portrayed as past and present enemies. See for example, Ven. Kotuguda Dhammawansa's two-part article (in English), 'Who are the Sinhalese?', *The Sunday Observer*, 10 and 17/ii/85, and H.F. Charles' analyses (in Sinhala) of cordial and hostile relations through history between the Sinhala and north and south Indians, respectively, *Dv*., 24/vii/85.

46 Jayawardena, 'Some aspects', p. 89.

47 *Dv*., 4/xi/84.

48 Jayawardena, 'Some aspects', p. 89.

49 *Dv*., 23/xii/84.

50 Jayawardena, 'Some aspects', pp. 83–5.

51 *Dv*., 4/xi/84.

52 In a later echo of the Sinhala Culture debate, both the polluting and western qualities of this brand of social science were combined in a derisive comparison of the 'foreign concept virus' to the disease, AIDS (de Silva in *Dv*., 6/x/85).

53 In 1978, the state attempted to institute a 'Dutugämunu cult' by officially recognizing what were popularly believed to be Dutugämunu's ashes. This symbolic appropriation of Dutugämunu by the state to legitimize its dedication to Sinhala-Buddhist nationalism did not go undisputed. In 1981, a Tamil scholar, James T. Rutnam, questioned the identity of the ashes claiming that they were not likely to be Dutugämunu's but his rival Elara's. A brief dispute over the archaeological record appeared in *The Island* in 1984, following the publication of Rutnam's investigations. Nevertheless, this dispute failed to provoke a row comparable to that which ensued later in the Sinhala press (*The Island*, 6 and 13/v/84; 10/vi/84 and 17/vi/84); see also Obeyesekere's comments in G. Obeyesekere, 'The conscience of King Dutthagamini Abhaya: or, the anthropologist as myth-maker', ms.

54 Ibid., W.I. Siriweera, 'The Dutthagamini–Elara episode: a reassessment', in *ESC*, pp. 54–73.

55 *Dv*., 4/xi/84.

56 S. Goonatilake, 'The formation of Sri Lankan culture: reinterpretations of chronicle and archaeological material', in *ESC*, p. xiv; also *Dv*., 25/xi/84.
57 Siriweera, 'The Dutthagamini–Elara episode'. As in the case of Dharmapala, earlier commentaries on the Dutugämunu myth had been published only in English and at a time when Sinhala identity was not as problematic, and perhaps for these reasons they remained uncontroversial. See, e.g. A. Greenwald, 'The relic on the spear: historiography and the saga of Dutthagamini', in B.L. Smith (ed.) *Religion and the Legitimation of Power in Sri Lanka*, Chambersburg, 1978.
58 *Dv*., 25/ix/84.
59 *Dv*., 16/xii/84.
60 *Dv*., 6/i/85.
61 *Mv*., 22: 76–86.
62 See Gunawardana, this volume.
63 *Dv*., 19/xii/84.
64 *Dv*., 30/xii/84.
65 *Dv*., 6/i/85; 13/ii/85.
66 Obeyesekere, 'The conscience'.
67 B.L. Smith, 'The ideal social order as portrayed in the chronicles of Ceylon'; R.T. Clifford, 'The *dhammadipa* tradition of Sri Lanka: three models within the Sinhalese chronicles'; both in Smith, *Religion and Legitimation*.

Chapter eleven

Afterword: scared places, violent spaces

E. Valentine Daniel

The authors of the chapters in this volume have not concerned themselves so much with the causes of the ethnic disturbances that have ravaged the island of Sri Lanka as with the conditions of their possibility. The one such condition that each of the chapters deals with is the subject of history, myth and mytho-history. In keeping with this theme and as a tribute to these chapters, I would like to examine the essential discursive practices that inform the mythic on the one hand and the historic on the other. I propose that that which fundamentally distinguishes the mythic from history is the following: the former provides a people with a way of *being in the world* and the latter a way of *seeing the world*. The first is an embodied discursive practice that is fundamentally ontic,[1] the second a theoretical discourse that is fundamentally epistemic. To be sure, neither history nor the mythic exhaust the epistemic and ontic realities but they constitute an important part of these respective realities. The principle argument of this chapter takes the form of an informed hypothesis, namely, that one of the structural conditions for collective violence is to be found in the discordance that obtains between epistemic and ontic discursive practices. This, I believe, is shown in all the chapters of this volume. Such discordance is not assured merely by the existence of a history that is antithetical to a people's mythic reality, but is to be found in those moments and contexts in which such a history comes face to face with, and demands to be incorporated into, that ontic reality. In this closing chapter, by means of an examination of the dynamic interplay between historic and mythic discursive practices in the context of six places of pilgrimage in Sri Lanka, I hope to submit evidence that makes such a hypothesis reasonable. Let us first take a closer look at history and myth, and the discursive practices within which they are embodied.

History/theory and myth

In order to appreciate my interpretation of what the mythic is, it is necessary for the reader to hold in abeyance some of the more familiar understandings of this human creation; and especially the one that aligns history and myth with that prejudicial pair known as 'true' and 'false'. An element of the mythic is inherent in all our intellectual activities, not only in what is commonly called myth. My use thus far, of the adjectival form, 'mythic' over the nominal form, 'myth', was intentional, meant to prevent the reduction of the mythic to myth. In fact, stories that we ordinarily identify as myths by virtue of their necessary (though not sufficient) narrative structure, are not the best embodiments of the mythic available to us. That honour goes to ritual, and that too, to rituals that are not readily available for reflective scrutiny. Now that I am done with cautioning the reader against any easy collapse of the mythic into the customary 'myth', I shall henceforth use 'myth' only in the sense of the 'mythic' enunciated above.

There is much that is common between myth and history, the most salient of which is that neither is factual but both are factitious. That is, their concern is fundamentally not with what can be discovered in reality but with how one comes to terms with reality. In this respect the craft of an excellent (perhaps even the most perspicuous) contemporary historian of Sri Lanka, such as R. A. L. H. Gunawardana, or the 'authors' of Mark Whitaker's seven histories, or the Mahavamsa's Mahanama, or even J. R. Jayewardene's claim to be the 193rd head of state of Sri Lanka are not different from one another.

But there are differences, important ones.[2] The assertions of history are logically future-oriented even though they may be about the past. The structure of these assertions, more explicit in the natural sciences, is implicitly present in the human sciences as well, including history. These assertions relate to actualities as potentialities; assertions that take the form of subjunctives, dispositionals and contrary-to-fact conditionals; that is, with what would be the case were certain conditions to be actualized. History, like all theoretical discourses, is in principle verificationistic. The assertions of myth, by contrast, insist that past actualities be cotemporaneous; that what is now is what went on then and what was then is what is going on now. It is this collapse of time, where past becomes present enactment, that characterizes myth. In a mythic world, the very same conditions that made past events possible still obtain.

A second feature that distinguishes history from myth is the 'aboutness' of the former and the 'participatoriness' of the latter. In any theoretical discourse, history included, its 'aboutness' is basic. Theory, true to its etymological link to the Greek root *thea* (to see), provides us with a way of *seeing* the world. In myth we find a way of *being* in the world, where participation is fundamental. The Malinowskian notion of 'myth as charter' fails to capture this important feature of myth's essence.[3] In the sense being developed here, a charter myth is less myth and more history to the extent that it provides one with a way of *seeing* the world. To repeat, history (including charter myths) is theoretical and therefore, predominantly epistemic, whereas myth is essentially ontic.

There is a third difference, one that can only be stated in the fashion of a parenthetical prolegomena. History is a theoretical discourse that is, in the main, simplex; held together by chronology and a logic of cause and effect. Furthermore, this kind of history, seen in its fullest bloom in the nineteenth century, – call it Hegelian, Rankeian, Micheletian or Marxian, (and think how exceptional Foucault is!) – is endogenous to European culture and civilization in a manner and to an extent that it is not to south Asia, especially to Hindu south Asia. I have argued elsewhere that Hindu India confounds the craft of the event-and-chronology-oriented historiographer by the manner in which it 'records' (if that be the word) events.[4] More than one European historian, mostly in keeping with the nineteenth century's understanding of history, has expressed his frustration with the 'Indian historical record' when attempting to write 'The History of India'. Perhaps, as Bernard Cohn suggests, the Europeans' attempts at writing *the* history of India rather than say, the *histories* of India, may have been the real problem.[5] But, according to the then dominant (and still alive) understanding of what 'history' is all about, anything but a simplex history would not have been history. Rather, it would qualify as a mélange of fact and fancy, a collection of contradictory legends; which indeed has been the dominant view of European historians of the Indian historical record. Be that as it may, it still merits noting that in this regard, as John Rogers has so finely demonstrated in this volume, thanks to the Mahavamsa, the Sri Lankan past proudly lends itself with an élan worthy of the European historiographer's tastes, and superior to anything Hindu India had to offer. For this reason it is easier to write 'The History of Sri Lanka' than 'The History of India'.

By homologous extension, it is much easier to write 'The History of the Sinhala' than it is to write 'The History of the Tamils', given the Tamils' cultural identification with Hindu south India rather than with Buddhist Sri Lanka. The Tamils do not have a simplex document and no great uncontested event comparable to the birth of Gautama Buddha. Their history, if the term be allowed, is multiple (as both Hellmann-Rajanayagam and Whitaker, more indirectly, have shown) and multiplex. It is only recently, and that too mainly in social history, that European historiography assimilated multiplexity into its craft. On the Indian scene we see similar acknowledgement and accommodation of the multiplex in records of the past in a recent paper by Romila Thapar and in a book by Nicholas Dirks.[6] In the greater tradition of historiography, in both the west and in south Asia, it is the simplex narrative that remains normative. In India, as Romila Thapar has shown us, in the history's very thinning out of the multiplex in the record of the past, in the reduction of its manifold forms to a single strand, communal violence finds its *raison d'être*.

If myth as a way of being in the world is multiplex, then on structural grounds alone, the likelihood of its striking up a discordant relationship with a 'single-minded' simplex history is greater than that of its generating similar discordance with a multiplex history. Multiplex histories are more easily accommodated within the multiplexity of lived experience. A simplex history is more likely to assert with impetuosity its independence. This is not to deny the violence that has emerged among the Tamils of Sri Lanka. Rather, it is to argue that the conditions that generate violence by and among Tamils ought to be sought elsewhere, not in Tamils' views of their past; at least not yet. A cruder way of (over)stating the same point is that no Tamil is likely to die or kill for history. But Sinhala do die and do kill because of and for their history, and especially when such a history contradicts the lived experience of myth.

Participation in myth is a matter of degree. A full participant in a myth is a participant in its ritual enactment as well. A ritual can range from being a simple performative utterance to a complex set of actions. Let us take President J. R. Jayewardene's claim to President Reagan, cited by Kemper, that he was Sri Lanka's 193rd head of state. When seen in the context of the general tenor of the pronouncements made between his election in 1977 and the beginning of the serious disenchantment that led to his retirement in 1988, this claim would qualify as 'mythic'. As one source who was close to President Jayewardene during these years put it to me in an interview in 1987, 'The President believes this [that he was the 193rd "king" of Sri Lanka] to be true in his very bones.' This is not to say that these bones did not rattle at times, and with increasing frequency towards the later years of his presidency. Some of this could be seen in the almost schizoid pronouncements he made when under stress. Within a span of a few days one finds him claiming that he was Asoka, the Prince of Peace, and also that he could, if he wished (and implying that he might choose to), wipe out the Tamils within a few minutes if he only so decided. On another occasion, while claiming to be a vessel of Buddha's compassion, he urged his supporters among the Tea Estate Tamils to use whatever work-instruments were at their disposal as weapons against any outsider who tried to enter the plantations to create trouble. The switch between 'India my first love' (being the land of the Buddha) and

'India our arch enemy' is yet another instance of myth under stress. On the complex side, the many elaborate 'rituals of development' described to us by Serena Tennekoon were, for at least some of the ministers intimately involved in them, more than mere strategies or ploys to dupe the masses.[7] A close study of the speeches of Gamini Dissanayake when he was the Minister of Lands and Land Development and Minister of Mahaväli Development will show that he deeply believed that he was engaged in the restoration of Sri Lanka to the glorious days of Parakramabahu the Great. These rituals are mythic in our sense, where, to use Evans-Pritchard's felicitous expression, 'ideas are imprisoned in action'; or in Peirce's pragmaticist phrase, 'mind [becomes] hidebound with habit'.[8]

In 1984 I interviewed two young brothers who had participated in the riots against the Tamils. They had been displaced from the town of Kotmale by the new hydroelectric dam and resettled in the Dry Zone where they were supposed to reap the benefits of the diverted Mahaväli river. They were resettled at the tail end of an irrigation canal beyond the reach of the sweet waters of the Mahaväli, depriving them of the promised green revolution of yesteryear. The excuse given to them by the minister's minions was that, even as the Tamil Colas had frustrated and destroyed the flourishing glory of the Sinhala people's hydro-agricultural past, the Tamil Tigers of today were frustrating and destroying the hydro-agricultural projects of the present and future. They were told that monies that had been set aside for building dams, sluices and dikes had to be diverted to finance the Sri Lankan army's war in the north. The emphasis here was not so much on an unbroken history but on the past become present and a present become past.

One may participate in a ritual without participating in the myth that informs it. That is when a ritual becomes a *mere* ritual. Such non-participation is often a matter of degree. The residents of Kukulewa studied by Brow appear to be further removed from participation than are the residents of Suduwatura Ara, as written about by Woost. The latter are beginning to be caught in 'a hegemonic vortex', even if that vortex is in a state of 'unstable equilibrium' or 'teeth-gritting harmony'. (The jarring metaphors are apt, given the state of discordance in Sri Lanka.) However, a narrative, even an imported one, that begins as theory, providing us with a way of seeing the world, can in time become embodied in practice, as when nineteenth-century European scientific racism (outlined for us by Rogers and Gunawardana), instantiated itself in 1983, with Sinhala 'Aryans' killing Tamil 'non-Aryans'. This is an instance of epistemic theory becoming ontic myth. Spencer is correct when he argues against the view that ideas about identity are primordial givens. Indeed, they are, in Spencer's words, 'painstakingly constructed, asserted, and argued about within specific historical and social conditions'.[9] To this extent they remain epistemic realities. But when thought sinks below the threshold of reflection, and ideas rise above the possibility of argument, then narrative history, as well as myth as narrative, become onticized bringing them in line with their mythic essence.

Before turning to look at the interplay between history and myth in the six places of pilgrimage I mentioned earlier, a few words on the nature of my own fieldwork upon which part of this essay is based deserve to be said.

A note on the field research

In late 1983 and again in early 1984, when it wasn't clear whether the biggest storm of violence was behind or before us, and at a time when the state and private machines of ideological-overproduction were operating at full and anxious throttle, I visited Anuradhapura, Polonnaruwa, Sigiriya, and Adam's Peak. All these places, still vaguely sacred for me, I had visited many times before, mostly in my youth. Two other places, or rather place-events, that I shall write about in this chapter that I did not visit in 1983–84 but am acquainted with from previous visits are the Kandy Asala Perahara and Kataragama.

Given the unusual state of affairs in Sri Lanka during 1983–84, my fieldwork was not harnessed to the planned, systematic, long-term, informant-centered, statistical sample-sensitive (even if not sample-bound), stay-put-in-one-place methodology that is the characterizing privilege of most conventional anthropological research. In my previous anthropological field research stints, information or 'data' (for those who prefer) came in controlled trickles towards the basically sedentary anthropologist. In 1983–84, even though I was (I had to be) constantly on the move, I was deluged with information on the ethnic conflict. The peripatetic genre of pilgrimage around which this chapter is built is metonymic in several respects to my entire fieldwork during this period. In my travels to and through the island's historic cities and scared places, my informants were many, all on the move – fellow pilgrims, tourists, tourist-guides, hoteliers, tour bus and tourist car drivers – mostly strangers. I, the anthropologist, was also a fellow pilgrim-tourist, at times a voyeur, an eavesdropper, and an interloper.

The ontic and epistemic in sacred places

In my study of a south Indian village I attempted to bring to light the sense concealed in the Tamil term, *ur*.[10] There I argued that unlike the referential equivalent, *kiramam*, *ur* is a place with which a people have a deep, even if diffuse, affinity. It is a place to which one 'belongs', in the full, affective sense of the term. An *ur* is defined through its centre.

I went on to argue further that the affinity that holds a people and their *ur* is a sense of shared substance. In the terminology of the current paper, I might have added that an *ur* and its people were bound together by ontic forces. *Kiramam*, by contrast, was a space, defined and demarcated by a boundary, and primarily served outsiders' interests, principally that of the revenue officer and other agents of the law. It was an epistemic space that provided the outsider with a way of seeing a part of the world, rather than an ontic place in which a people sought and found a whole way of being in the world. I am obliged to direct the reader's attention in more than passing to the difference between the pre-modern south Asian state and the modern nation state; the one is centrifocal and the other boundary-directed. In this chapter, when I use the term 'place' in juxtaposition with space, I do so to connote much the same as does the term *ur* in Tamil Nadu. A 'space', by contrast is an epistemic unit, marked by primarily non-ontic sentiments, be they of the revenue officer, the archaeologist, museologist, or historian.

Polonnaruwa, where once a medieval kingdom stood, was a locale that until recently, for all except most of its long-term residents, occupied the epistemic end in our proposed scheme. The story of Polonnaruwa was thoroughly historicized and epistemicized in Sinhala consciousness at large, made into an object of knowledge, available to be inquired into. It was a museum town which provided the Sinhala people with a story about the past. For the residents of Polonnaruwa, the town was a place that was constituted of sentiments and experiences other than those which were beginning to constitute the 'imagined community'[11] of growing Sinhala nationalism which reached the violent pitch of 1983. The residents of Polonnaruwa lived in its ontic centre; the tourists and pilgrims, from within and from without Sri Lanka, came to look at it. With the arrival of the Mahaväli waters to its environs, along with the attendant nationalistic rhetoric and settlers, Polonnaruwa has felt a certain rumble in its ontic core. A keeper of the Polonnaruwa Rest House whom I first interviewed in 1974 and then ten years later, revealed himself as one who had changed, from being a citizen of the city who did not give any more attention to its medieval monuments beyond their potential for supporting his livelihood, to one who claimed to be able to trace his ancestry to the courtiers of King Parakramabahu the Great. By and large, however, Polonnaruwa still (as of 1984) remained a space in the epistemic landscape of Sinhala awareness.

The same holds true for Sigiriya, the famous kingdom of refuge upon a rock, where there once lived a king who had passion enough to kill his father for a kingdom and then some to paint frescoes of his many ladies, all beautiful, all bare-breasted, and all carp-eyed. Contemporary Sri Lankans' reactions to these bare-breasted ladies are varied. Some, with Victorian sensibilities, titter with embarrassment behind cupped hands.

Some condemn with puritanical self-righteousness the decadence they represent.[12] But the English-speaking tourist guide I followed, called upon the guided to admire 'the lines of face, the sharp angles, and the sharp noses'. His often repeated refrain was, 'Look at the lines of face and the shades of colour.' To the frescoes of the 'dark ladies' (pointed out to us by R. A. L. H. Gunawardana in his essay in this volume) he did not draw our attention. He focused on the fair ones instead, remarking to his group how well the colours had been preserved, retaining their semblance to the skin colour of the ancient Sinhala people. This guide, in his mid-forties, an art historian by training, was an erudite Sinhala gentleman. Initially willing to let me cite his name in print, he has, since seeing an earlier draft of this chapter, opted for an anonymous code (which in my system turns out to be SP1-(2)84).

Polonnaruwa and Sigiriya, like many other places and objects in India and Sri Lanka, became victim to 'the major interpretive strategy by which south Asia was to become known to Europeans in the seventeenth, eighteenth and nineteenth centuries', namely, through a construction of the 'histories' of India (and Ceylon).[13] The interpretive interests of Europe varied over these centuries, but they established an enduring structural relationship between south Asia and the west. 'Europe was progressive and changing, India and Ceylon were static. Here could be found a kind of living fossil bed for the European past, a museum on which for the next hundred years (in the case of India) to impose Europe's own vision of history'.[14] Polonnaruwa and Sigiriya, like Anuradhapura, are nineteenth-century phenomena, subjects of 'discovery', first by British troops, then by British colonial officers and amateur archaeologists. Fortresses, palaces, bathing pools, gardens, stupas and temples, all of which had been rendered secure but irrelevant to the local inhabitants by the overgrowth of forests and time, were found, unearthed, and 'rescued from the jungle's snarl ... surveyed, mapped and prepared for labelling' (SP1-(2)84).

The historicization of place by transformation into space is accompanied by the historicization of a people by transforming them into a race. The sketch given us by Professor Gunawardana on the 'Aryanization' of the Sinhala people in the eighteenth and nineteenth centuries in the context of the spread of scientific racism to the colonies can scarce be bettered. And what is more, as Bernard Cohn has written, early British codifications of Indian languages in dictionaries and grammars 'began the establishment of discursive formation, defined an epistemological space, created a discourse (Orientalism), and had the effect of converting Indian forms of knowledge into European objects'.[15]

Anthropometry is alive and well in south Asia. How lasting the contributions of those pioneering physical anthropologists cited by Gunawardana are, is attested to by the fact that there exists to this day, an official museum monograph, published as late as the 1970s, titled *The Physical Anthropology of Ceylon*, which repeats the same anthropometric nonsense on race that served nineteenth-century European interests so well. It was this epistemicized history that was picked up by Sinhala nationalism in the first half of this century, and Sinhala chauvinism more recently, with which to bludgeon 'the decadence of the West', and the 'alien Tamils from the North', respectively. The little episode in Parliament cited by Serena Tennekoon about Jayewardene's Aryan nose and Amirthalingam's non-Aryan nose was followed by a flurry of letters to the newspapers. Most of these defended the 'Sinhala is an Aryan' theory, and many were from citizens well-read in the nineteenth-century anthropometric wisdom of the Sarasins, Virchow and others.

There are some ironies to the Sri Lankan appropriation of 'the lines of face and shades of colour', ironies that would have been charming if they had not turned out to be so deadly. In 1983, many a chocolate-coloured Sinhala apprehended a chocolate-coloured fellow-Sinhala, and, denying the victim's claim to his 'race' on the grounds that his skin was not of the shade that a Sinhala skin ought to be (like the Sigiri frescoes?) nor his face-shape that of an Aryan's (Mr Jayewardene's? Mrs Gandhi's?), beat him up and, in one instance known to me, even killed him for being a 'Tamil trying to pass as Sinhala'. By the same logic, several Tamils known to me escaped being killed, even when their pronunciation of Sinhala had all the giveaways of misplaced retroflexes and unaspirated h's, those distinguishing marks of Dravidian speech. They were excused as understandable speech impediments. Some of these stories constitute the growing collection of 'Jokes of the July Riots', told by Tamils. In the following example, a Sinhala rioter, holding up a handkerchief (*lensuva* in Sinhala) subjects a fair-skinned Tamil to a linguistic test:

Rioter: *Meka mokada*?
(What is this?)
Tamil: (stammering in fright) *Le-le-le-le ... Lenji*
(The Tamil counterpart of *lensuva*)
Rioter: *Tamuse mona jati da*?
(What race are you?)
Tamil: *Lal-Lal-Lal-Lal ... Lanji.*
(The Tamilization of the Sinhala word for 'Burgher', *Lansi*)
Rioter: *Nama mokada*?
(What is your name?)
Tamil: Jan-Jan-Jan ... Janji.
(Janz, a Burgher name; in fact the name of the then Commissioner of Prisons)

The victim is allowed to escape unharmed into an epistemic landscape because he is fair, and because the bully had either not noticed the non-Sinhala accent at all or had excused it as an understandable speech impediment becoming of one in fright, of whom he has by now known many, or of a Burgher, a category of persons he scarcely knows.

If Polonnaruwa, the museum town, and Sigiriya, the museum fortress, occupy the epistemic extreme in our typology of orientations towards the past, Kataragama with its ecstatic cult of Murugan or Skanda, has until recently, occupied the ontological extreme. So has the arduous southern approach to Adam's Peak (Sri Pada), in a more purely Buddhistic vein. Kataragama and Sri Pada are meaningless without participation. To merely observe is to be alienated at best and vulgar at worst. The eye alone is not enough, nor even the ears. The body must be involved in the climb, in the dance, in the singing, in the fire-walking, in the trance, in the believing. The myths that energize these places are not stories about their pasts but rather they are ritual enactments of their pasts. They provide 'structured contexts in which a people orders its moral life and against which it measures the worth of its endeavours'.[16]

The governing myths of Kataragama and Sri Pada implicate believers into conforming to the actualities practised in the rituals of these places. Whereas the theoretical constructs of history are predominantly referential, providing one with a way of seeing the past in epistemic discourses, mythic constructs are overwhelmingly performative and must be entered into for meaningfulness in ontic experience. The possible objection that theoretical constructs are also, after all, construable as performatives would miss the point of the distinction. Such constructs serve as instruments that inquirers (academic or otherwise) *use*, rather than modes of being into which they *enter*. Such theoretical constructs perform the normative functions of setting limits to ways of observing and suggesting what to look for. They do not provide us with ways of living. For the believer, by contrast, this is what Kataragama does.

Kandy and its annual Asala Perahara, the grandest procession of the land, is a curious blend of the two poles, with the epistemic dimension concealing an active ontic one. Here, one finds the re-enactment of a once-structured social order with all its attendant obligations of services, prestations and honours, bejewelled elephants, Kandyan dancers, drummers, aristocrats in full regalia, and the casket of the Tooth Relic. H. L. Seneviratne has argued persuasively for the persistent vitality of the Asala Perahara and the Temple of the Tooth as political symbols.[17] And it is indeed true that the Kandy ritual complex has provided legitimation to every Sinhala party and politician since Independence (including the Troskyites) who, on being elected to office, visit the temple to receive the blessings of the Triple Gem. To this extent we may concede that many of its discursive constructs are performative rather than predictive or referential (the two distinguishing features of theory). However, these performatives serve as instruments that politicians have used, rather than as modes of being into which they enter. It makes one recall Nietzsche's priestly class which can manipulate the herd only because they themselves do not participate in the drama that makes manipulation possible. As for the 'herd', there have not been many in Kandy. In fact, at least as far as the use of the Temple of the Tooth by politicians is concerned, the Sri Lankan populace in general has retained a healthy cynicism. If only the politicians could enter into the ritual complex as if it were a mode of being, and if they could be assured that the populace would follow them into it – as in the times of the Kandyan kings – then their conversion of epistemic symbol and pragmatic index into ontic icon[18] would be complete. However, there are ontic forces operating in Kandy and at the Temple of the Tooth. Indeed the Tooth Relic lies at the centre of such centripetalizing ontic forces, yielding myths that require one's participation in their understanding. It is no accident that the months closest to the Asala Perahara are the ones in which riots of all kinds, and ethnic riots in particular, have occurred. However, Kandy as a whole remains a spectacle, providing ways of observing the past (in addition to holding out the possibility of using it), yielding theories that are interpretations of 'objective' events of the past. It is this 'aboutness' of the theoretically coming to terms with the past that has been absent (until recently) in Kataragama and Sri Pada.

The Asala Perahara processes through designated streets. That much is not new. It happened this way even in the days of the kings. But, of course, the British made it more efficient. The ways in which 'crowds' (not believers or citizens) are 'controlled' is new. The language ('crowd control') is that of a new disciplinary order, a new disciplinary space. The 'spectators' are cordoned off on to the sidewalks, the streets are kept free for the 'performers.' Grandstands are provided for those who can afford them, mainly the tourists and the wealthy. Policemen stand at strategic points to keep the crowds disciplined. Participant and spectator are separated from each other; the one performs, the other beholds. Unlike similar ritual processions found all over India, the spectators cannot and do not join in and become part of the procession (except at the tail-end, almost as an afterthought). That would make them believers or citizens, and not spectators. In Peradeniya I was privy to a discussion about such processions in India – in Puri, in Madurai and in Tiruvandrum – among a group of middle-class Sri Lankans. These Sri Lankans found the contrast between the Kandy Perahara and its Indian counterparts (if indeed they were comparable at all) quite striking. They were proud of the discipline of their compatriots which stood in stark contrast to the indiscipline of the Hindu masses of India. Occasional stampedes have occurred in Kandy, but only when a mad elephant decided to break ranks with its hundred-plus fellow elephants.

The theatrical aspect of Kandy is enhanced by two modern phenomena. The more powerful of the two is the demands of tourism and the cultivated expectations of tourists. The show goes on in August, each year, every year. The second factor is the presence of a museum – an annex of the king's palace and the Temple of the Tooth – where objects of a now-extinct royality lie in labelled glass cases. Theory and theatre have epistemicized the past. Thus, despite the presence of the most sacred of relics in this town and the many devoted worshippers who do visit the temple during the Perahara, there is a characteristic tension in Kandy that makes this city neither Polonnaruwa nor Kataragama; a tension between the contemporaneity of ontic forces and the quaint and distancing picture painted by epistemology. The participation in the myth of Kataragama and Sri Pada is not merely a participation in the performance of their rituals, but entails the myth being somehow enacted for the pilgrim beyond the rituals. It is otherwise in Kandy. There, when the Perahara ends, the play comes to an end.

Enter Anuradhapura. The sacred bo-tree, Sri Maha Bodhi (believed to be a cutting from the tree at Buddh Gaya in India under which Gotama attained enlightenment), like the Tooth Relic of Kandy, generates sacred ontic forces that pull the pilgrim towards the conforming-participating centre, away from the validating-observing periphery. Until recently, however, the rest of Anuradhapura remained an epistemicized landscape even as its nineteenth-century 'discoverers' intended it to be. It had been the victim of the archaeologists' and historians' 'gaze' (to borrow a Foucauldian concept), a landscape that yielded theories to provide us with a way of seeing the world, a past world. If we were once again to take note of the shared etymology of theory and theatre and extend the play analogy to implicate historical and archaeological theorizing, we would find that the observer, however actively he or she may feel a part of the drama, must remain offstage.

Things have begun to change. In 1983 and 1984 I visited the cities of ancient Sri Lanka as tourist, pilgrim and anthropologist. In Anuradhapura I found a new phenomenon in the person of a Sinhala-speaking tour guide. On the face of it he may appear to be a mere extension of the English-, German-, French-, or Italian-speaking tour guide. The guide whom I followed was bilingual and had learned his craft from English-speaking tour guides and English-speaking tourists whom he had nonchalantly or otherwise followed in their meanderings.[19] Western tourists, after having read synoptic accounts of the ethnic conflict in their newspapers at home or in their tour books in flight, and who, using these reports, have already assumed that the conflict is based on religion or race, presume to ask 'informed' questions.[20] Some of them try to find out intelligently what it is in these two religions or races that is capable of inflaming so much animosity. The guide tries to answer, but only after having already bought into the premise of the question. Our Sinhala tour guide has learned these answers with a vengeance. His goal is to become as good a tour guide as his English-, French-, German-, or Italian-speaking counterpart. But in fact he becomes much more.

In Anuradhapura, our Sinhala-speaking tour guide's focus is not limited to the Sri Maha Bodhi. In fact the Sinhala-Buddhist tourist-pilgrims do not need a tour guide to understand the Sri Maha Bodhi. He becomes irrelevant in its presence. The faithful are drawn into devotion and held in awe by its power and centrality. As the pilgrims leave its presence, the tour guide takes over, pointing out its age and the fact that, for all the steel props that hold it up, its days are numbered. There is a palpable sadness among the believers and they resent the intrusion of time, of history. Indeed the seed of resentment against all intruders is sown. But not much else is said about this sacred place. Instead, our indigenous tour guide spends most of his time pointing out other ruins of a glorious past, a Buddhist past, with awesomely elegant stupas which are now in various states of decay and restoration; restorations that have been funded by western-based international organizations, thereby making the past glory into an internationally recognized one. He names and describes each one of the *dagaba*s: Thuparama, Ruvanveli-saya, Mirisavati, Abhayagiri, and the largest one of them all, Jetavana. And then there is Lovamahapaya, or the Brazen Palace, which once housed monks. In K. M. de Silva's words, which were quite closely paraphrased by our guide, this structure 'is believed to have risen on completion to nine storeys in all .... All that remains of this early skyscraper are some 1,600 weather-beaten granite pillars which are a haphazard reconstruction of the twelfth century, with some of the pillars upside down and not even on the original site'.[21] 'And who do you think built this?', our guide asks rhetorically. 'This great palace was built by that great king who vanquished (*Guti dunna rajjuruvo* [The king who gave a beating to]) the Tamil king, Elara.'

At this point, our guide repeats the 'charter' mytho-history of Sinhala nationalism in its entirety:

> Elara was a Tamil king who invaded this country 350 years after Lord Buddha attained *nibbana*. It was a time when the Sinhala people had forgotten the *dhamma* and began fighting among themselves. Elara ruled the country for 44 years. The Sinhala king was Kakavana Tissa. He was nowhere to be found in this area. He fled south to Ruhuna. He

had two sons, Tissa and Gamani. Tissa, like his father, was a coward. When Gamani was only sixteen – and you tell your sons not to join the army – ... when he was only sixteen, before he even had whiskers, he attempted to go to war against Elara. Three times he tried and each time his father stood in his way. He preferred to talk, sitting at the round table [an allusion to the all party amity-talks that were taking place in Colombo at that time]. Gamani was disgusted. So what did he do? He sent his father and brother a cloth and blouse (*redi-hatta*) to wear. We must send a few saris to our leaders in Colombo. [Laughter]. One day the prince was very sad. His heart was heavy. He was curled up like a baby in his mother's stomach, on the sofa. 'Son, why don't you stretch yourself and sleep in bed?' his mother wanted to know. 'How can I stretch myself when there are Tamils in the north and the ocean is to the south?' he replied. Only then she realized what was happening. She helped him gather soldiers and go to war. He killed one million and thirty thousand Tamils and Elara. Then he united the whole island and ruled it according to the ten kingly qualities laid out in Buddhism (*dasarajadharma*). But our king was still troubled. He could not sleep. He was a good Buddhist and had still killed so many human beings in order to achieve his great purpose. The *arahats* read his thoughts. They came to him in the middle watch of the night, alighted at the palace gates and said, 'Oh, great and noble king, protector of the *dhamma*, do not trouble yourself on account of the dead. Of the million and thirty thousand killed, only one had taken the Three Refuges and only one who observed the Five Precepts in addition. The rest were unbelievers and men of evil life; not more to be esteemed than beasts.' Thus it is said in the great history book of Professor K. M. de Silva.

Professor de Silva did not say it quite like that, but, as the British would say, 'bloody close', and close enough for our guide's purpose. The description of each *dagaba* and every ruin was followed by an account of how this once great structure was destroyed by Tamils from south India. Given the context of the current Sinhala–Tamil tensions, it was difficult to see how these 'closing statements,' buttressed by quotes from Professor K.M. de Silva's *History of Sri Lanka* could fail to fan the flames of passion.

Two days prior to my own guided tour of Anuradhapura, I met a family at Mihintale who had been guided by the same retired army sergeant whose acquaintance I was to make later. It was a teenager from this family who informed me of the ex-army sergeant's existence and expertise. What had drawn my attention to this young man was a couple of statements I overheard him make in conversation with the other members of his family. He was saying, 'The only thing left to do is to send them [the Tamils] back to where they came from.' And then he claimed that his school principal (of a leading Buddhist high school in Colombo) had made the following statement during school assembly: 'If you see a Tamil and a snake, kill the Tamil first.' After having met the guide in question, it was easy to understand how these pilgrim-tourists had had their fervour and imagination fired. And furthermore, another interesting process begins to take over: epistemic history becomes uninteresting and ontic myth begins to move in. Simultaneously, the affected tourist-pilgrim becomes less a spectator of history and more an actor in myth. For participation in myth involves the myth somehow being enacted for the person beyond the stage of mere theory, 'as though the actor, after playing his part in theatre, should find the play in a sense continuing when he is offstage'.[22] And this indeed is what is happening in Sri Lanka. The act continues beyond the peripheries of Anuradhapura.

The next day in Polonnaruwa, I found a scion of the group I had followed around in Anuradhapura under the guidance of the ex-sergeant. This was the site of the medieval kingdom that survived for over two centuries. I was near the ruins of the Siva Devale, labelled by archaeologists as Siva Devale No.1. It was built in the tenth century by the Colas of south India. Its walls are now stained and its surroundings reek of urine. True, there are no signs of worship, no joss sticks or jasmine, the *lingam* has long lost its oil-covered sheen. But urine? Just then a young man from the group walked towards me shouting, 'Never mind, sir, go ahead and urinate there. Why, it is written there, "Number One"' – a local euphemism for urinating. An older official in a khaki jacket overheard the remark and came towards me shouting out a warning: 'Don't soil (*narak karanna epa*) that place. It is a *devale* (temple)'. I was getting ready to protest that I was not intending any such thing, but was beaten to it by the younger man who shot back the defiant question to the offical, 'Did you think that our blood was Tamil blood? The blood that courses through this body is a lion's blood.'[23] The young man reached the wall of the ruin and began to urinate. I walked away from the place and past the women-folk of the group of pilgrims to which he belonged. The women were untying parcels of food and the young among them were amused by their male companion's bravado. Our young man may not have been a character in the myth, but because he had participated in the play of the myth he seemed constrained to act his life out in accordance with the orientation provided by the myth. The mythic play entered into at Anuradhapura had been carried on to Polonnaruwa and is likely to be carried into other contexts of life as well. As I passed the women, I caught the last few words of an older woman (they called her *acci*, or grandmother) as she admonished the younger ones with the words, 'This is not something to be trifled with. It is madness to play with the powers of the gods.' She represented a generation for whom Hinduism and Buddhism were not as demarcated from each other in practice as was beginning to happen in 1983.[24]

Let us return to our tour guide at Anuradhapura for one last time. He is engaged in a double move. On the one hand he brings the epistemicized peripheral ruins of the ancient city under the ontic and centripetalizing forces of the Sri Maha Bodhi. On the other, he holds for anxious contemplation the alarming possibility that the ontic center of the Sri Maha Bodhi itself may be epistemicized by history, or more ominously by historical forces let loose by Tamil armies, repeating history as it were.

Eighteen months later, Tamil separatists made their own contribution towards a further onticization of terror by gunning down 146 Buddhist pilgrims at the Sri Maha Bodhi, fulfilling thereby the worst fears of my fellow pilgrims of 1984.

What is the moral of this chapter, if indeed there is one? It may appear, given the last example, that the ontic and the mythic are to be viewed negatively; whereas the epistemicizing craft of theory-building and historicizing deserve to be viewed favourably. This need not be necessarily so. There are ontic rituals such as Ankeliya and Gammaduva described by Obeyesekere in his massive book, *The Cult of the Goddess Pattini*, wherein ritual contains violence, even ethnic violence.[25] I use 'contain' in both senses: to possess and to restrain. These two rituals are (about) a host of things; past and present, gods and men, male and female, immigrant and native, outsider and insider. Distinctions are made and differences recognized. There is even a part in it for a Muslim. The nineteenth-century discoverers of Anuradhapura and Polonnaruwa were not interested in these unwieldy dramas that kept moving and changing. Static ruins and royal processions were much more comprehensible and therefore manageable. Ethnographers (and Paul Wirz[26] is no exception) slighted these rituals. It took a Sinhala anthropologist, Gananath Obeyesekere, and an interest that spanned twenty-five years, to record these rituals in any detail. And, as might be expected, his account of these ritual dramas, even as truncated as they are, have given his book the appearance of unwieldiness and invited the characterization by one reviewer as, 'sprawling'.[27] Its fault (the book's, the ritual's) is its lack of self-containedness. For anyone who has participated in these ritual dramas in Sri Lankan villages, even Obeyesekere's book would appear to be too self-contained, even though insufficient to satisfy the economy of the ethnographic imagination.

Where the colonial encounter and the ethnographer's interest had failed to reduce the scope and size of these and many other rituals tourism has succeeded. The healing ritual known as *tovil* is such an example and so is Kandyan dance, which has been abstracted from its varied contextual manifestations which were primarily ritual. European (read, 'rich') spectators have been offered, by Europeanized middlemen, abbreviated versions of these rituals, trimmed to just the right size and length so they fit the auditorium stage of a three-star hotel, and the average tourist's time schedule and attention span, all at the same time. The choreographer, a man or woman acquainted with western tastes and patience, in collusion with 'middlemen' and 'financiers', reduces these rituals to a sequence of self-containedness which seals them into self-congratulation. Reflexively, these rituals (and here I am thinking of *tovil*) and ritual specialists are made fun of by the young in the villages as well.[28]

Since the beginning of the civil war in 1983, tourism has dropped precipitously, and with it, foreign exchange earnings. Over-built hotels are empty, Buñuelesque, and in the red. To the few locals, drawn mainly from the lumpen bourgeoisie, who have, thanks to the civil war, made fast and formidable fortunes, discount rates are offered to enable them to sleep in air-conditioned hotels, eat with knife and fork, be attended by waiters in clean white coats with brass buttons and black sashes, and served unfamiliarly pallid sauces, 'English vegetables', and potatoes (instead of rice), ice water, and puddings with funny French names. They have become affordable and desirable. Tour buses take them to see the sites; sequestered spaces, potentially desecrated places. Rituals, once performed in villages and which took days to wind down, have now been transformed into 'ritualettes', and performed on stages of hotel auditoriums. Erstwhile participants in rituals have been transformed into voyeurs.

Conclusion

Ontic and epistemic realities are fundamentally different. The particular manifestation of the ontic that I chose to consider was myth, and of the epistemic, history. Myth and history may coexist with neither friction nor conflagration under two conditions. The first is one in which the two are consonant with each other; the second, one in which (even though the two may be substantially antithetical to or contradictory of each other) they remain mutually indifferent and irrelevant. The latter was the case for most Sri Lankans, Sinhala and Tamil, during the greater part of the colonial period. Neither one of these conditions of equipoise can be guaranteed to remain so forever in any social order, especially in one that is caught in the currents of a rapidly modernizing (some may even say, postmodernizing) world. Forces, external and internal, are capable of changing the state of composure. An incendiary context is created when mutually dissonant history and myth are brought into engagement with each other. Such is currently the case in Sri Lanka.

History and myth have had their own favourite agents or repositories. In Sri Lanka the state has been the agent of history and civil society the repository of myth. As a rule, anthropologists have studied the various forms of civil society and likewise, historians have looked at forms of the state, including the nation state. An argument by analogy is in place here. Nissan and Stirrat have argued in their essay that the modern nation state is territorially defined through its boundaries, in contradistinction to the pre-modern states of South Asia which found their identities in their centres. Civil society[29] in south Asia has continued to define itself through its centre, whether the territorial unit of such a society is called an *ur*, a *gama* or a village. But the cultural topography of the modern nation state(s) and that of civil society have been at odds with each other, and in Sri Lanka the difference has come to a head. Even as history and myth are no longer unaffected by each other in Sri Lanka, the state and civil society too have been brought into active, even if explosive, engagement. However, this engagement has had a positive though long overdue effect on the crafts of anthropology and history respectively, as is made evident in the contributions of this volume. We witness here a healthy cross-over or hybridization: the beginning of an anthropology of the state and a history of civil society. In the face of the enormity of Sri Lanka's crisis and its people's anguish, even to acknowledge that our contribution to solving the ethnic crisis in Sri Lanka is modest at best is to be conceited. But the manner in which our own two disciplines, anthropology and history, have begun to lose their well-defined methodologies and theoretical boundaries in itself reflects a sympathetic appreciation of Sri Lanka's own transformation which we seek to understand. To this extent, I believe, we have made a start.

Notes and references

1 My use of the term 'ontic' is necessarily idiosyncratic; not intended in the best known and more elaborated Heideggerian sense. The fuller 'ontological' was the first alternative I considered, but the 'logos' of ontology is what I wish to efface. 'Praxical' and 'pragmaticistic' were two of the other alternatives I considered and turned down for reasons too complex and tangential for the purposes of this essay.

2 In making the distinction between 'myth' and 'history' I draw liberally from Thomas Olshewsky's 'Between Science and Religion', *The Journal of Religion*, 1982, vol. 62, pp. 242–60.

3 B. Malinowski, 'Myth in Primitive Psychology', in *Magic, Science and Religion and Other Essays*, Glencoe, Ill., 1948.

4 E.V. Daniel, 'Three Dispositions Towards the Past: One Sinhala and Two Tamil', in *Identity, Consciousness and the Past*, (1989) H.L. Seneviratne (ed.), *Social Analysis* (Special Issue Series) no. 25, pp. 22–41.

5 B.S. Cohn, 'The Transformation of Objects into Artefacts, Antiquities and Art in 19th Century India', paper prepared for NEH conference *Patronage in Indian Culture*, 10–13 October, 1985.

6 R. Thapar, 'Imagined religious communities? Ancient history and the modern search for a Hindu identity', MAS. 1989, vol. 23, pp. 209–31; N. Dirks, *The Hollow Crown: Ethnohistory of an Indian Kingdom*, Cambridge, 1987.

7 N.S. Tennekoon, 'Rituals of development: the accelerated Mahaväli development program of Sri Lanka' *American Ethnologist*, 1988, vol 15, pp. 294–310.

8 E. Evans-Pritchard, *Witchcraft, oracles and magic among the Hzande*, Oxford, 1937, p. 83; C.S. Peirce, *Collected Papers*, Cambridge, MA., 1963, vol. 6, p. 111.

9 J. Spencer, 'Telling histories: nationalism and nationalists in a Sinhala village', ms.

10 E.V. Daniel, *Fluid Signs: Being a Person the Tamil Way*, Berkeley and Los Angeles, 1984.

11 Benedict Anderson, *Imagined Communities*, London, 1983.

12 S. Ponnambalam, *Sri Lanka. The National Question and the Tamil Liberation Struggle*, London, 1983, p. 234.

13 B.S. Cohn, 'Transformation'.

14 Ibid.

15 B.S. Cohn, 'The command of language and the language of command', in R. Guha (ed.) *Subaltern Studies IV*, Delhi, 1985, p. 283.

16 Ibid.

17 H.L. Seneviratne, *Rituals of the Kandyan State*, Cambridge, 1978.

18 'Symbols' are signs of convention, 'indexes' are those implicated in the logic of cause and effect (*ergo* their 'manipulability') and 'icons' are signs determined by the qualities they share with the objects they stand for, a sharing which may range from similarity to identity. Thus a practising believer whose religious commitment is participatory and ontic, is drenched with the attributes of his or her ontic world, making him or her an icon of that world.

19 Our guide claimed to have served as a sergeant in the Ceylon–British army prior to Independence.

20 Tourists' queries and opinions are amply available for eavesdropping at the Tourist Information Centre in Colombo and the lobbies and coffee shops of tourist hotels all over the island. The company of my American wife, another American couple and a Canadian friend made this information-gathering method of mine as easy as picking green mangoes off the ground following a windstorm in August.

21 K.M. de Silva, *A History of Sri Lanka*, Delhi, 1981, pp. 53–4.

22 Olshewsky, ibid., p. 155.

23 About this time A. T. Ariyaratne, the founder and leader of the best known Sinhala-Buddhist grassroots development organization, the Sarvodaya Shramadana Movement (referred to by Woost) claimed in public that every last drop of blood in his veins was Sinhala-Buddhist.

Subsequently, Ariyaratne was awarded an honorary degree by Brown University.

24 It merits noting that in none of the anti-Tamil riots prior to 1983 had there been deliberate and wanton destruction of Hindu temple idols and desecration of Hindu temples. The priest of a Hindu temple in Colombo where the current President of the Republic, Mr Premadasa worships, informed me that 'the [then] Prime Minister was very troubled by this particular aspect of the riots'. Mr Premadasa is known to fervently beseech various Hindu gods for favours and regularly obtains the advice of at least two Hindu-Tamil astrologers regarding the disposition of the stars and planets towards him.

25 G. Obeyesekere, *The Cult of the Goddess Pattini*, Chicago, 1984.

26 P. Wirz, *Exorcism and the Art of Healing in Ceylon*, Leiden, 1954.

27 B. Kapferer, 'Review of Obeyesekere *The Cult of the Goddess Pattini*' *American Ethnologist*, 1985, vol. 12, p. 176.

28 Personal communication with Dr Kumari Jayawardena.

29 Even as I write these words I cannot help but note that civil society in Sri Lanka, in the north and the south, is being torn to shreds. 'The centre can not hold'.

Index

Abeygunawardana, V.W. 198
Abeysekera, Charles 210–11, 213–14
Adam's Peak 194, 136
Ähälepola 68
Alagiyawanna, Robert 220
All-Ceylon Buddhist Congress 194–5
Ananda, Kahawatte 215–19
Ananda, Muruttetuwe 196
Anderson, Benedict 24, 25, 206
Anuradhapura 10, 20, 22–3, 100, 238–40, 242
archaeology 32
Ariyaratne, A.T. 164–5
Arunachalam, Ponnambalam 75, 95–9, 111, 114
'Aryans' 22, 29–30, 32, 70–5, 94–7, 114, 215
Asala Perahara 236–8
Asoka, Emperor 20, 58, 100, 191–3
Ayyar, K.V. Subrahmanya 47

Bandaranaike, S.W.R.D. 2, 9, 35, 115, 191, 197
Bandaranaike, Mrs Sirimavo 36
Barnett, L.D. 51
Basham, A.L. 51–2
Batuvantudawe, Devarakkhita 189
Bechert, H. 21
Bertolacci, Anthony 88–9
Bhuvanekabahu I, King 73
Blazé, A.E. 74–5
Bloch, Marc 48
bo-tree 100, 194, 238–9, 242
Bopp, Franz 72
Brito, C. 109–10
Brow, James ix, 4, 10–11, 125–42, 231
Buddha 3, 14, 20, 48, 50, 57
Buddhaghosa 47, 54
Buddhavamsa 61
Buddhism: and colonialism 31–2, 189; Jayewardene and 194–8, 200–3; and kings 6–7, 190–1; monastic schools 197; teaching 188; 'village' 211
Buddhist Affairs Department 194–5, 198, 200–1
Budugunalankaraya 64
Burrows, S.M. 100

Caldwell, Robert 47, 72–3
Candraditya 53
caste system 31, 62–3
Catacivapillai, V. 110
Catholics 5, 8, 101
Centan Tivakaram 47
Childers, R.C. 74
Chitty, Simon Casie 109–10, 114
Clough, B.C. 71
Codrington, H.W. 75
Cohn, Bernard 229, 234
Colas 62–4, 112–13
colonialism 26–34; British historiography 87–92; and Buddhism 31–2, 76, 189; and conflict 5, 32–4; elite Sri Lankans 92–9, 103, 218; historiography 5, 87–103; and identity development 30–2; influence on Sinhalas 77–8; and language 70–5, 94, 96; and

politics 8–9, 28–9, 32–3; popular images of history 99–102; and progress 98–9; racial theory 8–9, 27–30, 39, 70–5, 95–7, 112, 234; and religion 94, 101; trust law 157–9
Committee for Rational Development (CRD) 13
communalism 33
conflict: growth of 32–4; historical assumptions 21–2, 40; origins 8–10; and religion 5, 8, 31; under colonialism 32–4
constitution 33, 37
Coomaraswamy, A.K. 111, 114
Culavamsa 5, 52, 59, 64, 67, 73, 190, 202; and colonial writers 88–9
Cultural Affairs Ministry 194–5, 200–1
Cumaratunga, Munidasa 199

Dalada-sirita 188
Daniel, E. Valentine x, 227–44
Davy, John 88–9
de Alwis, Anandatissa 192–3
de Alwis, James 72–3, 93–4
de Silva, C.R. 67
de Silva, John 101
de Silva, K.M. 21, 22, 208, 239–40
de Silva, Nalin 213, 220
Devadatta 212
Devanampiyatissa, King 20, 58
development, rural 165–81; and history 164–5, 171–8, 231; ideologies 167, 178–81
Dhammananda, Tallale 198
Dharmadasa, K.N.O. 68, 138–9
Dharmapala, Anagarika 34, 76–7, 95–6, 99, 101–3, 214–17
Dharmapradipika 61
dharmistha society 191–2, 194–6
Dhatusena 59, 62
Dingiribanda, A. 132–3, 137, 140
Dipavamsa 46; Vijaya myth 49, 50–1
Dirks, Nicholas 230
Dissanayake, Gamini 231
Divayina 13, 206–7, 217, 222; Dharmapala debate 214–17; Dutugamunu debate 217–21; Jaffna kingdom 207–10; Sinhala Culture 210–14
Divyavadana 49, 50–1, 56
Donoughmore Commission (1931) 29, 127
'Dravidians' 22, 30, 72–3, 75, 94, 97, 109, 114–15, 208–9
Dry Zone 91, 98; settlement of 10, 32, 117; villages 126
Dutugämunu, King (Dutthagamani Abhaya) 20, 21, 58–9, 97, 113, 214, 217–21

'Eelam' 114
Elara, King 20–1, 58, 97, 113, 218–19, 239–40
elections 1–2, 33, 35, 37
élites: historiography 92–9, 103, 218; ruling *vs.* rural 35
Engels, Friedrich 77
epistemic, sacred places 232–43
Europe 119, 229
Evans-Pritchard, E.E. 231

Fa-Hian 47
Federal Party 116
Fernando, C.M. 95–6, 98
Fonseka, Carlo 208–9
Forbes, Major John 89–90

Gajabahu II, King 64
Gamani, Prince 219, 240
Geiger, Wilhelm 52–4, 190, 219
Gellner, E. 10, 24, 25
Gnanaprakasar, S. 111
Gobineau, 70
Goldschmidt, Paul 74
Gombrich, R. 125
Gomis, P.L. 209
Goonatilake, Susantha 215, 218
Gramsci, A. 179
Gunasinghe, Newton 14, 210–11, 213–14
Gunawardana, R.A.L.H. ix, 4, 7–8, 45–79, 220, 228, 234

Gunawardene, D. 97
Gunawardhana, W.F. 75
Gurulugomi 63–4

Hall, Stuart 179
Helese movement 34
Hellmann-Rajanayagam, Dagmar ix, 4, 7, 107–20, 229
Hettiarachi, D.E. 198
Hinduism 5, 8; south India 59–60, 62
historiography: British 87–92; colonial period 5, 87–103; élite Sri Lankans 92–9, 103, 218; nationalism 7; and popular images 99–102; Tamils 7, 20–2, 107–20, 229
history 159–60; Europe 119, 229; India 229–30; *Mahavamsa (q.v.)* 5–6; ontic and epistemic in sacred places 232–43; and political power 187–91; pre-colonial 5–7, 22–4; pre-modern and modern 24–6; Sinhala villages 129–42, 165–81; Tamil east coast village 154–9, 161–2; theory and myth 227–32, 243–4
Hiuen Tsang 49–53, 56
'homogeneity' 26
Horombuwa 166, 169–75
Horsburgh, Benjamin 101
Hurulle, E.B. 194

identity 19–40; different views of history 20–6; generation of 30–2; origins 4–8
ideology, Sinhala 45, 48, 55–6
Ilam 46–7
Ilangasinghe, Mangala 213
'Ilankai' 114
incest, sibling 53–4
Independence 9–10, 33–4
India 2, 9; dynastic emblems 53; history 229–30; immigrants from 65–6; invasions of Sri Lanka 57, 62–3, 91–2, 112; pre-modern state 24–5
Indian Peace Keeping Force (IPKF) 1, 2–3, 13

Iriyagolla, Gamini 207–8
Isaacsz, Klaas 108

Jacobson, T. 78
Jaffna, history 23, 108–9, 110–12, 116, 118; controversy 207–10
Jainism 59, 62
Janata Vimukti Peramuna (JVP, People's Liberation Front) 1, 13
jatiya 205, 216
Jayatilaka, D.B. 101
Jayawardena, Kumari 214–17
jayawardhanapura 193
Jayewardene, J.R. 1, 12, 161, 187–203, 228, 230; and Asoka 192–3, 230; and Buddhism 194–8, 200–3; *Mahavamsa, Nutana Yugaya* 187, 198–203; and righteousness 191–6
Jennings, I. 157
John, Samuel 110
Johnston, Sir Alexander 28, 88
Jones, William 70, 72
Joyce, James 145

Kadirgamar/Kadirgamanathan, C.S. 116
Kakavannatissa, King 60, 219, 239
Kalubanda, U. 136–7, 139
Kandappu 135
Kandasami, K. 209
Kandathe, B. 136
Kandy: Asala Perahara 236–8; kingdom 23–4, 67–9, 89, 99, 210
Karunaratne, Vijita 219
Kassapa 63
Kasyapa I, King 55
Kasyapa V, King 62
Kataragama 132, 139, 236
katikavatas 190–1, 200–2
Kearney, R. 21
Kemper, Steven ix, 4, 5–6, 12, 187–203, 230
kings 6–7, 20, 23–4; and monks 6, 190–1
Kirala Sandesa 68
kiramam 232–3
Kirimätiyave 67

Kirti Sri Rajasinha/Rajasinghe, King 24, 69, 191
Knighton, William 71, 90–2, 95
knowledge 187–8
Knox, 70
Kokila Sandesa 66
Kotalawala 100–1
Kuhn, Ernst 74
Kukulewa 129–42; *gambadi rajakariva* 137–9; Village Awakening 129–32
Kulakkottan, Prince 111
Kulasuriya, Ananda S. 73
Kunte, M.M. 74
Kuruvaltampi, Mr 145–7, 151–2
Kuvanna 49–50, 56
Kuveni 130

Lala 51
Land Commission (**1928**) 127
language 9, 20, 26–7, 35–6, 109; and colonial racial theory 70–5, 94, 96; *Mahvamsa* 5, 89, 199
Lassen, Christian 71–2
Levi, Primo 1
lineage 46
lions 48–9, 52, 55, 57
Liyanagamage, Amaradasa 64, 198
Liyanage, Minuwangoda D. 216, 219

maccan 152
McGilvray, D.B. 156–7
Magha 64
Mahadevan, Iravatham 47
mahajanaya 48, 56
Mahalalasena 50
Mahanama 189–90
Mahapadaranga Jataka 66
Mahavali scheme 10, 231
Mahavamsa 5–6, 48; and Buddhism 188–90; and colonial period 88–90, 189–90; Dutugämunu 58–9; language 5, 89, 199; and nationalism 6–7; racism 220–1; updating of 12, 187, 189–90, 198–203; Vijaya myth 48–54, 56–8
Mahavamsa, Nutana Yugaya 187, 198–203
Mahendravarman I, King 59
Mahinda IV, King 52, 62
Mahinda 20
Maine, Henry Sumner 70–1, 126
Maitreya, Vidagama 64
Malabars 92, 97
Malinowski, Bronislaw 57
Manavamma 62
Mandur 145–62
Manikkavacakar 60
Manning, Governor 111
Manudharmasastra 73
Manuniticolan, King 113
Medhatithi 73
Mendis, G.C. 51, 75–6, 219
Menikrala, U. 139
MEP ('People's United Front') 35
Metcalfe, 126
Mill, James 90
Millave 88
Moggallana 61
Moore, M. 21
Moors 98
Movement for Inter-racial Justice and Equality (MIRJE) 13
Müller, Max 70–3
Murukan 155
Muslims 5, 8, 98
myth 228–32, 243–4

Nairn, T. 9
Namavaliya 66
Nandana 73
Nandhimitta 58–9
Nannurutun Minisannas, Prince 66
Narada 73
'nation' 205; and race 112; and state 25–6, 39, 244
nationalism: Europe 119; and *Mahavamsa* 6–7; and newspapers (*q.v.*) 205–22; process 10–14; rural 10–11; Sinhala-Buddhist 2, 3, 128–9; Tamils 113, 114–17; theory 40
Navalar, Arumuka 116
Nayakkar kings 23–4, 68–9

newspapers 10–11, 34, 205–22; Jaffna kingdom 207–10; nationalist discourse 221–2; Sinhala Culture 210–14; social scientists and national heroes 214–21
Nietzsche, F.W. 237
Nissan, Elizabeth ix, 4–5, 19–40, 148, 244
Nissanka Malla, King 65

Obeyesekere, Gananath 21, 52, 125, 211, 221, 242
Onesicritos 52
ontic, sacred places 232–43
'Orientalism' 234

Pali 5, 20
Panduvasudeva 54
Pannananda, Yagirala 189–90, 199
Parakramabahu I, King 63
Parakramabahu VI, King 66–7
Paramqi Hatana 67
Paranavitana, S. 46, 47, 60, 67
Parevi Sandesa 66
Pathmanathan, S. 116
Pavidi Handa 202
Pelliot, Paul 47
Percival, Robert 88
Perera, E.W. 95–6, 98–9
Perera, N.M. 197
Periya Puranam 59
Pieris, P.E. 68
pirivenas 197
Polamitta 50
Poliakov, L. 29
politics: under colonial rule 8–9, 28–9, 32–3; post-Independence 34–9; power and history 187–203; and use of history 114–17, 187–203
Polonnaruwa 10, 20, 23, 233, 241–2
Ponnambalam, G.G. 115
Ponnambalam, Satchi 20
Poor, Daniel 109
Portugal 98
Pragnarama, Yakkaduwa 197
Premadasa, Ranasinghe 1, 131–2, 197
Prevention of Terrorism Act 37
Pridham, Charles 71
processions, religious 101, 236–8
Ptolemy 52
Pujavaliya 64, 67
Pulavar, Mayilvakana 108
Pulindas 54, 56
Punyakumara 53

race 45, 110, 118; colonial theory 8–9, 27–30, 39, 70–5, 95–7, 112, 234; and nation 112
radala nobility 69
Rahula, Totagamuve 66
Rahula, Walpola 21, 197
Rajapaksa, C. 212
Rajasimha II, King 67
raksasis 49–50, 56
Ramanathan, Ponnambalam 98, 114
Ranawella, Sirimal 198
Rasanayagam, S. 111–12
Ratanasara, Daramitipola 202–3
Ratnaweera, A.E.R. 74, 77
Ratnayake, Nalin 198
Reagan, Ronald 193, 230
religion: colonialism 94, 101; and conflict 5, 8, 31; *see also* Buddhism
righteousness 191–6
riots 2, 36, 37–8, 205–6
Roberts, M. 21
Rogers, John D. ix, 4, 5, 8, 10, 87–103, 229
Rohanadeera, Mendis 213
rural society *see* villages

Saimhalaka 47
Saivism 59–60, 64
Sakka 57
Samadigama 132–7, 140
Samantapasadika 47
Samaraweera, Vijaya 21, 126–7, 208
Samarayanaka, M.T. 209
sangha 6
Sankili 110
Sannasgala, Puñcibandara 68

Sapumal, Prince 67
Sarasin, C.F. and P.B. 74
Sarath, Lionel 220
Sariputta 61, 63
Sarvodaya Sharamadana Movement 125, 164
Schlegel, Friedrich 70
Seelawathie, P.B. 133–6
Senadhira, Gunapala 198
Senanayake, D.S. 9–10, 117, 127, 197, 203
Seneviratna, Susil G. 209
Seneviratne, H.L. 236
Sigiriya 233–4
Sihabahu 48–9, 53, 56
Sihadipa/Sihaladipa 46–7, 57, 215, 216
Sihasivali 48
Simalankara 63
Simhala 49–51, 56
Singer, Marshall 206
Sinhala 45–79; and Buddhism 62–5; and colonial racial theory 67–8, 70–6; colour and appearance 60–1, 73–4, 234–5; Culture controversy 210–14; and Dutugämunu war 58–9, 76; government 2–3, 36; history 20–2, 87–103; ideology 45, 48, 55–6; and Indian invasions 57, 62–4; Jaffna kingdom denied 207–10; language 54–5, 66, 71–4; lions 48–9, 52, 55, 57; and *Mahavamsa, Nutana Yugaya* 187, 198–203; nationalism 2, 3, 128–9; and newspapers (*q.v.*) 205–22; origins 46–7; and Tamil culture 66–7; Tamil perceptions of 108, 115–18; Vijaya myth 45, 48–57; villages 125–42, 164–81
Siripala, 171–2
Siriweera, W.I. 219
Siva Devale 241
Social Scientists' Association (SSA) 13, 214, 218; Dharmapala debate 214–17; Dutugämunu debate 217–21
Somaratne, G.P.V. 67
Soulbury, Lord 116
Spencer, Jonathan ix, 1–14, 141, 231–2
Sri Lanka Freedom Party (SLEP) 2, 35, 38–9, 191
Sri Pada 194, 236
state 5; and identity 22; and 'nation' 25–6, 39, 244; pre-colonial 22–4; pre-modern and modern 24–6
Stein, Burton 24–5
Stirrat, R.L. ix, 4–5, 19–40, 148, 244
Suduwatura Ara 165–81
Sumanapala, U. 138–9
Sumangala, Hikkaduwe Sri 189
Sumitta 54
Suntheralingam, C. 115–16
Suriyaaracchi, Gunawardena 212

Tambapanni 52
Tambiah, H.W. 157
Tambiah, S.J. 13, 24, 25, 145, 192
Tamil United Liberation Front (TULF) 2, 37, 151
Tamils 1–2; and Buddhism 59–60; and colonial historiography 97, 101–2; colour and appearance 74; development of nationalism 113; disenfranchisement 9–10, 34, 117; dominant historical themes 117–18; and Dutugämunu war 58–9; history 20–2, 97, 101–2, 229; 'homeland' 117; independence demands 116; influence on Sinhala 66–7; Jaffna history 108–12, 116, 118, 207–10; kings 6–7 65; language 109; origins 47; perception of Sinhala 108, 115–18; perceptions of history 112–14; political use of history 114–17; villages 145–62
Tennekoon, Serena x, 4, 12–13, 14, 164, 205–22, 231, 235
Tennent, James Emerson 72, 90–2, 94–5
terrorism 2, 37–8
Thapar, Romila 53, 73, 230
theory 228–32

'Tigers' (Liberation Tigers of Tamil Eelam LTTE) 2, 13, 37
Tilakasiri, Dediyawela 220
Tirunanacampantar 60
Tiruvatavurar Puranam 59
Tissa, Prince 240
Tooth Relic 188, 236–8
trade union movement 33
transport 35
trust law 157–9
Turnour, George 88–9

Ukkubanda, A. 134–5, 137
Unambuve, Prince 68–9
United Front (UF) 37
United National Party (UNP) 1, 35, 37–9, 191–2
Upali Newspaper Group 206
Upham, Edward 88–9
Uppalavanna 48, 57
ur 232–3, 244

Vaduga Hatana 68–9
Vajiranana, Poruna 198
vamsa 187–8
Vamsatthappakasini 49–50, 52–5
Vanniyar kings 26
Vattagamani 60
Vatthuhamy, V.B. 76
Vayantimalaya 66
Veddas 75, 91, 97, 132, 154–5
Vesaturuda Sanne 61
Vijaya, Prince 20, 45, 48–57, 95–7, 108, 130
Vijayabahu I, King 63–4
Vijayatunga, Karunaratna 198
Vikramabahu 64
Village Awakening (*Gam Udava*) programme 125, 129, 167; Kukulewa 129–32
Village Communities Ordinance 95
villages 125–9, 148, 164–5; Kukulewa 129–42; Mandur 145–62; politics 10–11; Suduwatura Ara 165–81; Tamil east coast 145–62
Viraparakramabahu 67
Virchow, Rudolph 74
Vittipot 65
'Voice of the Clergy' 202

Wannihamy, K. 136
Weber, Max 27, 126
Welimada 166, 169–75
Whitaker, Mark ix, 4, 7–8, 11, 145–62, 228–9
Wijeratne, P.B. 133–7
Wijesekera, Nandadera 198
Wijesinha, C.A. 75
Wijesuriya, Sarath 212
Wijewardena, Upali 206
Wimalasena, 171–2
Wirz, Paul 242
Wittgenstein, Ludwig 159
Woost, Michael D. ix, 4, 10–11, 12, 164–81
Wright, A. 95–6

yakkhas 49–50, 56–7
Yalppana Vaipaya Malai 108–10, 112, 114